IRAQ &
THE EVOLUTION OF
AMERICAN
STRATEGY

IRAQ &
THE EVOLUTION OF
AMERICAN STRATEGY

STEVEN METZ

POTOMAC BOOKS, INC.
WASHINGTON, D.C.

Library of Congress Cataloging-in-Publication Data

Metz, Steven, 1956-
Iraq and the evolution of American strategy / Steven Metz. — 1st ed.
p. cm.
Includes bibliographical references and index.
ISBN 978-1-59797-196-6 (hardcover : alk. paper)
1. United States—Foreign relations—Iraq. 2. Iraq—Foreign relations—United States. 3. Iraq—Strategic aspects. 4. United States—Military policy. 5. National security—United States. 6. United States—Foreign relations—1989- 7. Iraq—Foreign public opinion, American. 8. Public opinion—United States. I. Title.
E183.8.I57M48 2008
327.730567—dc22

                        2008009001

ISBN: 978-1-59797-196-6

(alk. paper)

Printed in the United States of America on acid-free paper that meets the American National Standards Institute Z39-48 Standard.

Potomac Books, Inc.
22841 Quicksilver Drive
Dulles, Virginia 20166

First Edition

10 9 8 7 6 5 4 3 2 1

CONTENTS

FOREWORD

by Colin S. Gray

S teven Metz is one of the rare people who understands the military and its cultures, while remaining a civilian scholar of high repute. Although he has worked for the U.S. Army for many years he has never lost his independence of mind. Among other attributes, Dr. Metz's writings and behavior have shown a deep commitment to the proposition that strategic knowledge needs to be useful in the real world. When he theorizes, he does so for the clear constructive purpose of helping the realm of strategic practice. Carl von Clausewitz's disdain for scholars who theorize seemingly for its own sake, and who weave ever more elaborate architectures of theory, does not apply to Dr. Metz.

Unlike many of today's strategic theorists and commentators, Steven Metz has not staged a recent arrival in the messy and complex realm of insurgency and counterinsurgency (COIN), terrorism and counterterrorism (CT). He made his mark as an innovative analyst and theorist of the irregular forms of violence long before it was fashionable to do so. Unfortunately, what has happened is that the global security context and U.S. policy, grand strategy, military strategy, operations, and tactics have caught up with him. To people such as Steven Metz, who is truly expert in the principles, the practice and the malpractice of COIN and CT many years prior to 9/11, it has to be galling to observe the rediscovery of familiar nostrums by the broad defense community.

Dr. Metz has owed his talent and experience a major book, and here it is. This superb work attempts and achieves no less than three tasks. First, it unravels the tangled skein of U.S.-Iraqi relations since the early 1980s. In

viii ——————————————————————————————FOREWORD

great detail, the whole background to the contemporary troubles is explained. The book is especially revealing on the roots and continuing causes of mutual misunderstanding between Americans and Iraqis. Repeatedly, Dr. Metz advises wisely that the manifestation of culture on both sides has a great deal to answer for. With the publication of *Iraq & the Evolution of American Strategy*, there can be no excuse for anyone to remain baffled as to why and how the tragedy occurred. It is important to note that Dr. Metz has not written an angry book but rather a calm and balanced one. He recognizes that good American intentions have a way of producing undesired results.

Second, the book probes and exposes the problems Americans have with strategy. Indeed, the work is really as much about strategy making and execution in the American political and cultural contexts as it is about the U.S.-Iraqi nexus. The text can be read as a lengthy treatise on Americans and strategy, an analysis illustrated profusely by Iraq as a case study. It is somewhat ironic that America's strategy deficit, as I have termed it elsewhere, should be revealed today in so unmistakable a form vis-à-vis Iraq and Afghanistan. The irony lies in the fact that in the contemporary United States, "strategy has become an industry." Dr. Metz proceeds to argue that "[a]ll told this is truly a golden age of strategic discourse in the United States (if not of strategy itself)." If he is correct in this claim, one would expect American would-be strategic behavior to generate more benign effect than has been revealed thus far by events. Of course, it is entirely possible that although there is, or may be, a large and ever-growing band of American strategic cognoscenti, the country is prevented from achieving high strategic effectiveness by its culture. Specifically, it is not implausible to argue that America's public culture, strategic culture, and military institutional cultures work to constrain strategic, and hence political, effectiveness in some classes of conflict. The traditional American "way of war," to risk oversimplification, has favored regular over irregular warfare and a quest for decisive military victory. The conduct of complex and protracted conflict, where a military outcome appears impossible to secure, has not been the U.S. forte. As recently as 2003–06, it was commonplace to hear American soldiers complain that in Iraq they were committed to a struggle whose forms they did not understand and for which they were not properly trained, suitably armed, or appropriately organized. Matters have improved recently, but as the maxim has it, time lost is irretrievable. The grasp of doctrine required for effective COIN and CT behavior that is now widespread in America's military institutions does not enable Americans to reset the game clock back to 2003.

Third, Dr. Metz's book is a profound study of strategy itself. The historical subject happens to be the American experience with, and in, Iraq, but the text can be read as an extensive exploration of all aspects of the making and execution of strategy. The concept of strategy can be as hard for some people to understand as its attempted practice can be thwarted by a myriad of difficulties. Strategy is far more challenging to design, adapt, and carry into effect than is policy or operations or tactics. The latter categories are each substantially "pure" in military content, at least they should be. Policy sets political goals that operations and tactics should attain courtesy of the directing genius of strategy. If policy is about political judgment, while tactics are about fighting, and operations are concerned with the aggregation of tactical events into a campaign whole, what is strategy? Plainly, it is neither policy nor fighting. Instead, strategy is the bridge between the two. It is where theory and practice meet. Speculative policymaking, with probably a shifting set of political goals, has to be translated into behavior by the military instrument via strategy. The job of the strategist is to decide on the probable exchange rate of successful military threat and employment for political returns. When phrased thus, it becomes rapidly apparent why strategy is exceedingly difficult to do well.

History abounds with cases of countries leaping from policy decision to active military behavior, with little, if any, attention paid to strategy. Frequently it is just assumed that a heap of anticipated tactical victories will assume an operational significance that must, miraculously almost, produce the desired strategic result. It should be needless to add that this astrategic approach to the use of force for policy ends is near criminally irresponsible, even though it can succeed occasionally.

Dr. Metz's *Iraq & and the Evolution of American Strategy* is a book for which we have been waiting. This is a landmark text. Even though the strategic muddle of America's involvement in Iraq is far from over, Dr. Metz's history and analysis should stand the test of time.

COLIN S. GRAY

PREFACE

Writing a book is an adventure. To begin with, it is a toy and an amusement;
then it becomes a mistress, and then it becomes a master, and then a tyrant.
The last phase is that just as you are about to be reconciled to your
servitude, you kill the monster, and fling him out to the public.
—WINSTON CHURCHILL

Like most Americans, I thought little about Iraq before the summer of 1990. Having spent my entire adult life teaching and writing about national security I could not, of course, ignore it entirely. I knew a horrific war took place there in the 1980s, but its most intense images were of slaughtered Iranian youth, not the bluster of mustachioed Iraqi generals. Like most Americans, I was perplexed that a regime like the one in Teheran, inured to suffering and driven to barbarity by religious fervor, could exist in the modern world. It was so out of place, almost surreal, an echo of a different time. As a student of the Third World, though, I found Saddam Hussein lamentably familiar and, in Hannah Arendt's word, "banal." I knew of many more like him, from Mobutu to Ceausescu. They littered the world. But even this perception—as wrong as it turned out to be—was only a passing thought. I remained immersed in other regions, issues, and problems. Iraq was peripheral, best left for Middle East experts.

Then for the second time in a decade, Iraq invaded a neighboring state, bullying its way to the attention of the world. As Operation Desert Storm unfolded, I was on the faculty of the U.S. Army Command and General Staff

College. Not only did CNN make the war unusually vivid—I remember working in my garage, listening to play-by-play combat coverage on the radio as if it were a sporting event—the fact that some of my former students and current friends were in harm's way also made it personal. For a few months, at least, Iraq mattered greatly to me. But afterward, it faded again. I returned to other projects.

As another major war between the United States and Iraq approached in the late winter of 2003, I joined a study team from the U.S. Army War College. Our mission was to enter Iraq as soon as possible after combat subsided and undertake an initial strategic assessment. For a career academic, being issued military gear, fitted for uniforms (to the extent that the word "fitted" applies to the way the Army issues clothing), trained on chemical protection equipment, and inoculated against anthrax and a slew of other nasty things was strange but exciting. Our team established a base in Kuwait and then made five trips into Iraq. It was electrifying to see the country that had so dominated the headlines for the previous year, experience the immediate aftermath of a major war, and talk to military leaders and soldiers from both sides while their memories were fresh. The sight of exhausted U.S. soldiers, the jumble of feelings from relief to smoldering hatred on the part of Iraqis, nights spent in looted palaces, high-speed drives through liberated (or conquered) cities with absolutely no public order or security, and, in general, traversing a landscape littered with the detritus of war, much still smoking, were things few scholars experience.

My role in the study team was to analyze what was then called the "post-conflict" period. This was an afterthought to our project, added by a senior Army general after approving the study. Little did he or anyone else know that there would be more conflict in the "post-conflict" period than in the conventional war. As events in Iraq unfolded, the complexity of the project exploded beyond control. I worked frenetically just to keep abreast of breaking developments. My office filled with notes, articles, maps, briefing slides, reports, and transcripts. I could not finalize the report. Each draft was obsolete before I could distribute it.

Still, this was the right issue for me at the right time: I was one of a handful of scholars or analysts who had studied insurgency and counterinsurgency during the previous decade. This served me well as the insurgency in Iraq grew. But the idea that that I would spend a few months on the Iraq project and then return to my normal research and management concerns collapsed under the onslaught of events. Iraq became my life.

From the spring of 2003 until now I have worked on it nearly full time, collecting tens of thousands of pages of material. Clearly it was time to capture this in a comprehensive format.

Dozens of books and hundred of articles have been written about America's conflict with Iraq, the bulk since 2003. These cover a range of topics from policymaking to military tactics. But almost all share one feature: they concentrate on what the conflict has done *to Iraq* rather than what it has done *to America.* That realization inspired this book. The conflict with Iraq has changed us. A part of what we are, how we see the world, and how we define our role in the global security environment was born in this conflict. We must understand how and why. We must know whether Iraq has changed us for better or worse. We must use Iraq as a portal for introspection and use it to learn about the American approach to strategy. As such, it has much to offer.

I will undertake this in six primary chapters. The first, entitled "Ascent of an Enemy," will examine how Iraq became a threat to the United States and thus a strategic paradigm. The second is "The Test of Battle." It will cover Operation Desert Storm and the struggle of the first Bush administration to overcome the Vietnam syndrome and adjust the role that armed force plays in American strategy. This phase of the conflict demonstrated that the American military, honed through a decade of reform and improvement, was an effective tool of strategy, at least to the degree that the American strategic culture and zeitgeist would allow. This combination of effectiveness and constraints led to a strategy that could generate battlefield success but not ultimate strategic victory. The third chapter, called "Transformation and Containment," will assess American strategy toward Iraq and the process of military "transformation" between the two major wars. The "revolution in military affairs" plays a starring role here as the notion of quick and low-cost applications of military force was deified. But as Saddam Hussein's stubbornness demonstrated, this construct had severe limitations. The fourth—"Terrorism and Force"—will deal with how the September 11 attacks affected American strategy, particularly with the concepts that propelled the Bush administration to adopt a new, aggressive mode of American global leadership relying heavily on military force and then to intervene in Iraq. The fifth chapter, "Decision and Triumph," is an assessment of the decision to invade Iraq, the Bush administration's efforts to mobilize support for this, and the military campaign to remove Saddam Hussein from power. The symbolism here is dialectical: as the United States attained perhaps its most impressive battlefield victory, the contradictions and shortcomings of the Bush grand strategy became evident. The sixth chapter is entitled "Counterinsurgency." Again, I will focus on placing the U.S. efforts in their broader strategic context, stressing the peculiarly American approach to counterinsurgency as it was reborn in Iraq after a decade's hibernation. I will end with conclusions about with the process of selecting, interpreting, and using paradigms to drive American strategy, including an assessment of the strengths and weaknesses of this process and some ideas on how it can be made more effective.

ACKNOWLEDGMENTS

A s with every book, this one was made possible by contributions and, in some cases, sacrifices from a number of people. Professor Douglas Lovelace, director of the U.S. Army War College Strategic Studies Institute, was an indefatigable supporter and provided time and resources when he probably could have used me for other things.* Doug was also the source of significant ideas and material. Maj. Gen. David Huntoon, commandant of the U.S. Army War college, upon the recommendation of Dean Bill Johnsen and the College's Title 10 Board, provided the sabbatical during which I wrote a significant part of the book. It could never have been done without time away from the endless horde of meetings and management duties that swallow most days at the office. I leaned heavily on my colleague Andrew Terrill's encyclopedic knowledge of the Middle East. Suggestions from Raymond Millen, Bard O'Neill, Conrad Crane, Douglas MacDonald, Nathan Freier, T. X. Hammes, H. R. McMaster, Grant Hammond, John Martin, Antulio Echevarria, Peter Feaver, David Betz, and Douglas Johnson were invaluable. Andy Terrill and Doug Johnson read and commented on the entire manuscript. I owe much to them. Thomas Nelson and David Metz also provided useful insights. The contributions of these friends and colleagues made this a much better product. Flaws that remain do so despite their best efforts. Don McKeon and Hilary Claggett of Potomac

* I am an employee of the U.S. Army, but everything in this book is purely my own opinion and does not reflect official positions of the Department of Defense, U.S. Army, or the U.S. Army War College.

Books were immeasurably helpful during the editorial and publication process. Bohdan Kohutiak and his outstanding staff at the U.S. Army War College library helped in a multitude of ways.

I would also like to note the intellectual lineage of this book. My introduction to statecraft came at the talented hands of Robert W. Tucker and George Liska. I was first tutored in strategy by my colleagues on the Strategy Committee in the Department of Joint and Combined Operations, U.S. Army Command and General Staff College, particularly Dennis Quinn, Bob Walz, Don Vik, and Fred Downey. Ted Hailes at the Air War College picked up where they left off. During the course of my career, I have found endless inspiration from three friends radically dissimilar in their thinking but sharing a powerful and profound intellect—Colin Gray, Jeffrey Record, and Martin van Creveld. A nod is also due to the Starbucks and Macanudo companies without which this manuscript would never have reached fruition. My friends in the online discussion board "Small Talk" may not have known it, but they helped me get a better grasp on how the public sees national security, strategy, and the conflict in Iraq. Probably the only one who gained more from the writing of this book than he sacrificed is Max the golden retriever, who accompanied me on many long walks as I burned off stress and wrestled with various issues and problems. I'm sure he hopes the next volume follows closely on the heels of this one.

INTRODUCTION

History has many cunning passages, contrived corridors
And issues, deceives with whispering ambitions,
Guides us by vanities.
— T. S. ELIOT
"GERONTION"

This book is about strategy, particularly the way Americans undertake it, as much as it is about Iraq. My primary objective is not to provide new information about the long conflict itself—I am not a historian— but to use it as a single, time-series case study to explore and demonstrate points about American security strategy, particularly its evolution from the 1970s to the present. Given that, a few words to clarify what I mean by "strategy" are in order. While there is no shortage of definitions in the scholarly and professional literature, Barry Posen captured it succinctly and accurately:

> A state's grand strategy is its foreign policy elite's theory about how to produce national security. . . . A grand strategy enumerates and prioritizes threats and adduces political and military remedies for them. A grand strategy also explains why some threats attain a certain priority, and why and how the remedies proposed would work.[1]

In the broadest sense, strategy seeks to control risk, maximize effectiveness, and increase the chances of success during the mobilization and application of power—particularly but not exclusively military power—in pursuit of objectives or interests. It entails order extended in time, space, and milieus. Strategy attempts to impose coherence and predictability on an inherently disorderly environment composed of thinking, reacting, competing, and conflicting entities. It is built of interlinked general concepts, techniques, and repeated procedures. It is both a mode of thinking and the pattern that emerges from a series of discrete decisions if they are made in a particular way. Strategic decision making entails explicit or implicit priorities, preferences, assessments, and predictions. If a state takes a strategic approach to its security problems—and they can do otherwise—chaotic, ad hoc, and disorganized applications of national power are, to a varying extent, replaced with orderly ones. The *logic* of strategy holds that expected outcomes must be balanced against expected costs and risks, and expected short-term outcomes, costs, and risks against long-term ones. The *calculus* of strategy is a context- and cultural-dependent weighing and prioritizing of objectives, acceptable costs, and acceptable risks. When opponents utilize different strategic calculi, predictions and calculations are more complex, and thus strategy becomes even more difficult than it normally is.

Strategy has both horizontal and vertical dimensions. The horizontal seeks to augment order, add coherence, and synchronize actions across various domains of activity. The horizontal dimension, for instance, attempts to ensure that a nation's diplomatic, economic, and military efforts are integrated and all are applied in pursuit of common goals. The vertical dimension projects thinking and actions into the future. It is concerned with long-term and second-order effects. It is developed using systems that vary in complexity and formality. The American system for strategy development is complex and formalized. That of dictatorships is more personalized and informal. Strategy is shaped by a strategic culture—the way the individuals making or affecting strategy see history and time, the way they prioritize their objectives, the amount of risk they are willing to tolerate, and the role they accord force and conflict—and by a context, composed of personalities, political dynamics, specific issues, and specific conditions.

There are three other aspects of strategy that demand attention. First is the crucial role of assumptions. Assumptions allow strategy to take place when vital information is missing or unknowable. They can deal with the future; with the intentions of an opponent, partner, or unaffiliated actor; or with facts that cannot be discerned (such as the possession of nuclear weapons by a state that chooses to keep secret their possession or the lack thereof). Assumptions are necessary for strategy, but they are also a potential weakness. They reflect shortcomings in intelligence or understanding. As a general rule, the more a strategy is based on assumptions, the more fragile it is. The second aspect is the importance of perception and understanding, particularly across cultures. Third, strategy is and always will be a *human* endeavor. Ideas, concepts, principles, priorities, prejudices, and personalities matter greatly. Mine is not that variant of realism that sees states as faceless, soulless black boxes marching according to abstract rules, but entities of ambitious, talented, and flawed people. My roots run deeper in Thucydides than in Hegel.

The word "strategy" originated in the realm of armed conflict. It derives from the Greek word for military generalship. The most common meaning throughout history was the science and art of military command as applied to the overall planning and conduct of large-scale combat operations. Clausewitz, the most influential theorist of war, defined strategy as "the use of engagements for the object of the war."[2] Colin Gray, the most astute contemporary theorist of strategy, has expanded this to "the use that is made of force and the threat of force for the ends of policy."[3] But like many words and concepts, the meaning of strategy has expanded over time. Today it is used to describe any endeavor that seeks to control risk and maximize the chances of success during the mobilization and application of power in pursuit of objectives or interests. Businesses and other complex organizations thus can have strategies. It is not inaccurate to say that even some individuals approach life strategically.

I will use strategy to mean the mobilization and application of all national power resources but will concentrate on the traditional sense of the word—the preparation and use of armed force to promote or protect national interests. Conceived this way, strategy takes on several important characteristics. First is its importance. If a business adopts a strategy that fails, profits may decline. At worst, the company may go bankrupt, investors lose money, and employees lose jobs and benefits. This may be sad, even tragic, but is not disastrous. If a nation's security strategy fails, people are likely to die and the entire nation may suffer, perhaps to the point of obliteration. The stakes of security strategy are thus greater than the stakes of strategy in any other realm. In addition, strategy operates with what Edward Luttwak calls a "paradoxical logic"—most human endeavors involve a linear logic where what appears to be the best solution to a problem normally is.[4]

But since strategy pits two or more entities deliberately attempting to thwart the other, what appears best often is not, simply because the opponent will be prepared to counter it.

Security strategy entails the use or the threat to use armed force. In the broadest sense, American strategy has used force in three ways. One is to defend partners (and, to a lesser extent, the American homeland) against overt armed aggression or to reverse such aggression if it occurs. Because the moral and political structure of such situations is clear and unambiguous, it is easier to mobilize and sustain support for these uses of force. The situations have discrete beginnings and end points and are amenable to the type of warfare Americans are best at—the mobilization and application of conventional military power.

The second use of force in American strategy is to restore and strengthen stability in regions of interest. This embroils the United States in internal conflicts, often far away and often against irregular enemies. Such activities tend to be protracted, open ended, complex, and ambiguous. They do not play to American strengths even though the United States has often been forced to undertake them.

The third form—call it the "Kissingerian"—uses armed force as an element of diplomacy, seeking to compel an opponent toward a desired policy or to deter it from an undesired one. This creates problems in that it runs counter to the American perception that armed force should be used only to fight wars, and a condition of war either does or does not exist.

Rather than create strategy anew for each security problem faced, the United States, like all nations, uses paradigms. Thinking about new issues or problems is shaped by their resemblance to previous or parallel ones. What worked and did not work in those other situations is elevated to paradigmatic status. Again, this is simple in concept and difficult in application—strategy is a messy business. Something must inject focus. Because geography has not given America an enduring enemy to shape its security strategy and serve as a focus, a shifting series of protracted politico-military conflicts have done so. The classic example, of course, is the Soviet Union during the Cold War. For decades, American strategy was propelled by the conflict with the Soviet Union. The vocabulary, logic, and methodology of American strategy were derived from the bitter struggle with Moscow. Other challengers were viewed through a Cold War lens and treated as lesser variants of the Soviet Union. America chose its friends and enemies based on their relationship with Moscow. The enemies of our enemy were our friends.

While the Soviet Union has been the most important driver of American strategy, it was not the first (nor the last). The world has not seen the end of ideology nor the end of strategy. In the nintheenth century, Great Britain and, to some extent, the American Indians played a similar role. The American military was designed to defend against them; U.S. strategy was designed to counter them. All of these defining moments, precedent-setting issues, or strategic paradigms shared certain characteristics—they were the major threat at the time (or at least one of the major ones), and their conflict with the United States lasted long enough to resonate through the American political system and allow the development of a strategic response.

Without a central strategic paradigm, American security policy tends toward astrategic meandering and "ad hocery." Domestic politics shape defense spending and the configuration of the military. In such times there is little consensus on the essence of strategy—knowing why, where, and how national power should be used. Strategic debates become less intense because the stakes are lower. There is disagreement on the appropriate use of military strength (or even the need for it). This may not be fatal but is dangerous. The absence of a strategic paradigm complicates the task of reconstituting a coherent strategy and the power to implement it once changes in the global security environment demand greater energy and effectiveness. Having a central paradigm—particularly the correct one, properly understood—augments the coherence and, in most cases, effectiveness of American strategy. Since 1991, no paradigm has been more important for the evolution of American strategy than the conflict with Iraq.

Understanding the function of strategic paradigms in general and Iraq in particular requires first answering a series of questions: was the enemy, threat, opportunity, or issue, in fact, the most appropriate shaper or driver of strategy at the time it played that role? In other words, was it both prominent and emblematic, able to help shape a strategy and strategic resources applicable against other opponents or to other issues? How did a specific paradigm affect American strategy, to include not only the actual content of the strategy but also the way strategy is developed and strategic resources, particularly military force, are mobilized? What did the paradigm lead American leaders and the public to think about the global security environment and the U.S. role in it? What did the paradigm suggest to leaders and the public concerning the appropriate way to deal with the challenge or threat? Did policymakers, strategists, and strategic analysts fully understand a given paradigm and draw the right conclusions from it?

Context always matters. The American strategic culture is a peculiar one, blending impatience; pragmatism; a quest for permanent solutions to strategic challenges; a propensity to seek technological and legalistic solutions to security problems; a recurring lack of confidence in the exercise of power, which can only be ameliorated by moral clarity and support from partners; a belief that peace is the normal state of world affairs and armed conflict is abnormal and periodic; reliance on a small peacetime military bolstered during times of war with citizen soldiers; a tendency to "mirror image" and assume other cultures share the perceptions, perspectives, priorities, and value systems of Americans; a relatively transparent, open, and complex system for strategy formulation; coexistence of the urge to make the world over in America's image and to withdraw from it; and the belief that in ideological struggles or—to the use the more contemporary term— "the war of ideas," truth invariably wins. American strategy tends to vacillate between or intermix two traditions: realism, with its emphasis on creating and maintaining power balances among states, and idealism, or the idea that security is attained by spreading American values, particularly democracy, market economics, and rule by law. Taking shape not only in a democracy, but in a vibrant, raucous one in which the population is inherently skeptical of experts, American strategy relies on the creation and sustainment of public images by political leaders—"packaging," if you will, or, in the phrase popular in Washington today, "strategic communications."

In addition to the broad and enduring framework of strategic culture, the specific (and more fluid) political situation also shapes strategy. In particular, political and ideological myths—ideas that become widely accepted and used for political purposes but that may or may not reflect reality—are often translated into military strategy. For instance, part of the American ideology is the belief that regulated market mechanisms are the best method for distributing resources, whether consumer goods, money, or political power. Politically, this translates into a belief that pluralistic, open democracy with rule by law is the "best" political system and the only one that will remain stable over time. More important, the American ideology holds that people from other nations and cultures instinctively understand this. The only reason all do not adopt such systems is because evil elites with a vested interest in preventing the emergence of democracy seize power. From this flows a military strategy based on the idea of decapitation—remove the evil elites and the natural instinct for pluralistic democracy will flower. Of course, Americans are not the only ones who shape military strategy with political myth. In order to retain his grip on power after the military defeat of 1991, Saddam Hussein had to paint it as a victory. His armed forces, according to the myth, stopped their enemies at the Euphrates and thus saved the nation. This myth, created and propagated for the political purpose of sustaining Hussein's power, was translated into military strategy. Clearly the military strategy that worked in 1991, the dictator's thinking went, would work again in the future.

But military strategy reflects much more than simply existing political myths or conditions. All nations have a distinct "way of war" that shapes why, when, and how they use armed force. This phrase was coined by military historian Russell Weigley.[5] He contended that following the Civil War, the United States relied on a method of armed conflict that saw war as an all-or-nothing event, and sought victory by using America's massive industrial capability to grind down opponents through attrition. There was little subtle about it. America's reliance on citizen soldiers rather than long-serving professionals to provide the bulk of it troops made sophisticated or subtle military methods impossible. War was a matter of brute strength. In a real sense, Ulysses Grant, who destroyed Lee's Confederate Army despite the greater operational sophistication of the Southerners, was the founding father of the American way of war. Generals who have followed him carried the torch.

While this traditional American way of war worked when vital national interests or national survival were at stake and the enemy was a conventional state military—the Confederacy, the Germans in the world wars, or the Japanese in World War II—it was less useful in an increasingly interconnected and nuclear world, where the enemies faced by the United States were often not states and the stakes of armed conflict were less than vital. As a result, the American way of war has been changing. Max Boot argues, "Spurred by dramatic advances in information technology, the U.S. military has adopted a new style of warfare that eschews the bloody slogging matches of old. It seeks a quick victory with minimal casualties on both sides. Its hallmarks are speed, maneuver, flexibility, and surprise. It is heavily reliant upon precision firepower, special forces, and psychological operations. And it strives to integrate naval, air, and land power into a seamless whole."[6] The problem is, as Antulio Echevarria points out, this is more accurately a "way of battle" and not a comprehensive approach to the role of armed force within the larger framework of strategy.[7] To develop a true way of war appropriate to the contemporary strategic environment, he contends, American political and military leaders must become better at translating battlefield success into favorable strategic outcomes. More on this later: the evolution of the American way of war has played out in the conflict with Iraq and thus is a major theme of this book.

America's conflict with Iraq has also demonstrated one of the enduring problems in American strategy: the difficulty the United States has in developing sound assumptions when the opponent operates within a different psychological and cultural framework. For a diverse nation, Americans are notoriously poor at truly understanding other cultures. In part this is due to the lack of the sort of imperial tradition that gives a nation like Great Britain a cadre of people who have studied and lived in other cultures for extended periods of time. It is also a reflection of Americans' deep confidence in their own weltanschauung and culture. This leads to the belief that everyone else in the world must have similar perceptions, values, priorities, and goals as Americans. The net result is psychological "mirror imaging," reflected most deeply in the belief that everyone wants an American-style government and economy, and the only reason they don't have them is because evil men control power and prevent it. At a more concrete level, this has led to a series of flawed assumptions as the United States crafted its strategy toward Iraq. First, the Reagan and George H. W. Bush administrations assumed that Iraq was exhausted from its long war with Iran and would focus all its energies on reconstruction, moderating its behavior to attract outside help in this endeavor. Second, the Bush administration assumed the Iraqi elite would overthrow Hussein after his military defeat in the Gulf War and thus did not make plans to use American military power to do it. Third, the Clinton administration assumed that sanctions, other pressure, and a bit of covert support to anti-regime groups would lead to Hussein's overthrow. Fourth, the GeorgeW. Bush administration assumed the threat from Iraq was growing and the costs of ameliorating it were escalating. Fifth, the Bush administration assumed the Iraqi people would, in general, welcome a new, American-engineered political order. Finally, the Bush administration assumed that those who resisted the new American-engineered political order in Iraq could be cowed into submission by military might. All of these flawed assumptions can be traced to the belief that Iraqis saw the world and thought much as Americans do. Thus the United States assumed that Iraqis would respond to events the way they would in similar circumstances.

America's conflict with Iraq also has taken place when interest in and attention to strategy were high. The number of individuals and government organizations devoted to assessing and developing strategy has grown tremendously in the past two decades, particularly within the Department of Defense. For much of American history, few people would label themselves "strategists." Now many do. In the U.S. Army, it is a formal designation for officers who have acquired what are considered the requisite skills. The process for developing American strategy has become more formal. Documents like the president's annual National Security Strategy, mandated by Congress, and the report of the Quadrennial Defense Review establish public benchmarks. Those without security clearances have a much clearer picture of American strategy than in the past.

Because of this, strategy has become an industry, mostly in Washington but also in academia, particularly the policy-focused graduate schools of Johns Hopkins, American University, George Washington, Georgetown, Princeton, Harvard, the University of Pittsburgh, and Tufts. Washington's K Street corridor, Capitol Hill, and the Northern Virginia suburbs are awash with think tanks and consulting firms specializing in national security strategy and defense issues, many staffed by former military officers or government officials, all offering unsolicited or government-contracted advice, some partisan, some nonpartisan. There are too many strategy conferences, workshops, and symposia to count. Endless strategy experts fill the space created by the proliferation of twenty-four-hour news media. Commercial and academic presses add their contributions. All told, this is truly a golden age of strategic discourse in the United States (if not of strategy itself).

America's conflict with Iraq has been central to this explosion of interest in strategy. It has taken place during a time of great flux as the United States adjusted to a post–Cold War world, sometimes easily, sometimes with great, stumbling difficulty. That made Iraq important. America desperately needed a strategic paradigm and, for better or worse, Saddam Hussein and, later, the Iraqi insurgents provided it. Iraq may or may not have been the "only game in town," but it was treated that way. A full assessment of how and why this happened yields many insights about the process of evolution in American strategy. These can help us understand the past and, hopefully, suggest ways that strategic analysts might help future policymakers avoid some of the mistakes made during the long conflict with Iraq. My objective is not to provide another rehash of America's battles with Iraq or even to offer new tidbits of information about them, but to place the conflict in its broader strategic context, to see it as part of the ongoing evolution of American strategy. The conflict with Iraq can be, in a sense, a looking glass providing a new perspective on the American "self," at least so far as it is manifested in national security strategy. Throughout the various stages of the conflict, what it *symbolized*—the lessons and warnings about the exercise of power in pursuit of security—and what Americans learned mattered as much as the actual outcome. This has been true from the very beginning, from America's first tentative encounter with a strange Arab country that it little understood during the tumult of the 1970s.

1

ASCENT OF AN ENEMY

Americans can always be counted on to do the right thing
. . . after they have exhausted all other possibilities.
—WINSTON CHURCHILL

How did Iraq, so far away and alien to Americans, come to shape U.S. strategy? Neither geography nor history drove Washington and Baghdad to confrontation. Economic, political, and strategic trends may have made *contact* between the United States and Iraq likely, but the *conflict* between them was not inevitable. Yet, Saddam Hussein's pathological ambitions, paranoia, and belief that only raw power matters in the world of politics; wider changes in the global economy and strategic environment; bad decisions; misperceptions; faulty communications; and misunderstandings propelled the two toward—depending on one's perspective—one long war that lasted from 1990 to 2003 or two short wars with a period of low-intensity conflict in between.

This is all of recent vintage. The competition for security partners has long been a major component of American strategy. By the 1970s the scope and intensity of this contest increased in Southwest Asia, reflecting that region's mounting strategic and economic significance. The United States, wounded by Vietnam but unwilling to diminish its global security commitments, developed a new policy that became known as the "Nixon doctrine."[1]

This stated that America would assist a state facing aggression that did not originate from either the Soviet Union or internal subversion but the threatened state itself must provide most of the manpower for its own defense.[2] In practice this led to developing, strengthening, and relying on local surrogates to promote regional security. Although the Nixon doctrine originated as a new approach to Southeast Asia designed to avoid another Vietnam, it was soon applied to other regions, including Southwest Asia. While the Soviet Union built ties with nationalistic and socialist regimes, the United States found conservative, often monarchical governments most receptive. Saudi Arabia and Iran—which had been one of the first battlegrounds in the effort to contain Soviet influence after World War II—became important American security partners in what became known as the "twin pillars" policy. By the end of the Nixon-Ford administration, Teheran was the linchpin of American strategy in the Gulf.[3] The relationship with the shah of Iran provided a number of benefits to the United States, including a buffer against radical states like Iraq, which was already a concern to the Nixon administration. "Though not strictly speaking a Soviet satellite," Kissinger later wrote, "once fully armed with Soviet weapons Iraq would serve Soviet purposes by intimidating pro-Western governments."[4]

■ ■ ■

In 1979 a religious movement fanatically hostile to the United States overthrew the Shah. For the United States, the loss of its primary ally in the Gulf was catastrophic, representing, in the words of President Jimmy Carter's national security adviser Zbigniew Brzezinski, "the Carter Administration's greatest setback."[5] This setback showed that America must be concerned not only with the external policy of its Middle East partners, but also their internal stability. This was difficult for the United States, which, unlike the British, did not have a traditional interest in the cultures and societies of the Islamic world or a large cadre of Arabists. To compensate, American policymakers sometimes relied on émigrés from the region. Émigrés were not always the most effective guides for strategy because they either skewed American policy toward their own interests or operated with outdated information. A second tendency growing from the absence of extensive regional experience and expertise was adoption of a policy based on political realism. Emerging in academia, largely through the influence of European émigrés such as the political scientist Hans Morgenthau, it focused strictly on the

external behavior of states as they used power in pursuit of national interests. It did not require an astute understanding of other cultures, social
structures, or domestic politics, leading to a persisting uncertainty concerning the most effective way to press strategic partners for reform, and vacilla-
tion as to whether such pressure was even wise. Influential policy advisers
such as Henry Kissinger and Zbigniew Brzezinski—both comfortable with
realism because of their European roots—brought it to the corridors of power.
But realism and the more traditional American approach based on idealism
and legalism never fully melded; at best they coexisted in an uneasy truce.

A few months later the Soviet military intervened in Afghanistan to
prop up a client regime. This ended any doubts that Moscow was on the
strategic offensive and willing to use force to further its interests. Americans
feared that the next Soviet move would be toward the oil-producing Gulf. In
short order the administration promulgated what became known as the
"Carter doctrine"—a statement by President Jimmy Carter that "any attempt
by any outside force to gain control of the Persian Gulf region will be re-
garded as an assault on the vital interests of the United States of America
and such assault will be repelled by any means necessary including military
force."[6] Whatever the coherence and even necessity of the Carter doctrine,
America had only limited means to enforce it. To give his new doctrine some
teeth, Carter directed the creation of a Rapid Deployment Joint Task Force
(RDJTF) composed of existing military forces earmarked for a Gulf contingency. The Department of Defense (DOD) and the State Department were
instructed to obtain bases in the Gulf region and expand American air and
sealift capabilities. But the RDJTF remained mostly a paper force for the
remainder of the Carter administration; America's capability to project military power to the Gulf remained limited due to a shortage of bases and to
the extensive range of other security commitments. As sometimes happens in
American strategy, there was a gap between stated objectives and the means
to attain them.

In the broad sense, there are two solutions to a gap between strategic ends and means: adjust the ends by diminished objectives and responsibilities, or increase the means available to attain ends. Partnerships offer
one of the most economical means of augmenting strategic means. Initially
Iraq did not appear to have much potential as a partner. While it had been
one of America's closest allies in the Arab world in the 1950s, Gene. Ab-dul
Karim Qassim, who seized power 1958, moved Baghdad away from
Washington and toward Moscow. The Ba'ath Party in Iraq had cultivated a

relationship with the Soviet Union from the time it assumed power for the second time in 1968, largely as a counterweight to the West, which it considered inextricably linked to its archenemy, Israel. In 1972 Iraq signed a Treaty of Friendship and Cooperation with Moscow that provided Baghdad with extensive technical assistance and arms supplies paid for with petroleum or bought on credit. Baghdad was "transforming itself into a geopolitical challenge and was on the way to becoming the principal Soviet ally in the area."[7]

As the Carter administration attempted to reinforce its position in the Gulf and limit Soviet influence, it lowered the standards applied to potential strategic partners. The idea emerged that weaning Iraq away from Moscow would weaken such Soviet influence and help compensate for the loss of the shah. Administration official began to see Saddam Hussein, who had emerged as Iraq's paramount leader in the late 1970s, as a proponent of regional stability—a despot, but a coldly realistic one disinclined toward Iranian-style ideological fervor.[8] Initially Carter was hesitant to translate this into concrete policy changes, in large part due to divisions and disagreements within the administration. Some senior officials, like Secretary of State Cyrus Vance, remained concerned about Hussein's grim human rights record and feared that closer relations would run counter to the broader policy of stressing human rights. Others believed that the incompatibility of interests that had led to Iraqi-U.S. hostility in the first place remained intact. Eventually, though, Brzezinski and those favoring improved ties began to win out, bolstered by the seizure of the American embassy in Iran by students acting with the implicit if not explicit approval of the regime of Shiite cleric Ruhollah Khomeini. Carter opened channels of communication with Baghdad, moving to increase diplomatic contacts. A modest strategic shift had begun.

Iraq's strategic blunders soon turned this trickle to a torrent. In September 1980, after months of increasingly tense relations between Baghdad and Teheran, Iraqi troops entered Iran seeking to redress old border disputes and, if possible, to topple the Khomeini regime, which it considered both weak and threatening (given Hussein's fear that Khomeini might inspire Iraq's repressed Shiite majority). Hussein appeared to believe that his incursion into Iran would follow the pattern of the Arab-Israeli wars: a military strike would lead to a cease-fire and negotiations, leaving him with at least part of what he wanted.[9] But Khomeini refused to play along and moved toward a strategy of total warfare, something Iraq, with a much smaller population and economy than Iran, could ill-afford. Hussein's invasion soon became one of the twentieth century's "worst strategic miscalculations."[10]

Hussein, increasingly desperate as Iran poured resources into the war effort, looked for help wherever he could find it. The Carter administration did not immediately tilt toward either of the warring states given the sensitive negotiations with Iran concerning the American hostages. Much of the public and Congress thought that neither Iran nor Iraq, one led by a strutting, bloodstained dictator and the other by a rabid, hate-filled mullah, appeared worthy of support. Reflecting this, the Carter administration initially sought only to limit the damage from the war, push for a cease-fire, and return the region to stability, taking a "hands-off" approach to the combatants and increasing assistance to the Arab Gulf states. As always, Saudi Arabia, worried Iran would strike it after crushing Iraq, was the central concern.[11]

■   ■   ■

When Ronald Reagan assumed the presidency in 1981, his administration, driven by a blanket desire to reject any and all Carter administration policies, was skeptical of any relationship with Iraq.[12] While Carter had attempted to isolate problems in the Middle East from the Cold War, the Reagan administration focused overwhelmingly on the threat of Soviet invasion or aggression by Soviet-based radical states in the region.[13] Reagan could not easily overlook Baghdad's relationship with Moscow. But as the tide of battle swung against Iraq, the administration grudgingly concluded that an Iranian victory would be "a strategic defeat for the West."[14] Secretary of State George Shultz later wrote, "If Iraq collapsed, that could not only intimidate but inundate our friends in the Gulf and be a strategic disaster for the United States."[15] This was not a long shot: Hussein, according to the U.S. intelligence community, had "essentially lost the war with Iran."[16]

Facing the prospect of an ascendant Iran, the Reagan administration began a limited shift from strict neutrality to support for Iraq.[17] To implement the tilt, President Reagan instructed the State Department to remove Iraq from its list of state sponsors of terrorism, opening the way for a variety of ties. While Great Britain and France were Iraq's major Western sources of armaments and the Arab Gulf states provided most financial assistance, the United States gave credits, important intelligence, technical advice, and dual-use items, some of which Hussein diverted to his chemical and biological weapons programs.[18] In 1984 the Reagan administration restored diplomatic relations with Iraq, making a number of positive comments about Hussein's growing moderation.[19] "There were no stars in my eyes or in Ronald Reagan's," Shultz wrote, "I simply thought we were better off with diplomatic relations with Iraq."[20]

As the war wound down, the Reagan administration and the U.S. business community were enticed by the economic opportunities that Iraq's postwar reconstruction seemed to offer and thus were willing to overlook Hussein grievous abuses of human rights (including his use of chemical weapons against Iran and his own Kurdish population). As Ambassador Peter Galbraith writes, "The Reagan Administration was willing to overlook Saddam Hussein's gas attacks on the Kurds because it continued to believe that the dictator's behavior might be moderated and that Iraq could become a strategic asset."[21] Clearly there was little sense in Washington that Iraq was a potential enemy. Reagan's National Security Strategy statement made no mention of it. "Iran's continuation and escalation of the Iran-Iraq War, including its attempts to intimidate non-belligerent Arab Gulf states," the strategy stated, "poses the most serious, immediate threat to our interests, and provides the Soviet Union the opportunity to advance its regional agenda."[22] An assessment of regional threats by the U.S. Central Command (CENTCOM)—formed during the Reagan administration as an outgrowth of the RDJTF—stated, "Iraq is not expected to use military force to attack Kuwait or Saudi Arabia to seize disputed territory or resolve a dispute over oil policy."[23]

The strategic and scholarly communities did not see things differently. For instance, Anthony Cordesman, one of the foremost analysts of Gulf security, did foresee the change of a threat to America's allies in the region from Iraq, but only if radicals in Iraq hijacked the "trend toward political maturity and friendly relations with the Southern Gulf states" that Saddam Hussein and the Ba'ath Party had undertaken.[24] Adeed I. Dawisha, writing in the influential journal *Foreign Policy*, went so far as to argue that the stalemate between Iraq and Iran was a "fortuitous Western gain" because it stifled Hussein's attempts to become the leader of the Arab world and thus "could accelerate Iraq's Western trend." Dawisha stated, "Iraq's national interests are currently running parallel with those of the West in many areas."[25] Daniel Pipes and Laurie Mylroie, who later became two of the most vehement critics of Saddam Hussein, wrote in 1987 that "the Iranian revolution and seven years of bloody and inconclusive warfare have changed Iraq's view of its Arab neighbors, the United States, and even Israel . . . Iraq is now the *de facto* protector of the regional status quo."[26] Frederick Axelgard of the Center for Strategic and International Studies advocated moving toward a "more open dialogue" with Iraq, including discussion of a "limited, U.S.-Iraqi cooperation to maintain a strategic balance in the Gulf."[27] Axelgard contended that war fatigue would obligate the Iraqi leadership to concentrate on domestic, social, and economic programs once its war with Iran was over. Closer ties with the United States would encourage this "positive metamorphosis."[28] Edmund Ghareeb argued, "Iraq will have a strong interest in maintaining good and close relations with the Arab states of the Gulf, and it is unlikely that Baghdad would jeopardize the better ties it has found with its Arab neighbors by reverting to earlier, aggressive policies."[29] Robert H. Johnson, in a thirty-eight-page article on U.S. strategy in the Gulf, mentioned the threat of Iraqi aggression only in passing, noting that Iraq is a "traditional adversary" of Saudi Arabia—the only oil supplier truly vital to the United States—"but the Iraqi threat is limited by a combination of difficult geography and potential threats to Iraq from Iran, Syria, and the Kurds which preoccupy the Iraqis and tie down their forces."[30]

Within the Reagan administration, Assistant Secretary of Defense Richard Perle warned of Baghdad's continuing relationship with the Soviet Union and the threat its chemical and biological weapons programs posed to Israel, but this too ran counter to the administration's desire to use Iraq as a bulwark against Iran.[31] Toward the end of the Reagan administration, Zalmay Khalilizad, then on the State Department's Policy Planning Staff and later U.S. ambassador to Iraq, argued that the tilt toward Iraq during its war with Iran made sense but that Hussein's quest for regional hegemony remained intact, thus indicating that the United States should return to a policy of containment following the conflict. Again, senior policymakers, including Secretary of State George Shultz, rejected this idea.[32]

■ ■ ■

George H. W. Bush assumed the presidency during a time of historic change in the global security environment. The collapse of the Soviet empire was the precipitant. Among the many repercussions was an undercutting of the foundation of American national security and military strategy, depriving it of a paradigm. Everything the United States had prepared for was gone. This forced deep debate, revision, and introspection designed to stave off astrategic meandering and to find meaning and focus in the complex new global security environment. While the Cold War had ended, its psychological impact lingered. After decades of thinking of strategy through the lens of the Cold War, American policymakers and military leaders could not reinvent themselves overnight. As they struggled to understand the new security environment in which they found themselves, these leaders sought answers to four vital strategic questions: what is the appropriate American role in the world? Why and when should American military power be used? How should American military power be used? What is the appropriate size and configuration of the U.S. military?

The Bush administration (along with most of Congress and the American public) believed that even in the absence of the Soviet Union, the United States should remain actively engaged in the world, engineering or preserving stability. America was "a pivotal factor for peaceful change."[33] The president talked of a "new world order" with the United States as the only superpower, but one committed to democracy, human rights, and open economies. The goal, according to Bush, was a world "where diverse nations are drawn together in common cause to achieve the universal aspirations of mankind—peace and security, freedom, and the rule of law."[34] Freed from the Cold War stalemate, the president and his advisers thought, the United Nations could assume the role it was designed for and maintain the peace, particularly in regions with limited American interest. "The cold war is now drawing to a close," Bush said, "and after four decades of division and discord, our challenge today is to fulfill the great dream of all democracies: a true commonwealth of free nations."[35]

The "new world order," then, was one where the United States assumed a role as the world's preeminent power, was willing to use military power in regions of the world where it previously had not, would act to prevent aggression and preserve the balance of power, and would work in concert with both traditional and new partners, including the Soviet Union. But the intent was never to rely solely on international cooperation or the United Nations to manage conflict between states. During the Cold War, American power was used to *prevent* the rise of new problems such as the spread of communism and Soviet power. Now the idea was emerging that American power could be used to *promote* things, including U.S. influence and other values such as the promotion of human rights. But the question of whether a military configured to prevent things would be equally adept at promoting things remained open.

While the Bush administration was approaching agreement on *why* force might be used, the issue of *how* to use it remained. During the Cold

War, the primary task of the U.S. military was to prevent the expansion of communism by force. To do this, U.S. defense leaders developed an array of strategic concepts designed to block the Soviets and do so within a strategic culture that subjected the employment of armed force to public and congressional scrutiny and, in Marxist terms, sought to substitute capital for labor, using technology, qualitative superiority, and money to minimize American casualties. These included:

- Alliances and security commitments;
- Forward-deployed military forces to signal commitment to allies and defend them if necessary;
- The ability to augment forward-deployed forces through rapid, long-distance reinforcement and the mobilization of large reserve component forces;
- Air and naval superiority;
- Interoperability with allied forces;
- Extended nuclear deterrence;
- Reliance on qualitative superiority in equipment, technology, training, and doctrine to compensate for quantitative inferiority;
- Cultivation of clients or proxies in areas of less-than-vital concern, especially through security assistance;
- Counterinsurgency support to friendly regimes (and eventually support to insurgents attempting to overthrow unfriendly regimes);
- Limited use of the active component of the U.S. military in non-warfighting missions.

By 1990 the ongoing demise of the Soviet Union forced the United States to review the basic precepts of its strategy. The initial tendency was to err on the conservative side: President Bush and his key advisers remained wary of Moscow's intentions and capabilities, particularly its strategic nuclear weapons and large army. As Moscow's downward spiral continued, the administration concluded, "The enemy we face is less an expansionistic communism than it is instability itself."[36] "No communist hordes threaten western Europe today and, by extension the rest of the free word," Gen. Colin Powell, chairman of the Joint Chiefs of Staff, wrote. "So our new strategy emphasizes being able to deal with individual crises without their escalating to global or thermonuclear war."[37] The "new world order," in other words, was one where security problems were no longer inextricably linked to the global conflict between the ideological blocs.

In strategy, one must both forge the sword and decide how, when, and to what end it should be used. Sometimes this process is sequential: leaders and decide what they want to do with a military force then build one to accomplish these goals. Hitler's rebuilding of German military power in the 1930s and, earlier, the reconstruction of the Prussian Army after being crushed by Napoleon at Jena and Auerstädt are examples. More often—particularly for the United States—strategic concepts and force generation are simultaneous. Existing or anticipated enemies shape the military. What this means is that the American military in place at any given time is not always perfectly configured for the threats that emerged and for the missions assigned to it by political leaders.

Luckily, the Bush administration inherited a military that had undergone an extensive, nearly miraculous renaissance in the years after Vietnam. This task had been particularly pressing for the Army—the service most damaged and tainted by Vietnam. As an official U.S. Army history noted, "The American Army emerged from Vietnam cloaked in anguish. In the early seventies it was an institution fighting merely to maintain its existence in the midst of growing apathy, decay, and intolerance."[38] By 1990 military leaders had significantly increased the quality of troops entering the all-volunteer force. In its early days, it almost reflected eighteenth-century armies, which tended to attract recruits who had few other career options or who needed to flee from some sort of personal failure or misdeed. Eventually, the military learned how to function in a competitive labor market. Using a variety of incentives and savvy advertising, it was able to attract a high-quality recruit pool. Among both enlisted troops and officers, morale and a sense of honor and purpose were resuscitated. The 1983 military intervention in Grenada, while not without problems, showed that political inhibitions on the use of force were eroding and that the military was on the path toward renewed effectiveness.

Despite the rejuvenation of the military, unease with the use of armed force lingered among both Congress and the American public. Thinking in the Bush administration largely followed what was known as the "Weinberger principles." In a November 1984 speech at the National Press Club, Reagan's secretary of defense Caspar Weinberger contended that any use of military power must pass six tests: the vital national interests of the United States or its allies must be at stake; the United States must be committed to winning; there should be clearly defined political and military objectives; the relationship between the objectives and the forces committed must be continually reassessed and adjusted if necessary; there must be a reasonable assurance of support from Congress and the American public; and the commitment of U.S. forces to combat must be a last resort.[39] The most powerful advocate for this type of approach within the Bush administration was Colin Powell, who had been Weinberger's military assistant in 1984.

The military rejuvenation had come through increased defense budgets, new weapons systems, and new operational concepts, as well as through a renewed emphasis on conventional, state-on-state warfighting. Within the military the idea had arisen that while involvement in the "low-intensity conflict"—counterinsurgency, peacekeeping, counterterrorism, and support to insurgency—was necessary, it could be corrosive to the military and its relationship with the American people. The military would undertake low-intensity conflict when ordered to, but preferred to prepare for and focus on the less politically complex and ambiguous conventional, large-scale combat. Phrased differently, the military developed a "conventional mind-set." This had multiple effects that were only beginning to emerge at the end of the Cold War, including a personnel system where a concentration on conventional warfighting was the surest path to senior rank, a massive investment in advanced technology designed to defeat an opposing state military, and the first emergence of the idea that airpower had superseded land power as the most decisive component of armed conflict. All that was missing was a chance to demonstrate what the United States could do in pursuit of the new world order.

President Bush was not a conceptual thinker; he was a pragmatic problem solver. His extensive career in government was characterized not by major program changes or policy initiatives, but by "competent, day-to-day management."[40] He surrounded himself with similar people at the senior level, including National Security Adviser Brent Scowcroft, Secretary of State James Baker, and Secretary of Defense Dick Cheney. Even the concept of a "new world order" was more of a slogan than a strategic concept. It was never intended to be a rigorous concept or to define American policy. Bush, like Nixon, was a realist who believed in preserving the balance of power between states as they maneuvered in pursuit of their national interests. It is thus difficult to glean the logic and conceptual foundation of the Bush strategy—even a careful reading of the 561-page memoir written by Bush and

Scowcroft yields little but descriptions of a multitude of meetings, personal relationships, and specific problems, some resolved, some not. This absence of a conceptual framework amplified the deleterious effects of crafting strategy without a paradigm. For those who developed the Bush military strategy, this was a blessing in disguise. They often did not have firm and clear strategic guidance, but only a general approach to the world. When grand strategy is partially strategic, partially astrategic, there are limits to the coherence of military strategy.

■ ■ ■

In 1989 and the first half of 1990, dramatic events in the Soviet Union and Eastern Europe overshadowed the Middle East. Still, Southwest Asia remained a vital concern for the Bush administration, just as it had for the previous administrations. This was understandable since the strategic significance of the region was not determined by political events or the actions of external players such as the Soviet Union but by economics. In October 1989 the Bush administration's National Security Directive (NSD) 26 stated, "Access to Persian Gulf oil and the security of key friendly states in the area are vital to U.S. national security. The United States remains committed to defend its vital interests in the region, if necessary and appropriate through the use of U.S. military force, against the Soviet Union or any other regional power with interests inimical to our own."[41] The goal was to move from an alliance of convenience to long-term accommodation, continuing the "twin pillars" security policy through close ties with Saudi Arabia, but replacing the crumbled Iranian pillar with Iraq.[42] The thinking was that Iraq, exhausted by its war with Iran, would continue moderating its policies in order to gain access to debt relief and reconstruction assistance from the Arab Gulf states and the West.[43] The Bush National Security Strategy, while not explicitly describing the goal of normalizing relations with Iraq, noted only that threats to U.S. interests in the Gulf "come from a variety of sources" but did not mention Iraq as one of them.[44]

In hindsight, it is clear that both the Bush administration and the wider strategic community misread what now seem obvious indications that Hussein was becoming a threat. While there are multiple reasons for this, it reflected a misunderstanding of both his pathological personality—psychological "mirror imaging," which assumes that the priorities and likely responses of others are the same as one's own—and his system for retaining power, which relied on a bloated military and security services kept loyal by patronage. Iraq's massive war debt threatened his ability to sustain the patronage system and meant that there was no way to provide employment for demobilized soldiers, thus making them a potential threat to the regime. Hussein thus felt compelled to sustain a large military and security services, and needed the funds to maintain them. Americans, looking at Hussein's personality rather than the system that sustained his power, missed this.

While underestimating Hussein's desperation, the Bush administration overestimated its own ability to control him via diplomacy and the involvement of U.S. corporations in Iraq's reconstruction. It accepted the idea—espoused by the analytical and business communities as well as government officials—that Iraq's exhaustion made it malleable, despite Hussein's continuing, even escalating attempts to acquire chemical, biological, and nuclear weapons and ballistic missiles. Everyone knew that the grim human rights situation in Iraq showed little improvement. Hussein continued to bully and rail against the Arab Gulf states, which held extensive Iraqi debt, mostly incurred during the war with Iran. Iraq needed an estimated $30 billion to repair damage from the war, and $5 billion of the country's $14 billion annual income went to servicing debts.[45] To encourage or coerce Kuwait into debt relief, Hussein became increasingly belligerent on the long-standing border dispute between the two countries. "In early 1990," wrote Brent Scowcroft, "it gradually became apparent to me that Saddam had made an abrupt change in his policy toward the United States. The relative moderation he had adopted earlier, perhaps mostly to curry favor with us, was abandoned."[46]

By the summer of 1990 the situation approached the point of crisis. In July, Hussein's intimidation of the Arab Gulf states reached a new level of intensity. He accused Kuwait and the United Arab Emirates of overproducing oil and driving prices down, and Kuwait of stealing Iraqi oil from the Rumayla oil field, which straddled the border between the two nations. Iraqi foreign minister Tariq Aziz sent an angry letter to the Arab League, slamming Kuwait's unwillingness to resolve ongoing territorial and financial disputes in a satisfactory way for Iraq. At the same time, Hussein, in his annual speech on the Ba'ath Party's Revolutionary Day, attacked unnamed states for stabbing Iraq in the back. All listeners understood that he meant the Arab Gulf states, particularly Kuwait.

In mid-July, both the Defense Intelligence Agency and the Central Intelligence Agency (CIA) warned that Hussein was concentrating troops on Iraq's border with Kuwait.[47] By the beginning of August, eight Iraqi divisions—around 100,000 troops—were deployed.[48] This included elite Republican Guard units, some of the best in the Iraqi army. American policymakers, though, did not know what to make of this. Swayed by Arab leaders such as Hosni Mubarak of Egypt, King Hussein of Jordan, and King Fahd of Saudi Arabia, who advised that Saddam Hussein would never invade Kuwait, the Bush administration waited.[49]

Unfortunately, the Bush policy toward Iraq was, in Bob Woodward's words, "muddled," combining tough talk on some issues with blocking congressional efforts to impose sanctions or cut U.S. assistance.[50] A meeting between Hussein and U.S. ambassador April Glaspie attempted to defuse the situation but, by erring on the side of conciliation, misled Hussein into believing that he had American approval. Tragically, he did not understand Americans any better than Americans understood him. In his brutal world, politics was not a process of compromise and cooperation leading to mutual benefit, but a Hobbesian struggle where the powerful ruled and the weak lost. Hussein and American officials did not speak the same language, and no effective translator stepped into this void.

On August 2, 1990, Iraqi forces invaded Kuwait. They quickly routed the small, unprepared Kuwaiti military and occupied the country. After briefly installing and then dissolving a puppet government in Kuwait, Hussein attached part of it to Basra Province and declared the rest to be Iraq's nineteenth province. He also threatened missile attacks against Israel and Saudi Arabia if challenged.[51] The United States had a strategic paradigm. The question was what to do with it.

2

THE TEST OF BATTLE

Beautiful that war and all its deeds of carnage
must in time be utterly lost.
—WALT WHITMAN
"RECONCILIATION"

T he United States began its long conflict with Iraq with a strategy, a
military force structure, operational concepts, technology, equipment,
perceptions, and a mind-set forged by the Cold War. The immediate
challenge was finding which of these could be adapted to the Gulf and which
were obsolete. Whenever American leaders become innovative in the face
of new challenges, they do so within the confines of strategic culture and
tradition. This defines the possible while revealing and sometimes ruling
out alternatives. For instance, the United States is a democracy where the
public influences national security policy (indirectly if not directly). Even
when polls do not directly shape strategic decisions, public opinion—often
expressed through Congress—looms in the background, influencing decisions. This is not the only source of connection between the public and
strategy. The U.S. military has deep roots in the community through the
important role of Reserve forces and the tradition of citizen soldiers. Traditionally the American military is "America's military"—something not always
true in other countries where the armed forces are seen as separate from,

even alien to, society. This means that sustaining public and congressional support for any use of force is vital.

Moral clarity eases this task. The American strategic culture has a powerful crusading element: the public tends to see the world in ethical categories. Actions are either right or wrong. Despite the brief Kissingerian foray into passionless realpolitik, the public and its elected representatives are likely to support the use of force when they are convinced the United States is on the side of right. Reversing the aggression of an evil regime or movement fulfills this condition and thus is the preferred American mode of war. Unfortunately, moral clarity is rare in statecraft and national security affairs, leaving America constrained, even hobbled. Even in conflicts with moral clarity, the American strategic culture is imbued with an essentially defensive view of military power. Armed action is to prevent an enemy from forcibly altering the power balance, not to reengineer a power balance or redesign an existing regional security configuration or its constituent political systems. This idea assumed even greater importance during the Cold War when conflict had the potential to escalate to superpower confrontation and nuclear war. The defensive approach to military force was no longer a preference, but a survival mechanism. "Limited war" entered the American strategic lexicon and became part of the nation's military strategy. U.S. grand strategy, derived from George Kennan's initial conceptualization of the Soviet threat, assumed that communism's inherent weaknesses would destroy it if it could not expand. The West did not need to destroy communism militarily, only contain it. Liberating Soviet-controlled regions through force—"roll back"—was discussed, even advocated, but never gained traction among American leaders or the public. In nearly all war games and war plans, whether for Europe, Korea, or other regions of conflict, the outcome was the restoration of the *status quo ante bellum.* As the Department of Defense described U.S. military strategy:

> The US purpose is to prepare for war so well that aggression is successfully deterred. If deterrence fails, US strategy seeks to secure all US and allies interests and to deny the aggressor any of his war aims. The United States would seek to terminate any war at the earliest practical time and to restore peace on terms favorable to the United States and its allies.[1]

The phrase "earliest practical time" is telling. While official statements did not specify what determined the "earliest practical time," the implication was that it was determined by conditions on the battlefield. Wars ended with an enemy's armed forces could no longer resist, not when the conditions that spawned aggression were altered.

The support of partners and allies during a military operation also helps sustain public and congressional support. Partners allow the United States to promote security around the world without bankrupting itself and reassure Americans that they are on the side of right. This is America's deep democratic instinct at play—widespread support confirms that a policy is sound. The United States is an unconfident superpower. Thus the larger a coalition backing U.S. actions, the more confident Americans feel. Even partners with little or no military capability—Antigua and Barbuda, Barbados, Dominica, Jamaica, St. Lucia, and St. Vincent in the 1983 intervention in Grenada, for instance—validate American decisions. The fact that only a few other states provided significant military forces to support South Vietnam contributed to the erosion of American confidence. U.S. military strategy is designed to sustain public and congressional backing for the use of force. American casualties, civilian deaths, and protracted conflict can erode public support for a military operation. The military thus seeks to avoid these things.

■ ■ ■

As the Bush administration scrambled to respond to Iraq's invasion of Kuwait in the summer of 1990, the pieces were falling into place for the use of force. There was moral clarity and a growing group of allies. The fact that the conflict entailed external aggression rather than internal war avoided the sticky question of deciding whether the Kuwaiti regime deserved support. Had the specter of Vietnam not hovered over every American decision concerning military force, the Bush administration probably would not have debated how to respond. Ultimately, though, the sheer stakes of the conflict forced the administration into action. Even if Washington's more extreme concerns—that Iraq would deny oil to the United States or engineer massive petroleum price increases if allowed to occupy Kuwait permanently—were unlikely, Hussein's actions challenged the most basic strategic goals of the Bush administration. It upset the balance of power in a vital region, undercutting a decade of American efforts to restore stability after the Iranian revolution.

Since the horrors of World War I, Americans had believed that collective security based on cooperative action by the major powers was possible and desirable. The inability of the League of Nations to prevent World War II and the paralysis of the United Nations during the Cold War were seen as context-specific anomalies rather than evidence that the concept of collective security itself was flawed. The collapse of the Soviet Union changed that. As Bush stated in an address to Congress, "The crisis in the Persian Gulf, as grave as it is, also offers a rare opportunity to move toward an historic period of cooperation. Out of these troubled times . . . a new world order can emerge: a new era freer from the threat of terror, stronger in pursuit of justice, and more secure in the quest for peace."[2] The invasion was, the president said, "the first assault on the new world that we seek, the first test of our mettle." With such lofty ambitions forming the backdrop, the Soviet Union, the United Nations, the Arab League, and the European Economic Community quickly condemned the invasion, assuring that the United States had international support.

The Bush administration was also aware that vigorous action would reassure partners and potential partners of America's resolve, something questioned after the failures in Vietnam and Iran. It was particularly important to convince the cautious Saudis that the United States would stand by them. The Bush administration, then, saw "nested" objectives. The immediate goal was preventing Saddam Hussein from controlling more of the world's oil than he did. The broader goals were to renew America's domestic confidence and international influence, and to use these to establish precedents that could contribute to a new world order more amenable to U.S. national interests.

Saddam Hussein made the use of force viable because of his inability to read the Bush administration or the American public. He did not understand that Iraq's historical claim to Kuwait—which mattered in the Arab world with its intense sensitivity to historical grievances and injustices—meant little to the United States. For Americans, historical claims to territory have a short lifespan (given that a sizable portion of the United States was taken by force from someone) and armed force is not a legitimate means to redress even legitimate claims. Hussein, by contrast, emerged from a culture and political system in which brutality and intimidation were effective tools. He had not learned—as Stalin eventually did and Hitler did not—that the United States is difficult to intimidate and must be managed in other ways, often with more carrots than sticks. By invading a small neighbor and then brutalizing it, Hussein stripped the conflict of any moral ambiguity that he might have used to blunt the American response. Still, it was not immediately clear exactly what the Bush administration's response would be. The questions of *what* to do and *how* to do it remained unanswered.

■   ■   ■

Neither the Bush administration nor the national security bureaucracy had given the conventional threat from Iraq much thought. "The Persian Gulf," Bush and Scowcroft later wrote, "had not been among our major concerns early in the administration."[3] When a new threat emerges, policymakers normally search for a historical analogy that can be used to craft understanding, develop strategy, and explain the issue to the public and its elected representatives. But, in the late summer of 1990, there was not a perfect analogy for Saddam Hussein. No "X" article explained Baghdad's behavior and galvanized official thinking. The Hitler analogy was bandied about—President Bush even used it—but this was as much to stir passion as for accuracy. Hussein might approach Hitler's level of personal evil, but Iraq was no Germany in terms of national power. Stalin might have been an equally good comparison—at least in terms of brutality, paranoia, ruthlessness, intolerance, and territorial ambitions—but it did not have the same emotive impact among Americans as the Hitler one. In any case, Iraq was no Soviet Union. American leaders had mobilized public support for opposition to Hitler and Stalin because both despots posed a threat to the fundamental American value of freedom. It was hard to make a case that a strutting Arab tyrant seizing a medieval sheikhdom was a threat to freedom.

Historical analogies also shaped the debate over precisely what the appropriate American response was. In simple terms, the Bush administration, Congress, and the public had to decide which historical "lesson" applied. Was it the Hitler "lesson," which implied that if not checked early, aggression by evil dictators becomes worse and more dangerous? Or was it the Vietnam "lesson," which suggested that American involvement in complex Asian struggles and strange cultures can easily become quagmires, eroding U.S. confidence and influence? This was an extraordinarily important choice. The Hitler lesson led to a renewed confidence and activism, the Vietnam lesson to a continued lack of confidence, perhaps even disengagement. But the utility of American military power was depending on exorcising the ghosts of Vietnam. Reagan's 1983 intervention in Grenada and Bush's

1989 restoration of democracy in Panama had helped. They had not, however, fully erased the memories of Vietnam. The standards for using force
remained high as illustrated by the Weinberger and Powell "principles."
President Bush knew this. He believed that a major military failure could
revive the Vietnam syndrome, further hobbling American security policy.
As he contemplated action against Iraq, Bush was driven by the desire to
avoid repeating the mistakes of Vietnam, at least the military ones.[4]

The armed forces were ready if called on. Reversing a successful, large-
scale, cross-border invasion in a faraway land is challenging, but American
military leaders had examined every nuance of it at one time or another.
For decades the American military had refined ways to mobilize and deploy
forces to Europe in order to join with those already there in deterring or
reversing Warsaw Pact aggression. Annual exercises tested the plans and
provided military leaders with valuable experience. Much of the U.S. military's
doctrine was designed for precisely this sort of task. American military leaders believed that a war to expel Iraq from Kuwait would look much more like
an envisioned NATO campaign to blunt Warsaw Pact aggression than it would
the Iran-Iraq War with its protracted, grinding attrition.

When Iraqi forces first began massing on the Kuwaiti border, Colin
Powell had instructed U.S. Army Gen. Norman Schwarzkopf, the commander
of U.S. Central Command, to begin developing military options to deter or
counter an Iraqi incursion even before the president had opted to use force.
The pace and intensity of military planning increased dramatically after the
Iraqi forces invaded Kuwait. Just as the administration did not start with a
blank sheet of paper when facing the crisis but, instead, looked for and
adapted analogies, CENTCOM began with the most relevant existing plan—
Operations Plan (OPLAN) 90–1002 for defending Saudi Arabia against external aggression.[5] Modeled on plans for defending West Germany from the
Warsaw Pact, this was a typical OPLAN that assumed the United States was
in a defensive role. It was divided into three phases: deter, defend, and then
seize the initiative.

Using an existing plan sped the process, but 90–1002 had a significant shortcoming: like most plans developed with the Soviets in mind, it
assumed that the United States would have at least twenty-one days of warning to prepare and deploy forces before the onset of hostilities. Iraq's invasion of Kuwait had caught the United States unprepared. Thus the revised
plan had to pay significant attention to mobilization and deployment. Transportation and logistics would be crucial and challenging. In the primary

theaters of American military strategy during the Cold War—Europe and Korea—the United States had forces, equipment, and supplies in place. If an invasion occurred, units already deployed would hold the line until reinforcements arrived. But the United States did not have significant forward-deployed forces or prepositioned equipment and supplies in the Gulf. Luckily, though, Washington had provided Saudi Arabia with extensive air bases, port facilities, and bunkers during the 1980s. "Knowing that with their tiny population they would never be able to defend their riches against greedy neighbors," John Keegan wrote, "the Saudis created the best military infrastructure money could buy."[6] They were about to reap the return on this investment.

While the military wheels turned, the president and his top advisers struggled to place the intervention in a broader strategic context. What did it mean for wider U.S. national interests? What were the long-term and second-order effects of various actions or the absence of action? What conclusions would friends, enemies, and potential friends and enemies derive from America's actions? Clarity came quickly. After only a few days, Bush, steeled by a meeting with British prime minister Margaret Thatcher during which she compared Hussein's actions to Hitler's aggression of the 1930s, concluded that the invasion was intolerable. The debate over whether Iraq should be treated as Nazi Germany or Vietnam tipped toward the former. "This will not stand. This will not stand, this aggression against Kuwait," President Bush told reporters on August 5, 1990.[7] The question was precisely how to keep it from standing. The options were limited, particularly military ones. Schwarzkopf briefed the president on August 4: "While we could do nothing to stop the invasion . . . we could make certain moves with our air and sea power to demonstrate U.S. determination and, if necessary, punish Iraq."[8] But the president's mind seemed made up. He had become "the biggest hawk in Washington."[9]

In ensuing weeks, two possibilities emerged: use military power in a strictly defensive mode to keep the Iraqi military where it was or forcibly expel the Iraqis from Kuwait. President Bush did not immediately opt for military liberation, hoping political and economic pressure would compel Hussein to back down. But the initial concern was Saudi Arabia. The CIA warned that armed intervention in Saudi Arabia was imminent, and if it occurred, Iraqi forces could be in Riyadh in three days.[10] According to the U.S. Department of Defense's official history of the Gulf War, such an invasion was "deemed possible both by the United States and Saudi Arabia."[11]

President Bush himself later wrote, "It seemed incontrovertible that Hussein planned to invade Saudi Arabia."[12] Control of even the northern oil fields of Saudi Arabia would give Hussein a stranglehold over the world's petroleum supply and thus pose a dire risk to not only the United States, but the rest of the world as well. With all this in mind, Bush committed the American military to the defense of the Saudi kingdom.

Immediately after the invasion, Bush had frozen all Kuwaiti assets in the United States to prevent Hussein from gaining control of them, implemented other sanctions, and sought action from the United Nations. "While I was prepared to deal with this crisis unilaterally if necessary," Bush later wrote, "I wanted the United Nations involved as part of our first response, starting with a strong condemnation of Iraq's attack on a fellow member. Decisive UN action would be important in rallying international opposition to the invasion and reversing it."[13] As he told Congress, "We're now in sight of a United Nations that performs as envisioned by its founders."[14] No longer paralyzed by an intransigent Soviet Union, the United Nations did act. Security Council Resolution 660 condemned the invasion and demanded withdrawal; four days later Security Council Resolution 661 invoked economic sanctions against Iraq.

In the administration policy debates, Vietnam hovered in the background even if unmentioned. Colin Powell, at meeting of the National Security Council, raised the question of public support for the liberation of Kuwait.[15] "We can't make a case for losing lives for Kuwait," Powell argued, "but Saudi Arabia is different."[16] The president saw things differently. Events would show that Bush's reading of the American public and Congress was more accurate than Powell's. The moral clarity of the crisis did not hinge on whether the Kuwaiti regime was worthy of support but on the brazen nature of Iraqi aggression. Had Saddam Hussein been clever enough to de-velop a fifth column of Iraqi sympathizers in Kuwait and then intervene to protect them, the morale clarity would have been eroded, perhaps enough to cause the United States to hesitate, perhaps even to tolerate the intervention.

■   ■   ■

On August 4, Schwarzkopf advised the National Security Council (NSC) that it would take nearly three months to deploy all of the forces needed to defend Saudi Arabia and up to twelve months before enough troops were in place to expel the Iraqis from Kuwait should the president decide on offensive action.[17] This was not good news. Much could happen during that time: the Iraqis would strengthen their defensive positions, the will of the world community might temper, or the anger of the American public and Congress might subside, weakening support for the tough policy Bush wanted to pursue. There was a more immediate problem: both the defensive and offensive military options required access to Saudi airfields and harbors. The regime in Riyadh had a nearly pathological mistrust of outsiders and had not yet offered access despite what had happened to its fellow monarch in Kuwait. The NSC considered using only long-range and sea-based airpower, but this had both military and political shortcomings. There was no precedent for airpower alone reversing an attack by major armored forces, and as Scowcroft pointed out, such an approach would cause the Saudis to question American seriousness. "Ground forces," he noted, "are the best symbol of our commitment. . . ."[18] General Powell made a similar argument to the president.[19] The problem was convincing the Saudis of the danger they were in, the need for an American presence on the ground, and U.S. determination to support them. On August 6, following a briefing to the Saudi leadership by Secretary of Defense Cheney, King Fahd agreed to allow U.S. ground and air forces into the kingdom. This was a monumental step for the Saudis and solved at least one of Schwarzkopf's most pressing dilemmas.

CENTCOM began to deploy combat forces on August 7 in what it called Operation Desert Shield. The first major units to arrive on Saudi territory were U.S. Air Force planes and a brigade of the Army's 82d Airborne Division. The U.S. Navy sent the aircraft carriers USS *Independence* and USS *Dwight D. Eisenhower* to the Gulf. As the Saudi army established a thin defensive barrier along the border with Kuwait, initial U.S. ground units secured facilities needed for further deployments, particularly ports and airfields such as Al-Jubayl and the Dhahran complex. The American buildup continued at a breakneck pace throughout August. On August 11, B-52 heavy bombers arrived at the Indian Ocean island of Diego Garcia, giving them a shorter run to strike Iraqi targets in Kuwait or Saudi Arabia than if they had to fly directly from bases in the United States. Several days later, the 101st Airborne Division (Air Assault) began deployment and the 7th Marine Expeditionary Brigade (MEB) arrived. Day by day, the American force became more capable of withstanding an assault. Each new unit helped but only with the September arrival of the U.S. Army's 24th Infantry Division (Mechanized) equipped with the state-of-the-art M1A1 Abrams tanks, along with additional

Marine and Air Force units, did Powell feel that the United States had adequate military forces in Saudi Arabia to defeat an Iraqi thrust.[20] In October, Schwarzkopf advised Powell and Cheney that he could successfully defend Saudi Arabia if the Iraqis invaded. The window of vulnerability was closed.

The failure of Iraq to enter Saudi Arabia in August and September when the opportunity was there suggests this was never Hussein's intention. As Michael Palmer notes, he was not inclined to boldness in strategy, preferring what he considered low-risk options (even though he was often wrong in his assessment of risk).[21] Most likely, Hussein concluded that any political, economic, and military pressure arising from his seizure of Kuwait would be tolerable since that nation was, in Bob Woodward's words, "small, unpopular, and an afterthought in the region."[22] But he understood that Saudi Arabia was different. There he had no historical claim to cloak his aggression. And, he probably thought, the Americans might accept his seizure of Kuwait but were less likely to remain passive if America's Saudi allies were threatened.

Saddam Hussein planned a reprise of his war with Iran, not understanding that the enemy was different this time. His army constructed two major defensive belts in Kuwait plus fortifications and obstacles along the coast, expecting that the Americans would assault these head-on. The defensive belts would trap them in "kill zones" where they could be destroyed with artillery.[23] Hussein's strategy was similar to that of the Japanese in the opening months of World War II: seize territory quickly through surprise strikes, then dig in, and make recapture so costly that the United States—seen as averse to casualties—would negotiate a settlement. That was exactly what Iraq had attempted in its war with Iran. As Michael Gordon and Bernard Trainor noted, "Iraqi commanders intended to fight the same type of war they waged against Iran, a grinding battle of attrition with high casualties on both sides that would nullify the American hopes to win a quick victory with high-technology weapons."[24] An astute strategist might have pointed out to them that this hadn't worked when the Japanese tried it. Both the Japanese and the Iraqis underestimated American will, assuming that a democracy did not have the stomach for a tough war. Hussein also failed to grasp the ability of the American military to avoid casualties. But at least Hussein did not, like the Japanese, overextend while flush with initial victories. His mistakes were equally deep and deadly, but they were of a different nature.

■ ■ ■

By October, President Bush had reached a point of decision. Saudi Arabia was safe, but diplomatic efforts by the United States, Arab nations, the United Nations, and European states (including Russia) had failed to sway Hussein.[25] Bush was increasingly skeptical that sanctions and diplomacy would work, and had become convinced that military power was the only effective tool or, at least, the only one that Hussein understood. But General Powell advised the president that offensive action would require more troops. By that point Hussein had twenty-seven divisions, including all eight of the elite Republican Guard formation, in or near Kuwait. Bush authorized another deployment of an additional 200,000 troops. In Powell's mind, that was enough to liberate Kuwait.[26]

Meanwhile, CENTCOM continued to refine its war plan. Planning a complex military operation is always arduous. This one was made all the more so by the need to incorporate a growing range of allies, each with varying capabilities. Again, the U.S. experience in NATO was valuable, since that had given military planners experience with a heterogeneous coalition. A major war plan goes through many iterations, each reflecting changing conditions on the ground, shifting political guidance, and the need for refinement and detail. Following the August 4 meeting at Camp David at which Schwarzkopf presented his initial military assessment to the president, Cheney had instructed Powell and Schwarzkopf to begin work on an offensive plan and force package that would be ready if the president later requested it. Within a few weeks CENTCOM headquarters in Tampa, Florida, had a four-phase plan: a strategic air campaign against leadership and military targets in Iraq; an air campaign against Iraqi forces in Kuwait itself, a ground operation to neutralize Republican Guard forces and isolate the Kuwait battlefield, and a ground attack to expel Iraqi forces from Kuwait. This sequential approach characterized all major U.S. war plans at the time.

In an October 11 briefing, Bush, Cheney, and Powell indicated to Schwarzkopf that they were satisfied with the first three phases, but concerned that Phase IV called for a direct ground assault on the entrenched Iraqi forces. This seemed to play directly into Hussein's hand and risked significant American casualties as they battered against prepared defenses. Cheney requested a different option based on bypassing the Iraqi defenses by outflanking them to the west rather than attacking them head-on. This would surprise and confuse the Iraqi commanders—large-scale armored movements through untracked desert were difficult and thus not something that Hussein's cautious generals would expect. By the end of October,

CENTCOM had followed instructions and developed a new plan integrating what later became known as the "left hook" (after Schwarzkopf described it that way in a televised briefing), using a larger, two-corps force for the land assault rather than one as in the original plan.

Within the military, debate flared over the relationship between airpower and land power. Strategic bombing of leadership, command, and control targets deep in Iraq was an important part of CENTCOM's war plan. But the question was whether it should be, in military terms, the *main* effort or a *supporting* effort. This was the latest battle in a conceptual and theoretical struggle covering many decades. Airpower theorists, beginning with the Italian Giulio Douhet and the American Billy Mitchell in the 1930s, contended that strategic bombing—attacking an enemy's infrastructure, industry, leadership, and population deep in its territory—could win wars without the grinding, bloody engagement of land armies. World War II did not bear this out. The intensive strategic bombing campaigns against Germany and Japan were militarily vital but not decisive. It took invasion by ground forces or, in the case of Japan, the threat of invasion to force surrender. But the true believers in airpower continued to support their concept. The problem, they felt, was that the technology to implement it was not yet mature. By the 1950s, the development of intercontinental bombers, intercontinental ballistic missiles, and thermonuclear weapons revived the notion of a military strategy based heavily, perhaps even exclusively, on airpower (or, later, aerospace power). Eisenhower's "New Look" strategy reflected this.

The idea of relying on strategic bombing did not die even when it again proved indecisive in Vietnam. Airpower advocates argued that Vietnam had not disproved the concept but simply shown that it required improved technology and a free hand for military professionals. By the 1990s, they believed that the technology for target acquisition, precision strike, air defense suppression, and radar evasion had matured to the point that Douhet and Mitchell's vision was within reach. Iraq's invasion of Kuwait provided an opportunity to confirm this. Lt. Gen. Charles A. Horner, whom Schwarzkopf had named Joint Forces Air Component Commander (JFACC), assigned Air Force Brig. Gen. Buster Glosson to plan the air campaign. Headed by Col. John A. Warden III, who had published a theory of air campaigning the year before, a small group in the Air Staff under Glosson's direction began work almost immediately after Iraqi forces moved into Kuwait. They sought an approach that would attain CENTCOM's military objectives using both strategic and tactical applications of airpower.[27] Ultimately Schwarzkopf and

Powell neither rejected nor fully embraced the strategic airpower idea, but allowed it to coexist in parallel with the other parts of the campaign.

While continuing to seek nonmilitary solutions to the crisis—including a personal meeting between Secretary of State James Baker and Iraqi foreign minister Tariq Aziz—Bush recognized that only a realistic threat of force would influence Hussein. This required overcoming congressional hesitation. Intensive lobbying paid off on January 12, 1991, when Congress passed a resolution supporting the use of force.[28] By that time there were nearly 1,800 combat aircraft from twelve countries and 540,000 ground forces from thirty-one countries in Saudi Arabia. President Bush recognized that delay could allow the Iraqis to strengthen their defensive positions in Kuwait and eventually would require that some American units be rotated and reserve mobilization extended. Time was limited.

The war opened with strikes to blind and confuse the Iraqis, sever their communications, and suppress their air defenses. On the night of January 17, Air Force MH-53J Pave Low special operations helicopters, army AH-64 Apache attack helicopters, F-15E Strike Eagle fighters, and British Tornado GR-1-fighter bombers struck Iraq's air defense, radar, and command and control systems. Air Force B-52s launched cruise missile strikes, F-117A Nighthawk stealth aircraft attacked targets in Baghdad, and Navy vessels launched Tomahawk Land Attack Cruise Missiles (TLAMs) at a range of Iraq targets. Operation Desert Shield had given way to Operation Desert Storm.

■   ■   ■

The air campaign lasted throughout the forty-three days of Operation Desert Storm. Coalition forces crushed the Iraqi air forces and gained air superiority on the first day. They then destroyed Iraq's extensive air defenses and attacked other military targets. Coalition airpower was instrumental in blunting Iraq's only foray into Saudi Arabia—the Battle of al-Khafji from January 29 to January 31—decimating two attacking divisions.[29] By early February coalition airpower was isolating and destroying deployed Iraqi ground forces. The only major shortcoming in the air campaign was the failure to find and destroy Iraq's mobile Scud missile launchers and nuclear facilities. This demonstrated that when airpower advocates said, "If we can find it, we can kill it," it might have been true, but the "if" was a big one. The technology for *finding* small, moving, or camouflaged targets was not nearly as mature as the technology for striking them once they were found.

Ground operations began on February 24, 1991.[30] This sequence reflected a mode of warfare which originated in the seventeenth century and was often used by advanced, industrial nations: long-range fires, whether artillery, missiles, or aerial bombing, "softened up" defenses and weakened the enemy's will. They were followed by direct, close engagement. The American military had long preferred this method since it minimized U.S. casualties. Desert Storm was thus the linear descendent of battles such as the island assaults in the Pacific during World War II in which hours, days, even weeks of naval bombardment and aerial bombing preceded direct invasion by Army or Marine forces. What did distinguish Desert Storm from its forebears, though, was the precision of the long-range fires and the resulting efficiency, all derived from technological advances in target acquisition and the attacking systems themselves.

Schwarzkopf's ground campaign combined a feint toward the center of the Iraqi defenses, a supporting attack toward Kuwait City, and a sweep to the west of the Iraqi prepared defenses. Again, this was not a new concept; using superior mobility, discipline, and situational awareness to outflank a static opponent in a defensive posture is one of the oldest techniques in land warfare. It could work at the tactical, operational, and strategic levels. Examples in American experience include Robert E. Lee's flanking sweep at the Battle of Chancellorsville, which collapsed the Union forces; Grant's large-scale flanking maneuvers around the Confederate defenses of Richmond during the 1864 and 1865 campaigns; and Douglas MacArthur's operational flanking swings against the Japanese in New Guinea and, later, North Korean forces by way of the amphibious landing at Inchon. Despite isolated resistance, both axes of advance exceeded expectations. Surprisingly the thrust toward Kuwait City that was intended as a supporting attack to pin down Iraqi forces while the "left hook" struck the decisive blow, penetrated the defensive belts, and moved quickly toward the city. This allowed CENTCOM to accelerate its timetable for the "left hook" by fourteen hours. On February 28, the Iraqi forces, hindered from the beginning by poor morale, ineffective leadership, and rigid operational methods, and mauled by weeks of air attacks, were shattered by the ground offensive, with most retreating or surrendering.

Since war is undertaken for political purposes, military strategy must reflect and be shaped by policy objectives. While military leaders sometimes believe that a defeated enemy should be annihilated if possible, President

Bush and his top advisers were concerned about the adverse political reper-cussions of appearing to kill Iraqis for killing's sake once they had left Ku-wait. As images of the shattered Iraqi forces streaming north or dying while attempting to do so appeared on televisions around the world, Saudi Arabia and Egypt—sensitive to Arab solidarity and honor at the same time that they sought to punish Saddam Hussein—pressed for an end to the fighting. The Bush administration was less concerned with Arab honor but hesitant to be seen as the architect of a senseless massacre. Its political goals were not only to liberate Kuwait but to set a precedent where the use of force in the inter-national system is limited and constrained and to solidify a new security order and power balance in the Gulf with the United States at its center. An Iraq mired in chaos or civil war would be an obstacle to regional stability, as would the idea that America cared little for Arab lives.

On February 28 President Bush declared a cease-fire—exactly 100 hours after the beginning of the ground war. "Kuwait is liberated. Iraq's army is defeated. Our military objectives are met," he told the nation. On March 3, coalition and Iraqi military leaders met in the town of Safwan, just north of the Kuwaiti border, to work out terms. After months of briefings from CENTCOM and warnings from a range of security analysts that the size and combat experience of the Iraqi army would make for a tough and po-tentially bloody campaign, the speed and completeness of the collapse sur-prised everyone.

■   ■   ■

Desert Storm elevated America's conflict with Iraq to the role of stra-tegic paradigm, in part because of its timing. Had Saddam Hussein invaded Kuwait a few years earlier when America's conflict with the Soviets was still the primary strategic paradigm or a few years later when something else had replaced the fading Soviet threat, things might have been different. But his timing was impeccable in terms of clarifying thinking in Washington. The war occurred precisely at the point of flux in the global security environ-ment as its central organizing structure—the competition and conflict between East and West—subsided. The United States needed a strategic paradigm. In the post–Cold War uncertainty about the purpose of Ameri-can power, particularly military power, Desert Storm provided an instant perception of clarity. American political and military leaders found light in the darkness and concluded that they understood the most important type of threat in the new security environment. Equally important, they knew how to deal with such challenges. The new strategic paradigm was a comfortable one.

The Gulf War formalized the geographic shift in the focus of American strategy from European and Northeast Asia to Southwest Asia. While this had been under way for decades, Hussein's invasion of Kuwait showed that the region was not only important but also unable to manage its own security without external assistance. The security structure of the Middle East had long been weak compared to other regions. Formal organizations—effective in other parts of the world—played a minimal role. The region may not have had a security *vacuum* but it certainly had a security *shortfall.* Hussein's invasion of Kuwait forced Gulf leaders to recognize their own vulnerability, thus paving the way for a new regional security order with the United States at its center. This required an America that was both willing and able to intervene. As Bush and Scowcroft later wrote, "The Gulf War had far greater significance in the emerging post–Cold War world than simply reversing Iraqi aggression and restoring Kuwait. Its magnitude and significance impelled us from the outset to extend our strategic vision beyond the crisis to the kind of precedent we should lay down for the future."[31]

A precedent it was then. Perhaps the most important point the administration derived from the war was that the post-Vietnam paralysis in American strategy had been transcended or circumvented. The Gulf War, coming on the heels of an effective and relatively low-cost intervention in Panama, showed that the American people and their elected leaders would support the use of armed force when given moral clarity, clear national interests, and the prospect of a quick campaign with limited friendly casualties. As Harry Summers later put it, even though American military power remained significant after Vietnam, what he called "military authority"—the perception by other nations that the United States was willing to use force—declined. The liberation of Kuwait reinforced this.[32] "American political credibility and influence," Bush and Scowcroft contended, "had skyrocketed."[33] The "unipolar moment" in world history was formalized, giving the United States political capital to spend constructing the new world order.[34]

For the Bush administration, Desert Storm confirmed that the primary role of the American military in the new security environment would be to control aggressive dictators, mostly in Asia, and to address regional power vacuums and imbalances which gave rise to aggression. As the

National Security Strategy released a few months after Desert Storm noted, the U.S. military must by able "to combat not a particular, poised enemy but the nascent threat of power vacuums and regional instabilities."[35] Activism is the best way to combat nascent threats. The National Security Strategy explicitly rejected the idea that the United States should be the "world's policeman" but advocated a leading role. It was to be *semi*-collective security, an orchestra with a single maestro. While Bush had espoused this idea since the fall of the Berlin Wall in 1989, Desert Storm gave it teeth: "In the Gulf we caught a glimmer of a better future—a new world community brought together by a growing consensus that force cannot be used to settle disputes and that when that consensus is broken, the world will respond."[36] The negative perspective on armed force enshrined in the American strategic culture—that its sole purpose is to prevent an aggressor from altering power balances or security structures rather than being used by the United States to alter power balances or security structures—was codified.

The Gulf War showed that to be effective, the United States needed both U.N. authorization and active support from allies and partners, at least outside its traditional North American area of concern (where the rules were different). Assuring such support took work. "Our first priority in foreign policy," the Bush strategy stated, "remains solidarity with our allies and friends."[37] What the administration overlooked was an emerging dissonance between the *political* importance of partners and the growing ability of the American military to operate unilaterally. There was a mounting capability gap between the U.S. military and its partners, including those from NATO states. While George Bush talked of de-legitimizing armed force, the Europeans had begun to act as if it were an accomplished fact, cutting military spending and force size and postponing or canceling many major acquisitions. Bush sought to de-legitimize armed force but, in the interim, wanted to guarantee that the United States remained good at it. The European approach was to assume that the erosion of its military capability—unilateral disarmament—would accelerate the de-legitimization. Immediately after the Gulf War this had not yet become a major problem, but it soon would be.

The Bush administration immediately began incorporating lessons from the Gulf War into its military strategy. In the broadest sense, this signaled the end of the "limited war" concept in American strategy that had emerged early in the Cold War, and it was replaced—at least for a while—with the "all-or-nothing" approach advocated by Weinberger, Powell, and most other top military leaders.[38] From this perspective, the conditions for the use of military force were stringent, but once they were met, the United States would hold nothing back.

The Bush administration derived two additional strategic concepts from the Gulf War. Both were important because they generated force structure and acquisition requirements for the military. One was "forward presence." Bush and his advisers recognized that Iraq's invasion of Kuwait might have been deterred or more easily reversed if the United States had a robust military presence in the Gulf beforehand. Saddam Hussein had underestimated American commitment to the region and thus blundered into aggression. If the United States established a military presence there, future aggressors would not repeat the miscalculation. Bush administration officials and U.S. military leaders recognized that they could not permanently station massive numbers of American troops in the Gulf. There could be no mid-sized American towns plopped down in Kuwait or Saudi Arabia as there were in Germany, Japan, or South Korea. Forward presence was thus different than the old notion of forward defense. It needed to be something more than no involvement at all, engaging in at times even short-term deployments but something less than Cold War–style large-scale, long-term deployments.

The second (and linked) strategic concept was "crisis response"—projecting power with little or no advance warning. Gone were the days when military planners could count on weeks or months before a deployment. Deterrence is contingent on having a demonstrated capability to respond to aggression—the greater the capacity to project power, the greater the credibility. Crisis response generated a range of requirements including more transportation aircraft and sealift ships, more aerial refueling aircraft, an increased ability to operate in austere environments, greater intelligence and surveillance capabilities, and some adjustment of the active and reserve components of the military so that the response to a crisis would not be delayed by mobilizing Reserves. The emphasis on crisis response in the new National Security Strategy was a direct result from the "lessons" of the Gulf War, extrapolating general requirements from that specific conflict.

For the U.S. military, Iraq's invasion of Kuwait bolstered its argument that even a world without the Soviet threat remained perilous. The military had not worked itself out of a job. As Army Chief of Staff Gen. Carl Vuono phrased it, "While the risk of a major conflict with the Soviet Union has certainly ebbed to a forty-five-year low, Iraq's aggression against Kuwait clearly demonstrates that the international environment remains dangerous and is in many respects growing more complex."[39] This was not surprising. All bureaucratic organizations have a survival instinct and strive to justify their own existence and find rationales for the resources devoted to them. In the post–Cold War period, the U.S. military's survival instinct kicked in. The Gulf War helped. The notion that military strength, particularly land power, is a temporary expedient necessary during only in wartime faded. The American strategic culture had shifted, embracing the idea that military strength has enduring value for deterrence and conflict prevention as well as for winning wars.

What was not yet clear was exactly how large the post–Cold War military should be or how it should be structured. That was where Desert Storm came in. Pointing to the Gulf War, the military argued that the United States needed a military organized, sized, equipped, and trained much like the one it had. Why tweak success? The Gulf War, in other words, was portrayed as validating everything the military's leaders had done after Vietnam. It illustrated the effectiveness of what Harold Brown, Carter's defense secretary, called the "offset strategy" in which technological and qualitative superiority countered an enemy's quantitative advantages.[40] It showed that techniques developed for European battlefields worked in other environments (at least against proto-Soviet adversaries).[41] It showed that the seminal shift in American military strategy begun in the 1970s was successful. The grinding approach of Grant and Eisenhower gave way to a mode of fighting where finesse, speed, and precision bewildered the enemy; avoided his strengths; capitalized on his weaknesses; and, eventually, shattered his will. Ironically, though, precisely because of the military success of the Gulf War, this style of military operations became so deeply etched in the American mind that later change was difficult. Americans (like most people) have a difficult time grasping the paradoxical logic of strategy and knowing that what worked yesterday may not work tomorrow.

American technological superiority did not, in itself, *cause* battlefield success in the Gulf War, but it certainly enabled it, amplifying the skill differential between the U.S. and Iraq forces.[42] All of the new high-tech systems performed at least as well as expected, in some cases much better. The U.S. military also felt that the Gulf War confirmed the success of a decade of effort toward improved "jointness," or cooperation between the services, some self-instigated and some imposed. One of the major lessons of previous military operations, such as the abortive 1980 attempt to rescue the American hostages held by Iran and the 1983 intervention in Grenada, was that the services had problems operating closely together. Sometimes this was as simple as radios that could not communicate with each other or as complex as radically different service cultures.[43] Congress had addressed this problem via the 1986 Goldwater-Nichols Department of Defense Reorganization Act.[44] While not yet seamless—the Army was particularly concerned about the slowness that ground commanders experienced when requesting air operations because of the complexity of the daily air tasking process—cooperation and synchronization among the services was the best it had ever been.

The Gulf War also validated the military's "Total Force" concept, which treated the active and reserve components as a seamless team, placing much of the support, transportation, and logistics capability in the Reserves. For the Army in particular, this was not only a matter of cost-effectiveness, but also a deliberate political move. Gen. Creighton W. Abrams Jr., who led the drawdown from Vietnam from 1972 to 1974, was convinced that Lyndon Johnson's refusal to mobilize the Reserves, with its ties in nearly every American community, contributed to the public's disassociation with the war and eventually played a role in the collapse of public support. Because it was largely fought by the lower class (at least among enlisted personnel), Vietnam was never "America's war." When serving as Army chief of staff, Abrams redesigned the Army so that future presidents would be forced to activate the Reserves in order to go to war, and thus could not use armed force without public support. Desert Storm showed that this worked. Despite a few problems getting Reserve units ready, about one-fourth of the U.S. forces in Desert Storm were reservists. More than 70 percent of the Army support units were from the U. S. Army Reserve and National Guard.

Desert Storm also slowed the planned post–Cold War drawdown of the U.S. military. Just before the invasion of Kuwait, Secretary of Defense Cheney proposed reducing the force by 25 percent over five years but with only a 10 percent budget cut. Congressman Les Aspin (D-WA), one of the leading military experts among Democrats, countered that real defense spending could be decreased by 18 to 27 percent over five years. The Gulf War prevented a showdown between the Pentagon and congressional Democrats, tempered this debate, and led to smaller cuts than would have occurred.[45] A move to shift additional combat forces from the active component to the Reserves was shelved. Crisis response made rapid deployment more important than ever. The military thus retained its old system in which two-thirds of the combat units were in the active component. Plans to shift a number of "heavy" Army units with extensive armor and mechanization to more mobile "light" ones were also scrapped. Beginning in 1984, the Army instigated a light infantry initiative to create more mobile forces for "contingency" missions. With the Soviet threat receding, there had been pressure to push this even further, shifting more heavy units to light ones. But Desert Storm was seen as evidence that the United States still needed heavy divisions in the new global security environment or, at least, a "middleweight" force capable of taking on armor-heavy enemies. As a result the Army retained its existing three-to-one ratio of heavy to light divisions. Air National Guard units performed well during the war and eventually took a proportionally smaller cut than active tactical Air Force units. Rejecting a cost-cutting idea for a tiered readiness system, the Pentagon opted to keep all active forces at the highest level of readiness.

The success of advanced technology in the Gulf discredited any plans to delay or drop major new high-tech systems. The general consensus among the military, defense analysts, Congress, and the public was that advanced technology saved American lives and allowed quick resolution of the conflict. In war, as in shopping, they felt "you get what you pay for." Despite a persuasive argument later made by defense analyst Stephen Biddle that the skill differential between American and Iraqi forces—amplified but not caused by technological superiority—accounted for the outcome rather than technology itself, the U.S. military and most of the defense and strategic communities decided that the technological asymmetry determined the outcome.[46] Moreover, the American technological advantage augmented deterrence since, it was assumed, potential aggressors were wedded to conventional military aggression and the United States had shown it could defeat this with relative ease. Programs such as the B-2 Stealth bomber, Advanced Tactical Fighter, advanced medium air-to-air missile, the C-17 transport aircraft, JSTARS, and the Army's Tactical Missile System received a breath of life and sustained funding. Little thought was given at that time to possible adverse political effects or unintended consequences of increasing America's already huge military advantage over potential state opponents. Americans saw their own power as benign and assumed others would too (except, of course, for aggressors). The United States was "in a unique position of trusted leadership throughout the world," the Pentagon triumphantly wrote. "Old friends view us as a stabilizing force in vitally important regions, and new friends look to us for inspiration and security."[47] No one seemed to consider whether that was transitory or permanent. And equally little thought was given to potential enemies who did not undertake conventional cross-border aggression.

■　■　■

Interservice competition normally intensifies as defense budgets shrink. Extensive and rapid declines can turn competition into outright conflict as the services scramble to protect their share of a smaller pie. The end of the Cold War sparked one of the most intense bouts of interservice competition since the 1950s. While strategists debate whether the United States would face another "peer competitor" after the demise of the Soviet Union, wags quipped that the U.S. Army had, in fact, found a peer competitor—the U.S. Air Force. Like many jokes, this one reflected a serious issue. After Desert Storm, each service used the war to support its vision of the emerging security environment and future war, as evidence of its continued importance, and of proof that it needed a constant or increased share of Pentagon resources. The services knew budget cuts were coming, but each made a case that the others should shoulder most of them.

For the Air Force, Desert Storm showed that airpower could be decisive on the battlefield: the reason the ground campaign lasted a hundred hours was not because of the prowess of the Army and Marine Corps, but because air attacks had destroyed the Iraqis physically and psychologically. As Dennis Drew expressed it, "The stunning performance of coalition air power symbolized both the maturity of air power and its dominant position in late twentieth-century warfare. Most important, victory in the Gulf War symbolized the need to reevaluate and reform traditional ways of thinking about the art and science of war."[48] The "traditional ways" were those that held that airpower prepared for the decisive application of land power. For the Air Force, the Gulf War demonstrated a discontinuity or paradigmatic shift in military strategy. Hence they argued that resources devoted to the further development of airpower (including the acquisition of new technology) were well spent both in terms of battlefield effectiveness and in minimizing U.S. casualties (thus making armed force politically usable).

The Army, of course, drew decidedly different lessons from Desert Storm. Its leaders and their political allies believed that that the conflict verified one of the oldest rules of war—only land power could trump land power. Even if future conflicts were not exact replicas of the Gulf War, the failure to prepare for land power–based wars would encourage aggressors to

THE TEST OF BATTLE ——————————————————————— 37

emulate Hussein. The Army's argument had three components: the Army was the most versatile service, able to undertake a range of missions from peacetime engagement with partner militaries (most composed primarily of land forces) through low-intensity conflict, deterrence, and conventional fighting; only land power could decisively defeat an opponent (airpower could weaken them but not fully break their will); and land power was the ultimate and necessary symbol of American commitment to an ally or friend. If the United States was to be the engineer and guarantor of regional security, the argument went, it must have effective land power. In a sense, this too was a historical discontinuity since the American tradition was to demobilize its Army after a war.

The Navy and Marine Corps offered a third perspective on the Gulf War. The sea services felt that the war demonstrated how much the United States needed a combination of standoff firepower and rapidly-deployable, expeditionary land capabilities that could operate independently of local infrastructure (as would have been required if Iraq had overrun Saudi facilities). Of course, this was precisely what the Navy–Marine Corps team offered. It was the only "stand alone" force—the Army needed the Air Force for deep strikes and close air support, while the Air Force needed the Army to protect its facilities near the front. The Navy–Marine Corps team, its leaders held, could apply a broad range of conventional military capabilities without support of the Air Force or Army. At least it could do so anywhere near the oceanic littoral (which, the sea services pointed out, included most of the world's population and vital economic areas). Based on Desert Storm and the end of the Cold War, the Navy was shifting from its traditional focus of fighting fleet actions *on* the sea—the inheritance of Alfred Mahan—to projecting power ashore *from* the sea.[49] To complement this, the Marine Corps developed a concept it called "operational maneuver from the sea."[50] Again, the Gulf War was portrayed as validation of changes already under way.

■   ■   ■

Outside the government, the lessons of Desert Storm were more complex, ambiguous, even disconcerting. Beyond the idea that American power was still needed in the post–Cold War world, there was little consensus. Many analysts pointed out that the conflict left important qualities and capabilities of the American military untested. It provided incomplete validation, at best, of recent reforms and policy shifts. For instance, the Bush administration indicated that as the focus of the global security environ-ment moved away from the inter-German border to the developing world, the U.S. military would often be used in what were called "austere" ope-rating theaters—ones with limited existing support infrastructure. While the Gulf was certainly less developed than Germany or South Korea, it was not exactly "austere." Saudi facilities were modern and extensive. What if they had not been? Could the U.S. military truly undertake a large-scale opera-tion in an austere environment? How could the Air Force undertake sustained strategic bombing or provide close air support to ground forces without bases in the theater? How could the Army sustain the massive logis-tics flow that a high-tech force required for fast-paced operations? Could the Navy–Marine Corps team really provide enough combat power from the sea to be decisive against a powerful enemy?

At the level of grand strategy, the war did not demonstrate that the United States could—as the Bush administration claimed—use military power unilaterally or with limited international support. Was U.N. approval and support from allies and partners a preference or a requirement when the United States went to war? Similarly, Desert Storm did not show whether the public and Congress actually would tolerate high casualties. The standard wisdom among defense analysts was that the public and Congress would accept casualties if the stakes of the conflict were clear and important and if U.S. strategy aimed at a successful outcome with a definitive end state. Bush indicated that he was willing to accept thousands, perhaps even tens of thou-sands, of American casualties. But whether the administration actually could have sustained public support under such conditions remained unclear. Certainly Saddam Hussein thought not. He based his strategy on making the blood cost of liberating Kuwait so high that the United States would lose its will to fight. This may have been accurate in concept but simply flawed in execution.

The war also did not test the idea that military systems and methods developed to counter the Soviets would work against dissimilar enemies. What if the enemy had not been mostly equipped by the Soviets? And the Gulf War did not prove that America's all-volunteer force could sustain a protracted, tough war, particularly one that required extensive mobilization of the Reserves. The United States had never reached a point in Desert Storm where it was forced to rotate large numbers of units exhausted by a lengthy deployment or long bouts of combat, or extend the mobilization of the reserves with all of the personal strains that causes.

In an even more general sense, the war with Iraq did not test America's ability to confront a skilled or astute opponent. In many ways, Hussein was the perfect enemy—both brutal and strategically incompetent. His vicious-ness allowed the Bush administration to demonize him. His pathetic attempts to appear benign—for instance, a famous televised episode with a cringing British boy—angered the world rather than place it. Ultimately, Hussein could not transcend the environment that spawned him. His grasp of con-cepts such as legitimacy, justice, and moral right were diametric to the Ameri-can view of these same things. His world was one where only raw power, exercised through fear and patronage, mattered. He was not creative enough to adapt in the heat of crisis. He did not realize that those in an inferior position must develop a deep understanding of their opponents' psycho-logical weaknesses and manipulate them if they are to have any chance of success. He assumed that the strategy used against Iran—the creation of static defensive positions with extensive armor and artillery, leading the en-emy to take massive casualties as they crashed against the defenses—would work against the United States. This showed an unbelievably deep ignor-ance of American military capabilities, strategy, and operational methods. As Jeffrey Record phrased it, Hussein's "appreciation of warfare was one-dimensional, and mired in the paradigm of the Battles of Somme and Passchendaele as revisited in the Iran-Iraq War seventy years later."[51] World War I was dominated by what became known as a strategy of attrition. Vic-tory came by bleeding the enemy beyond the point of tolerance, normally by massing huge amounts of firepower, particularly artillery. The Central Powers lost the war because they exhausted their manpower. World War II returned movement to warfare. The adversaries sought to break their oppo-nents by placing them in an untenable position from which resistance was futile. The classic operational maneuver of blitzkrieg was a deep penetra-tion by a fast-moving armored force, heavily supported by air attacks, which disrupted the enemy's ability to replenish its supplies and reinforce its front-line units and, eventually, led to the encirclement and annihilation of en-emy units. Somehow Saddam Hussein had missed this revolution in military strategy. He still fought World War I while the Americans utilized a vastly improved variant of blitzkrieg. Desert Storm was the first war in history, ac-cording to William Taylor and James Blackwell, where one side relied exclu-sively on a strategy of attrition and the other on a strategy of maneuver.[52]

Saddam Hussein was incapable of recognizing his own shortcomings. Like Hitler and Stalin, Hussein made most important military decisions himself rather than delegating authority to his generals. Because of this, Iraq's command system, like the Soviet one, was highly centralized. Local commanders did not have the authority to innovate and seize opportunities. In fact, to do so could be fatal. Only cautious sycophants survived, thus breeding an utterly incompetent senior leadership. This amplified the effects of coalition attacks on the Iraqi command, control, and communication systems. Units cut off from higher echelons often sat passively. Attacks and defenses were uncoordinated, again the result of destroyed communication grids, inadequate training (particularly in large unit operations), and poor leadership. Iraqi forces were particularly inept at night operations, one of the strengths of the American forces. Was, then, the Gulf War a paradigm on which American strategy should be built?

U.S. political and military leaders missed what may have been the most important lesson from the Gulf War: the United States had a military strategy that led to battlefield success but not necessarily to strategic victory defined as the attainment of long-term political objectives. As soon became evident, the conflict left Hussein with significant military capability, at least enough to repress internal opposition if not to invade his neighbors. On February 15, 1991, President Bush said, "There's another way for the bloodshed to stop, and that is for the Iraqi military and the Iraqi people to take matters into their own hands and force Saddam Hussein, the dictator, to step aside and then comply with the United Nations resolutions and rejoin the family of peace-loving nations."[53] Bush himself later described this as a "hurriedly added" comment.[54] But in one more tragic instance of the mutual miscomprehension that shaped U.S.-Iraqi relations, the Shiites and Kurds saw this as instructions from the world's dominant power and thus launched uprisings to remove Saddam Hussein's yoke. Brent Scowcroft scoffed at the idea that an "impulsive ad lib . . . would have gotten to Iraqi malcontents [sic—a strange choice of words for opponents of Saddam Hussein] and have been the motivation for the subsequent actions of Shiites and Kurds."[55] But, as Peter Galbraith points out, that is exactly what did happen.[56] Iraqis did not understand the communication style of American politicians, and Bush did not understand the seriousness with which Iraqis would take his statements. This both contributed to a humanitarian disaster in Iraq and came back to haunt the United States twelve years later when Iraq's Shiites showed little trust of American intentions in the post-Hussein stabilization of their country.

Nor did Bush force Iraq to implement a U.N.-based program to destroy its chemical, biological, and nuclear weapons and production facilities. Despite the administration's stated desire to see Hussein replaced, he retained power. A U.S. Army plan to overthrow Hussein did not receive serious consideration by the administration.[57] A year after the war, even the Pentagon was admitting that that "decisive military victory in regional conflict does not necessarily bring permanent peace."[58] Eventually Desert Storm was called "triumph without victory" or a "hollow victory."[59]

Why did this happen? Militarily, the United States could have consummated strategic success. When President Bush stopped the offensive, the U.S. Army had two corps deep in Iraq, the coalition had complete control of the air, and the Iraqi military was in disarray. The official U.S. Army history of the Gulf War states, "Despite the fact that many combat units were nearing exhaustion after days of uninterrupted fighting and moving, CENTCOM could have sustained operations considerably longer. The Iraqis, on the other hand, reached their culminating point when the Republican Guard was destroyed."[60] But Schwarzkopf and Powell did not push for a march on Baghdad. Military leaders were worried that the units in the field, many of which had been deployed for months under difficult conditions, were approaching exhaustion. They were also sensitive to political concerns. After the public vilification the military suffered after Vietnam, it enjoyed its revived stature and did not want to put it at risk. If the Hussein regime was removed by external force, someone would have to occupy and stabilize the country. The military knew it was the most likely candidate. Its leaders believed that the tremendous boost in morale, respect, and public support that followed the liberation of Kuwait might be frittered away during occupation duty in Iraq. As Strobe Talbott put it, "Much of the U.S. military wanted to quit while it was ahead."[61]

Bush and his top political advisers were no more inclined for renewed combat to topple Hussein, but had different motives. They were particularly concerned about the long-term political effects of continuing the war. Bush believed further offensive action would endanger the coalition, potentially damaging America's ability to construct a postwar regional security structure in the Gulf. The Arab coalition partners—sensitive to what they saw as a century-long humiliation of Arabs by Westerners—did not want Iraq occupied by American forces. And the administration believed attempts to move deeper into Iraq or remove Hussein by force might lead to the collapse or breakup of that nation, thus creating a power vacuum that would benefit

Iran (still seen as more of a long-term threat than Iraq). The remnants of Vietnam syndrome also played a role: if public support crumbled, the United States would be unable to use military power to promote the new world order. The U.S. military was a terrible, swift sword, but one that could be used under special conditions.

One more consideration also shaped the outcome: President Bush was determined to avoid inordinate civilian involvement in military decisions which, he believed, had contributed to America's problems in Vietnam. To compensate, he erred on the side of deference, particularly on issues he considered purely military. As is always true in civil-military relations, the trick was defining exactly which issues were purely military and which were not. No civilian official or diplomat accompanied Schwarzkopf when he negotiated the cease-fire. Focused on immediate military concerns, he made, without political advice or assessment, decisions that proved to have immense political importance. These included allowing the Iraqis to fly helicopters over the southern no-fly zone (which they then used to repress the Shiite uprising) and what Michael Gordon and Bernard Trainor call "an extraordinary assurance" to withdraw American forces from Iraqi territory quickly, thus giving away the leverage that might later have been used to force Hussein to adhere to the cease-fire terms and comply with U.N. resolutions.[62] To a large extent, Bush rendered more unto the military than it was due.

In a sense, though, the problem ran even deeper. It reflected the enduring issue of strategic assumptions when Americans deal with other cultures. The Bush administration assumed that military defeat would shatter Hussein's authority and charisma, thus leading to his overthrow, probably by members of his military. The idea was—to replicate the thinking of a few years earlier—that a new military dictator would be more "rational" (with rationality defined as "thinking like Americans") and thus interested in moderating Iraq's behavior to curry favor with outsiders who could help with reconstruction.

At a broader level, the decision to stop the war short of ultimate, long-term success reflected the Bush administration's contradictory weltanschauung, with Wilsonian idealism—the desire for a new world order—and Kissingerian realism in an uneasy, even tempestuous coexistence. Idealism dictated that aggressors be replaced or at least severely punished. It also implied that sustaining collective security was nearly as important as the outcome of any specific application of it. Force is used in a collective security system when an aggressor breaks the rules of the system. It is the act of aggression itself that generates a response. But the realist instincts of the Bush administration told it that the only way to preserve long-term security was through functioning power balances. In a balance of power system, decisions to use force are based on the damage that a state's action poses to the balance itself. Even evil leaders like Hussein sometimes contributed to a functioning balance. Internal chaos in Iraq—a likely outcome if Hussein was removed—would lead to a power vacuum. And few things were more upsetting to a power balance than a vacuum. Ultimately the Bush administration never reconciled the tension between its idealism and realism, and thus it never crafted a fully coherent grand strategy. The absence of a coherent grand strategy prevented using military power for the attainment of strategic victory.

Bush's decision to stop the war when he did also reflected the defensive or negative attitude toward the use of military force in the American strategic culture. The notion that military action was solely a means to prevent an enemy from opposing its will on America or its friends unlinked force and diplomacy. In its extreme form, Americans saw diplomacy as something that stopped when a war began and picked up again after the enemy was vanquished. Occasionally national leaders such as Henry Kissinger and George Shultz had pushed for a tighter linkage between military action and diplomacy. Shultz, for instance, wrote "better to use force when you *should* rather than when you *must*."[63] But those who advocated a nuanced approach to the use of force and its seamless integration with diplomacy swam upstream against the mighty current of American tradition.

Even had the administration opted to continue the fight, it was institutionally unprepared for a prolonged military occupation of Iraq. The United States had not dictated peace terms to a defeated state since the end of World War II. Even that precedent provided little guidance: there are important differences between imposing terms on a fully defeated enemy and on one who still had the capability to renew the fight if pushed too hard. By 1945 the American public had paid a high enough cost during the war that it had no qualms about imposing terms on the defeated enemies. Attitudes were different in the late winter of 1991. Post-Vietnam America, concerned about being perceived as a bully, was less inclined to impose its will on other states, particularly at the point of a bayonet. As a result, the Bush administration did not push Saddam Hussein nearly as hard as it could have. As Jeffrey Record wrote, "Rarely in history has a victorious army unilaterally stopped fighting—*in the absence of any request for terms by the vanquished*; and a man with Saddam Hussein's mentality almost certainly interpreted Bush's haste in unilaterally calling of the war as a sign of weakness."[64]

In the broadest sense, the Bush administration's response to the invasion of Kuwait set the direction for post–Cold War American strategy, assuring involvement in the security affairs of all the world's regions. But as the decision to stop before crushing Hussein showed, the United States was still a hesitant, even unconfident, power. As Niall Ferguson points out, the United States has always been an empire, even though it is an "empire in denial."[65] This is particularly accurate if imperialism is defined as a willingness and ability to affect security arrangements outside traditional state boundaries. "Like it or not," Ivo Daalder and James Lindsay wrote, "the power and reach of the United States have already turned it into an empire."[66] The question was what form of imperial management would the United States pursue?

For most of history, American imperialism emulated the British model. Growth of the empire—of influence—was driven by the desire to secure certain regions in order to protect economic interests. Like imperial Britain, the United States only played a direct role in the governance and security affairs of certain key regions (traditionally North America, later expanded to Western Europe and Northeast Asia). Like imperial Britain, America preferred to promote security through control of the seas and regional power balances rather than direct imperial policing. Problems and threats were to be contained when possible and only ameliorated when absolutely necessary. But the American empire had always had some vital differences with the British one. It was more like the modern French empire or the ancient Roman one in its proselytizing dimension, or its lack of tolerance for political systems significantly different than its own. Imperial Americans, unlike their British counterparts, drew a direct connection between a state's culture and internal political system and its external behavior. The British were willing to tolerate all sorts of internal systems and rulers—sheikhs, pashas, sultans, chiefs, rajahs, maharajahs, shahs, emperors, khans, and a slew of motley kings—so long as a state's external behavior did not endanger their interests or upset important power balances. Americans felt that states with flawed internal systems would invariably stoke aggression or instability. The rub was that this model of imperialism required a different sort of military, one that was land power intensive rather than reliant on a standoff force, and one capable of both defeating enemies in war and undertaking occupation, stabilization, and reconstruction duties—ameliorating threats rather than simply containing them. It would be more of a Roman military than an imperial British one (which also saw land power as a temporary wartime expedient, relying on local forces when it was necessary to stabilize the core regions of the empire). By taking the Gulf War to the point of battlefield victory but not ultimate strategic success, the Bush administration avoided having to confront the problem of having a military that was not optimized for ameliorating security threats and instead contained them.

■ ■ ■

Some of the massive literature about the Gulf War that exploded in its aftermath warned against using it as a paradigm for future armed conflict. Jeffrey Record called Desert Storm "the mother of all anomalies," Michael Mandelbaum advised that the Gulf conflict was not "a preview of international politics beyond the Cold War," and so forth.[67] These were largely disregarded within the government. The U.S. military and its supporting defense community accepted Desert Storm as a model for America's wars in the new security environment. Colin Powell expressed the military's thinking when he warned, "Today there are other Saddam Husseins in the world."[68] The implication was that there might be other Desert Storms. Few military leaders or policymakers questioned the elevation of the conflict with Iraq to the role of strategic paradigm.

The United States thus began to change its military basing system, force composition, acquisition, concept development, war gaming, military education, and experimentation based in large part on Desert Storm. Conventional, cross-border aggression by an evil, unscrupulous, but somewhat stupid dictator became the standard planning scenario. It evolved into a generic concept known first as a "major regional contingency" (MRC), later "major theater war" (MTW). MRCs and MTWs became the central force-sizing construct for the U.S. military. They were assessed in a plethora of war games and staff exercises, most of which—not coincidentally—involved a rogue state (sometimes named, sometimes generic) armed by the Soviet Union undertaking cross-border invasion in a desert environment. In most of these, the United States was caught somewhat by surprise but was able to deploy enough military force to the region to restore the status quo ante bellum. The enemy was always qualitatively inferior yet relied on conventional military forces. Economics, politics, and social factors such as culture and ideology played a limited role. On the conventional battlefield divorced from politics and culture, it made no difference whether a T-72 tank was driven by an Islamic radical pursuing a new caliphate, an Iraqi Ba'athist seeking to dominate weak neighbors, a Bosnian Serb out to eradicate Muslims, or a communist in quest of a worker's paradise. As grizzled soldiers say, "A kill is a kill." Political subtlety and cultural understanding, if not wholly irrelevant, were nearly so. The American military was most comfortable with warfare where culture did not matter but professionalism and technology did.

At one level, this is understandable. The military had gone from a historic low to a historic high in fifteen years. Naturally it wanted to sustain this. Its leaders had thought about conventional cross-border invasion for their entire professional careers and were good at stopping and reversing it. Other dynamics also drove the concentration on Desert Storm–style MRCs. Without lapsing into simplistic Marxist explanations, it is true that many powerful commercial organizations had a vested interest in preparing the United States for high-tech, conventional war. These included producers of military systems, providers of supplies and services, and the burgeoning defense analytical and consulting industry. The "military-industrial complex" Eisenhower warned about was real and was influential. Desert Storm–style warfare required the purchase of increasingly complex and expensive military systems. Put bluntly, MRCs were good for business.

For the U.S. military, Desert Storm proved the worth of deliberate, controlled, and focused change. After the war, the military was even more enthusiastic about this process beginning, in Trotsky's phrase, a time of "permanent revolution." But during the reforms of the 1970s and 1980s, the military had responded to clear political guidance and a well-defined grand strategy. In the post–Gulf War period, these were missing. The problem, then, was how to structure further reform and change. In a perfect world, policy and grand strategy should drive military strategy, force development, and acquisition. The reverse held for the United States immediately after the Gulf War—it was the military that was most active in thinking strategically and assessing the future. The administration's contradictory instincts toward idealism and realism had a particular impact. A military devoted to preserving power balances need only deter and reverse aggression by one state against another. A military designed to occupy, stabilize, reconstruct, and govern shattered states would need different capabilities and, to a large extent, a different mind-set.

The lack of clarity in American grand strategy—its tensions and contradictions—allowed a rejuvenated and confident U.S. military, supported by a web of industries and corporations, to set its own path to transformation (or, more accurately, a number of vaguely similar paths defined by the services). Since civilian leaders did not instruct the military on what the nation would demand of it in the future, the military made it own assumptions about future requirements and undertook change itself based on them. For the military, there was nothing insidious or even wrong about this—if there is culpability, it lay with the civilians who failed to provide adequate long-term strategic guidance. But the results were far-reaching, helping define the parameters of strategic feasibility. For a variety of reasons, the trajectory of change set by the military and its supporters relied heavily on technology. Within months of the Gulf War, defense analysts both in and out of uniform began to talk of a "military-technical revolution" and eventually a "revolution in military affairs."

The Bush administration instinctively understood that America's military prowess was a good thing but was not completely clear on how to use it. Two hundred years of history ingrained the idea that military power is to prevent bad things rather than engineer desired results, a negative force rather than a positive one. Having found a mode of warfare it was good at and comfortable with, the United States sought a grand strategy in which this could be a centerpiece. With no serious challenger left standing in the security environment of 1991, this posed few problems, but more would come. Among other things, strategy entails defining conditions under which a state chooses to exercise power, particularly military power, and exercising restraint when those conditions are not met. Admittedly, sometimes this is impossible. On occasion states must fight wars they are not prepared for and do not want—Great Britain when forced to undertake massive land warfare in World War I, the French when facing insurgency in Algeria and Indochina, and so forth. But the preference is to avoid types of war the state is not good at or not prepared for.

As the United States adopted the imperial role of managing world order, it became difficult to resist conflicts the American military was not designed for. Eschewing involvement had high, sometimes unacceptable political costs. An architect and guarantor of world order cannot pick and chose among crises. So while the United State preferred replays of Desert Storm with their moral clarity and militarily inferior opponents operating in precisely the way the U.S. military was best equipped to counter, it did not find them. The great irony of Desert Storm was that America's prowess at the particular type of warfare it involved helped ensure that enemies—most of whom were not as prone to mistakes as Saddam Hussein—would not undertake it. In a complex, ambiguous security environment and with the United States in the midst of a defense drawdown, there was a great need for a paradigm to preserve strategic focus and coherence. Iraq was a flawed strategic paradigm, but it was the only one available.

For better or worse, it remained so. Despite predictions by America's Gulf allies that Hussein would lose his grip on power when stigmatized by military defeat, he held on, because of both his utter ruthlessness and skill at manipulating Iraqi opinion. This allowed him to make resistance against the United States, even though it had been a military disaster, seem a psychological and political victory. As with the Egyptians in the 1973 war against Israel, to resist and survive were touted as success—an idea that resonated with Iraqi (and other Arab) publics accustomed to crushing defeats and foreign domination. Hussein neither moderated his behavior and complied with the conditions imposed by the United States and the United Nations nor fell from power. The Bush administration did strengthen containment after it became clear that the Gulf War had not resolved the Iraq problem, increasing its military ties to the Arab Gulf states (reinforcing Hussein's claims that the United States sought a permanent foothold in the Arab world, at least among some), launching some air strikes after Iraq challenged the southern no-fly zone and blocked U.N. weapons inspectors, and, after watching Hussein pummel the Shiite uprising in the south, creating a protected enclave in the Kurdish north. Even contained, Hussein remained a threat, helping further drive the evolution of American strategy.

3

TRANSFORMATION
AND CONTAINMENT

For now I see
Peace to corrupt no less than war to waste.
—JOHN MILTON
"PARADISE LOST"

T he Clinton family had barely unpacked in the White House before
the Iraq problem confronted the new president. The Bush administration, despite its best efforts, left the conflict unresolved, making
little progress toward forcing Saddam Hussein to comply with the 1991 settlement during its last year in office. The question was whether Clinton could
do better. Was this a shortcoming of Bush and his close advisers, or did it
reflect deeper factors in the American approach to strategy?

While Saddam Hussein had made disastrous miscalculations about
the Americans in 1991, he learned quickly. He realized that intimidation,
fear, and brutality—his instinctive methods when pressured—did not work.
The key to ending the U.N. sanctions, the Iraqi dictator concluded, was
chipping away at the will of the American public and the coalition by portraying Iraq as the victim of Western aggression and making containment
distracting, annoying, and costly. To do this without crossing the point at
which the United States would remove him from power, he had to paint
himself as a victim. This required a partner, albeit an unwitting one. The

role of the United States in this great charade was to hurt Hussein without destroying him, providing psychological ammunition to win sympathy in the Arab world—always sensitive to "abuse" of a fellow Arab, even a badly flawed one—and within the political Left in Europe and North America. This was the game—Hussein provoked, and the United States struck but never hard enough to destroy him.

With his highly personalized view of politics and power, Hussein had assumed that his problem was not with the United States as a nation and certainly not with the American people, but with G. H. W. Bush himself. When Clinton assumed office, the Iraqi dictator declared a cease-fire as a "good will gesture," beginning a "charm offensive" aimed at the United States and key coalition partners. But as was often true with Hussein, actions did not match rhetoric. Within two days of Clinton's inauguration American warplanes, acting on standing orders established by the Bush administration, attacked an Iraqi surface-to-air missile battery that had illuminated them with air defense radar. The new president indicated that he would continue responding to provocation.

Beyond that, it was not immediately clear how Clinton would approach the Iraq problem. The president himself had given little thought to the issue. Colin Powell, still serving as chairman of the Joint Chiefs of Staff, saw Hussein as more of a nuisance than a major threat. He suggested that the United States refocus its attention on more pressing security concerns. Secretary of State Warren Christopher and National Security Adviser Anthony Lake followed a similar line. Other members of Clinton's new national security team, by contrast, advocated more forceful options, including arming the Kurds and expanding the no-fly zone to the entire country.[1] They seemed to subscribe to the Bush administration's idea that constant and escalating demonstrations of Hussein's weakness would undercut his support. All that was needed was finding the right pressure point and the right amount of pressure to apply. They showed little concern for what came after Hussein, assuming that whoever assumed power would be an improvement. President Clinton did not immediately embrace either position. He did seem interested in depersonalizing the conflict, initially suggesting that the sanctions might be lifted even with Hussein in power. But after a detailed policy review, Clinton opted to retain most of the Bush strategy of containment, seeking an extension of U.N. Security Council sanctions. While scaling back the covert program to overthrow Hussein, Clinton did decide to sustain it. Hussein's "charm offensive" soon ended.

In June, tensions reached a post–Desert Storm high. Faced with evidence that Hussein had attempted to assassinate former President Bush in Kuwait, Clinton order a major cruise missile strike against the headquarters of the Iraqi Intelligence Service in Baghdad. "We should not be surprised by such deeds, coming as they do from a regime like Saddam Hussein's," Clinton said, "which has ruled by atrocity, slaughtered its own people, invaded two neighbors, attacked others, and engaged in chemical and environmental warfare."[2] Any desire on the part of the United States to deescalate the conflict was shattered. Iraq was to remain a central element of the Clinton strategy.

■ ■ ■

President Clinton did not bring a refined notion of strategy with him to the White House. At a time of crucial flux in the global security environment, the new administration was forced to think on the fly. Having spent most of his political career as governor of Arkansas, Clinton had little background in foreign policy or national security. After twelve years of Republican presidents, the Democrats did not have a deep pool of experienced talent to draw from. Anthony Lake, Clinton's primary foreign policy adviser during the 1992 campaign, his first national security adviser, and the key architect of his strategy, however, was a brilliant and cerebral thinker. His early career was in the State Department and the National Security Council staff. He had served as director of the State Department's Policy Planning during the Carter administration. Following the pattern first established by Henry Kissinger and Zbigniew Brzezinski, Lake's most recent experience before joining the administration was in academia. Les Aspin, the secretary of defense, was also a former college professor educated at Yale and the Massachusetts Institute of Technology. While he had become a specialist on military issues, particularly the defense budget, he had held no senior executive branch experience and proved more of a conceptualizer than a manager. The initial inclination of Clinton and most of his senior advisers, then, was to diminish the role military force played in American statecraft, relying more on diplomacy and economic power.

But the administration found—like most of those before and after it—that it is extraordinarily difficult to make radical shifts in American strategy. Policy can be changed, but strategic culture, the configuration of the national interest, and the political process by which strategy is made change

with glacial slowness. There was much that the Clinton administration inherited and could not change. In the broadest sense, the overarching goal
of American strategy was such a constant. The United States sought a global
security system or a constellation of regional systems where armed force was
not used to resolve disputes or to alter political systems and power balances.
However paradoxical, American strategy sought to transcend strategy. Given
this, America's strategic opponents were states or non-state actors that used
violence to resolve disputes or alter political systems and power balances.
The cast of enemies changed over time, but their defining characteristic—
the use of violence for aggression—remained constant.

Throughout history, great powers have sought to simultaneously address extant threats and reengineer their security environment. It is a defining characteristic of a great power. States vary, though, on the degree to
which they emphasize the two tasks. Obviously great powers facing significant extant threats must focus on them; those with few extant threats have
the option of devoting energy and resources to the engineering of their
security environment. By contrast, the strategy of lesser powers seeks to
counter, contain, deter, or defeat enemies. Great powers can also seek to
shape or alter the security environment so as to prevent the rise of enemies.

Once the United States became a great power in the decades after
the Civil War, it attained the ability to do this. Initially this was focused on
the traditional area of concern—North America and the Caribbean—and
later in an expanding segment of the world to include South America and
parts of the Pacific Rim. At times this process took its most traditional form:
replacing hostile leaders with friendly or, at least, pliant ones. But like many
great powers from the Romans onward, the United States also saw replicat-
ing its values and methods of political and economic organization as a useful way to both create partners and make itself more secure. This "civilizing"
mission was often wrapped in morality with themes of obligation and duty,
but it was also sound strategy. For the United States, it meant promoting a
set of liberal political and economic values: responsible, transparent governance; democracy; market economic systems; rule by law, and peaceful procedures for conflict resolution.

While many American presidents actively sought to shape the security environment, the presence of a real and dangerous enemy meant that
America's Cold War strategy had to focus more on countering extant threats
than on shaping or reengineering the security environment. By the time
Clinton assumed office, the Soviet Union had fallen. Thus his administra-

tion was freed from the fetters of a threat-based strategy. The administration's leaders saw unbound opportunity. As Warren Christopher, the secretary of state, put it, "We stand on the brink of shaping a new world of extraordinary hope and possibility . . . We can shape the future knowing that the United States is more secure now than at any time since early in this century."[3] William Perry, who replaced Aspin as Clinton's defense secretary, wrote of "defense in an age of hope."[4]

Reengineering the security environment had an internal rationale as well—America needed a "mission" to sustain public and congressional support for activism abroad. Since the early years of the American republic, its leaders have considered access to markets and trading partners abroad an important national interest, crucial to both the economic and political well-being of the United States (since the stability of American democracy is based on providing economic opportunity, which is contingent on economic growth). There is, however, an enduring dilemma. While America's political and business elites understand the importance of foreign markets and trading partners, much of the public does not. And because public opinion, expressed directly or through Congress, matters in American statecraft, national leaders have always been forced to craft strategy in a way that will maximize public support. While a variety of techniques lend themselves to this, two of the most effective are the crusading nature of American policy—putting the United States on the side of "good"—and minimizing the blood and financial costs of overseas engagement. A particular policy could be sustained with either of the two methods, but the strongest support came when both were at place. And a policy with neither was not long for this world.

Clinton and his top advisers—particularly Anthony Lake—were concerned, almost obsessed, with the idea that the end of the Soviet threat had taken away America's global mission, leaving public and congressional support for continued engagement fragile. Thus, they feared, there would be pressure for less involvement outside traditional geographic areas such as the Caribbean, Western Europe, and the Pacific Rim. The public understood the need to counter extant threats and stand by old friends, but convincing Americans to bear the costs of reengineering the security environment, particularly in regions without a tradition of involvement, was a harder sell. "There is," Lake stated, "a dangerous isolationist backlash in the air . . . Our policy of engagement in world affairs is under siege and American leadership is in peril."[5] Persuading the public of the need for the exercise of U.S. military power was especially challenging. Americans traditionally avoided involvement in the security affairs of faraway places during peacetime, mobilized and undertook great exertions during times of war, and then withdrew once the enemy was vanquished. Episodic involvement was appropriate for an insular, middle-range power, but not for a superpower on which global security depended. The Truman administration revised the tradition by convincing the American public and its elected leaders that the United States was at war, albeit a new kind, "cold" rather than "hot." For Clinton, though, there was no war, either hot or cold. Global leadership and engagement in the absence of war was a complete break with tradition rather than simply a Truman-style revision of it.

While Clinton was convinced of the need for American engagement and leadership in the world, he assumed office without a clear notion of the role that military power should play—or at least without a clearly articulated one. As part of the generation shaped by Vietnam, Clinton mistrusted the use of armed force. The absence of ideas about the appropriate (and inappropriate) use of force was exacerbated in the opening year of the administration by the personal antagonism between some of its appointed officials and a military that had grown extremely fond of the Republicans in the preceding twelve years. Many officers simply did not like Clinton on a personal level, seeing him as the personification of the anti-military liberals who had shunned service during the Vietnam conflict and then blamed the military for the outcome. Military leaders recognized that further defense cuts were inevitable, but they had trusted President Bush and Secretary Cheney to modulate this process. They were uncertain that Clinton and Aspin would do the same. There were fears that the major assessment of defense posture and programs that the new secretary of defense began soon after taking office—which became known as the "Bottom-Up Review"—would lead to extensive cuts in force structure or programs.

After this rocky start, Clinton and his top advisers developed a more refined notion of the role of armed force in American strategy, and the U.S. military became less overtly suspicious of the administration. But this was an extended process. It took several years for the administration to develop a coherent strategy integrating the military element of national power in addition to political and economic means. Throughout this process, the enduring challenge was to craft a military strategy for a nonideological age—in Edward Luttwak's term, a time for "post-heroic warfare." This meant that the use of force had to be relatively quick, relatively cheap (in blood terms), and had to generate tangible gains. As Clinton himself said, with the Cold

War over, the primary challenge was to "secure the peace." Knowing how to deter or defeat enemies was one thing. Understanding how to use force to secure the peace was another. From the Clinton administration's perspective the strategic errors of the past—particularly Vietnam—were made because American policymakers lost sight of the need to balance expected costs and risks against expected gains. Clinton, like his immediate predecessors, was determined not to repeat this. Disengagement would have minimized costs and risks, but left the world a disorderly place and thus put important national interests at risk. That left two other methods: sustaining and expanding the qualitative superiority of the American military over its enemies and placing greater reliance on partners, whether other states or international organizations. President Clinton pursued both.

■   ■   ■

The way the Clinton administration chose to deal with aggressor states was much the same as the Bush approach and only a modest deviation from the Cold War. The primary mission of the American armed forces was to deter aggression and, if deterrence failed, defeat them on the battlefield, restoring the status quo ante bellum. Any change to regional power balances or the internal political structure of aggressor states would come through diplomacy rather than being imposed by force of arms. The purpose of military power was to create a "space" for diplomacy. Clinton also adopted the core military strategy concept of the Bush administration's "major regional conflicts" (MRCs)—meet cross-border aggression by a hostile regional power with significant conventional military capability. Iraq, North Korea, and Iran were considered the only states with the capability and willingness for such aggression, hence most planning and war gaming for MRCs dealt with them.

While the three states were heavily armed dictatorships, the likelihood of any of them launching a cross-border invasion was small, at least after Desert Storm. The official explanation was that even though such a contingency was unlikely, it would be the most taxing conflict that the U.S. military might face. If the military was prepared for an MRC (or, actually, two simultaneous MRCs), it could handle anything else it might face. Given that MRCs were based on a short campaign against a conventional Army, this was a stretch. It assumed that a military configured for a short, intense campaign against a conventional enemy can also deal with a protracted irregular campaign. But in the opening years of the Clinton administration, few policymakers or military leaders anticipated involvement in a large-scale, protracted irregular campaign. The military configured for MRC was, in fact, able to handle participation in multinational peacekeeping in the Balkans fairly well, thus validating the idea. Civilian defense leaders and the military favored an MRC-based strategy, and the inclination of the Clinton administration was to defer to them. The fiasco in Somalia should have given some warning that the military had shortcomings when undertaking missions other than Desert Storm–style conventional wars, but it didn't. It was seen as an aberration, the result of bad decisions by policymakers and tactical commanders rather than as an indication of structural flaws in the military or conceptual shortcomings in American strategy.

The focus on MRCs reflected the pressures and constituencies the administration faced. Since MRCs entailed reversing overt, cross-border aggression, they were politically and morally unambiguous. Who could oppose stopping a Saddam Hussein or a Kim il-Sung or Kim Jong-il bent on invading their neighbors? The public and Congress would naturally support sustaining the military capability to do this. Military spending for operations other than war, on the other hand, were always a more difficult sell. Focusing on MRCs also placated other powerful constituencies including the military itself and the defense industry. MRCs required a large force structure and complex systems—things both the military and defense industry liked. From the perspective of the U.S. military and the industries that supported it, Iraq and North Korea had one other advantage: because both relied heavily on Soviet-style equipment, organization, and operational methods, the equipment, organization, and operational methods of the United States, which had been developed to defeat the Soviets, were appropriate. The American military, in other words, had only to keep doing what it had been doing. Saddam Hussein (and his fellow "rogues") thus helped mute those calling for radical change or deep cuts in the U.S. military. Moreover, treating Desert Storm as a paradigm through the focus on MRCS convinced the public that the use of armed force would entail few American or civilian casualties. They assumed all of America's future wars would be like the Gulf War. This helped sustain its utility but also created unrealistic expectations. It also meant that any investment in the continued qualitative superiority of the American military was strategically worthwhile.

■ ■ ■

With rare exceptions, Americans only took strategy seriously during armed conflict. Wartime presidents, particularly Lincoln and Franklin Roosevelt, developed an understanding of strategy despite having little background in it and then found generals and admirals who could complete the grand strategy by crafting a military strategy and armed force to actualize it. The Cold War forced a break from this tradition. It was enough like a "real" war to inspire a community of strategic thinkers, some of whom held political office while others provided ideas and criticism from think tanks, universities, and other bastions of the national intelligentsia. A few serious strategists also emerged in Congress, supported by a greatly expanded cadre of staff assistants, including a crucial group specializing in national security. This led to greater concern for strategy within the military. Its leaders sought to be more than simply the tool of strategy, but also a partner in its development. In the post–Cold War period, the military's role in strategy formulation increased even further, with an assertiveness that led some observers to warn of a "crisis" in civil-military relations.[6] In large part, this was a reaction to Vietnam. The uniformed military had played only a minor role in the strategic decisions that led the United States to involvement in Southeast Asia. Whether openly stated or not, the military seemed to believe that if it were more active in educating civilian policymakers on the uses and misuses of armed force, they would be less likely to make such strategic blunders or miscalculations. Perhaps, as the old saying goes, war is too serious to be left to the generals, but strategy was also too serious to be left solely to politicians. This reached an apogee during the Clinton administration. The uniformed military virtually became the equal of civilian policymakers in influencing where and how the military would be used. The primary method of doing this was by shaping the type of military the nation *had*. The toolmaker, in a sense, influenced how the craftsman went about his work.

As the Clinton strategy took shape, the military was determined to retain its strategic relevance, further augment its qualitative superiority over anticipated opponents, and continue the improvements begun in the dark days of the 1970s. To do this, it needed both a rationale and a road map. This emerged from what became known as the "revolution in military affairs" (RMA). As it developed during the first Clinton administration, the RMA was both a philosophy of strategy and, eventually, a framework for the evolution of the military. American strategic thinkers derived the RMA concept from Soviet military writing of the 1970s and 1980s. The basic idea was that the history of armed conflict was characterized by periods of stability or modest change in operational methods, technology, and organizations interspersed with short periods of rapid and extensive change leading to significant increases in the combat effectiveness of armed forces. What made this particularly important was that states that embraced and capitalized on these military revolutions often gained strategic advantage over those that did not. Thus the political stakes of military revolutions were immense. After observing the 1973 Arab-Israeli War, Soviet Gen.Nikolai Ogarkov (later chief of the General Staff) contended that the world had again entered a period of military revolution. For other Soviet theorists, the 1991 Gulf War reinforced and clarified this idea, showing that new forms of information technology, computing, and networking were allowing unprecedented operational speed and complexity, much greater precision of fires than in past wars, and a vastly improved battlefield awareness on the part of advanced militaries.

The idea that a military revolution was under way and that the United States should embrace and master it found a receptive audience within the Pentagon and American defense community. Even though the United States faced no immediate military challenger, the early advocates of an RMA-based strategy believed, history suggested that one would invariably emerge. Unipolarity always had a finite lifespan. "Although current U.S. military capabilities are superior to any existing threat," as a Pentagon study phrased it, "our supremacy will rapidly diminish over time if we do not continue to enhance our military prowess."[7] By embracing the military revolution, the United States could sustain and even increase its military advantage over potential competitors. A military revolution based on information technology also appeared to offer a solution to another problem American strategists faced: sustaining the political usability of force in an era of diffuse threat and global information saturation that could undercut public support by making military conflict more vivid and real. When the public saw the horrors of armed conflict and the pain of those whose family members were injured or killed on a daily basis, its tolerance was fragile. But the RMA, by augmenting the ability of a military that embraced it in order to limit the human costs of war by precise strikes and rapid operations, might provide a palliative. The benign global security environment of the immediate post–Cold War period provided not only an imperative for embracing the RMA, but also an opportunity.

The RMA concept first took root in the Pentagon's Office of Net Assessment—often called the Department of Defense's "internal think tank."

Its long-serving director, Andrew Marshall, was, in a real sense, the founding father of the movement.[8] The Office of Net Assessment was small—its previous task was monitoring the Soviet Union—but it had the autonomy to explore new strategic concepts and the money to fund research, analysis, and discussion. All revolutions need birthplaces, whether the taverns of colonial America or the radical universities of the modern era. The American RMA was born on the third floor of the Pentagon and in the consulting firms, think tanks, and war colleges that participated in the development of strategic concepts. It quickly caught on among senior military leaders, most important of whom was Adm. William Owens (who later became vice chairman of the Joint Chiefs of Staff).[9] Within a few years the revolutionary cadre and its allies had convinced senior political leaders in the Department of Defense and Congress that America's security depended on mastering the ongoing RMA.

The idea that armed conflict evolves through periodic revolutions did not imply the direction that the revolution of the 1990s should take. Several were feasible—a revolution focused on irregular conflict, on robotic warfare, and so forth. What actually happened was that RMA advocates harnessed the idea of military revolutions to a view of global security focused on force projection for conventional combat against aggressive states. In other words, the RMA did not provide an alternative to the idea of a military strategy built on major regional contingencies but was merged with it. The result was a peculiarly American notion of the ongoing military revolution. This was first fully articulated in a 1997 document entitled *Joint Vision 2010* (soon followed by a revision known as *Joint Vision 2020*).[10] This contended that the key to success in an "increasingly lethal" battlespace would be "dominant battlespace awareness" growing from a "system of systems." Operational concepts like massed force and sequential operations were to be replaced by massed effects and complex simultaneous operations made possible because of networking and information technology. Technological advances, according to *Joint Vision 2010*, "will continue the trend toward improved precision. Global positioning systems, high-energy research, electromagnetic technology, and enhanced stand-off capabilities will provide increased accuracy and a wider range of delivery options."

While the basic conceptual framework for what can be called the "Joint Vision" RMA took shape quickly, Department of Defense leaders recognized that implementing it could be more of a challenge. Eventually, the bevy of actions designed to master and implement the revolution in military affairs became known as "defense transformation."[11] The word itself entered the lexicon of American defense policymakers and experts in 1997. Congress—which often instigated major Pentagon reform, most famously the 1986 Goldwater-Nichols Department of Defense Reorganization Act—had directed the secretary of defense to conduct a periodic "comprehensive examination of America's defense needs" with the first due in 1997. The initial Quadrennial Defense Review (QDR) appeared in May of that year.

Expecting that the QDR would not produce new thinking, Congress used the fiscal year 1997 Defense Authorization Act to require that the secretary of defense also commission an independent, senior-level National Defense Panel to provide another (and hopefully more creative) perspective.[12] The main theme of this group's report was that the United States should undertake "a broad transformation of its military and national security structures, operational concepts and equipment."[13] Transformation, then, was harnessing, directing, and controlling the RMA (along with similar management changes labeled the "revolution in business affairs"). The word and the ideas it included immediately burst into major Department of Defense documents. In the preface to the 1997 *National Military Strategy*, Gen. John M. Shalikashvili, chairman of the Joints Chiefs of Staff, wrote, "We must begin to transform . . . now by exploiting technological advances that are changing warfare."[14] The 1998 *National Security Strategy* stated, "We must transform our forces by exploiting the Revolution in Military Affairs."[15] But despite the rhetoric, what was proposed was reform packaged as revolution. The strategy called for "a carefully planned and focused modernization program" to "replace Cold War-era equipment with new systems and platforms," give U.S. forces greater capability and flexibility, and make the Department of Defense more efficient.[16] The final Clinton National Security Strategy developed this in more detail, noting that "transformation within the military requires integrating activities in six areas: service concept development and experimentation; joint concept development and experimentation, robust processes to implement changes in the services and the joint community, focused science and technology efforts, international transformation activities, and new approaches to personnel development that foster a culture of bold innovation and dynamic leadership."[17] The phrase "integrating activities" is instructive: transformation at that point was primarily the coordination of ongoing reform initiatives.

Each military service recognized that resisting change was a losing proposition but, they believed, change might be shaped to their advantage.

Ideas about the emerging security environment and the nature of future war provided the ammunition in this war. By the late 1990s, each service had its own "strategic futures" division. Not surprising, these produced dramatically different visions of future war. For the Air Force, the key to victory was long-range, precision strike—aerospace power utilizing the latest technology.[18] It placed great emphasis on "effects-based operations," which held that effectiveness and efficiency in war came from a deep understanding of the nature of an enemy's systems and sources of strength, and then seeking to disrupt those.[19]

The Navy's favorite concept was "network-centric warfare," in which American forces were tied together in a seamless web rather than fighting as individual platforms or units.[20] A military that masters network-centric warfare, according to its adherents, will achieve information superiority, reach out long distances with precision weapons, and collapse an enemy's will through the shock of rapid and closely linked attacks. This was important— the Navy, like the Air Force, saw destroying targets the essence of warfare.[21]

The Marine Corps developed its own themes related to its role in expeditionary warfare.[22] One of the more innovative ideas emerging from the Marine Corps in the 1990s was the idea of "fourth-generation war" in which a low-tech enemy "uses all available networks—political, economic, social, and military—to convince the enemy's political decision makers that their strategic goals are either unachievable or too costly for the perceived benefit."[23] This, however, was a radical divergence from the Joint Vision view of the RMA, so it remained confined to the pages of *Marine Corps Gazette* and a few other publications at that time. More central, though, was the idea of the "three block war" developed by Gen. Charles Krulak, commandant of the Marine Corps.[24] This stressed that many modern military operations would involve humanitarian assistance, peacekeeping, and warfighting, often simultaneously. Krulak was particularly concerned with the challenges this posed to junior leaders—what he called the "strategic corporal"—facing the complexity of such an operating environment.

Finally, the Army made its case with the growing complexity of the global security environment and the emergence of what became known as "asymmetric" challenges.[25] It argued that land power would remain crucial in the future security environment, largely because most military operations would fall on the lower and middle portions of the operational continuum, most foreign militaries would remain land power oriented, and land power makes permanent "the otherwise transitory advantages achieved by air and naval forces."[26] But while emphasizing the role of land power against asymmetric threats, the Army did not abandon large-scale conventional war. For instance, *Speed and Knowledge*, the first annual report of the Army After Next Project, singled out the persisting threat from a "major military competitor" and the role that the Army would play in attaining decisive victory against such an enemy.[27]

There were four military services, at least three and a half visions of future warfare, and, by implication, three and a half trajectories of change. The Navy and the Air Force built their future on precision strike; the land forces—the Army and the Marines—on more integrated and closer involvement in a conflict. If there was a revolution under way, it was a tumultuous, even chaotic one. Transformation had become one more venue in interservice conflict made more intense by declines in the size of the U.S. military and defense budget.[28] As Adm. William Owens notes, "History reveals a tendency for the services to diverge rather than coalesce during periods of relative fiscal austerity. That is, each service tends to put planning priority on assuring and protecting core competencies at the expense of those capabilities that support and facilitate operations of the other services. It is easier to be joint in word and deed in times of fiscal largess; parochialism is stronger when budgets draw down."[29] Like most revolutions, then, the RMA spawned factionalism among the revolutionaries. But for all of the debate and dissention, the element of the Clinton military strategy designed to counter threats remained focused on major conventional war against aggressor states. The RMA was preparing the U.S. military to fight Desert Storm more effectively than it had the first time.

■ ■ ■

The Clinton administration sought to shape the security environment using two methods. One was enhancing the military capabilities of partners, augmenting their ability to work in conjunction with U.S. forces, and assisting with the reform of civil-military relations during the transition to democracy. This became known as "engagement." It included the stationing or deployment of U.S. military forces abroad, a broad range of defense cooperation and security assistance programs, training and exercises with allies and friends, and educational exchanges that brought members of foreign militaries to U.S. military schools from service academies to war colleges and that sent U.S. service members to the staff and war colleges of some foreign militaries. Engagement became one of the most important peacetime functions of the regional combatant commands (the Pacific, European, Southern, and Central commands). The Department of Defense created a constellation of regionally focused schools to encourage regional collaboration and help the militaries and defense establishments of states building democracy.

The second method of shaping the security environment was involvement in multinational peacekeeping. This had first developed under the aegis of the United Nations, initially inspired by Secretary-General Dag Hammarskjöld. After the Congo crisis of the early 1960s, participation by the permanent members of the Security Council was seen as an invitation to turn an operation into proxy conflict. Thus the American military gave it little attention. But with the United Nations reinvigorated by the end of the Cold War and a spate of internal wars breaking out in Asia, Europe, and Africa, peacekeeping again became a component of American strategy.

Peacekeeping was never popular within the U.S. military. It tended to drag out into long deployments that interfered with training for warfighting. More important, it involved the armed services in the kinds of ambiguous, politicized activities that could erode morale within the military and public support. There were no victory marches after a peacekeeping operation as there were after short, glorious wars like Desert Storm. The military had learned from its Vietnam experience and its subsequent renaissance that it was better off focusing on warfighting than on low-intensity conflict of any form, including peacekeeping. Many political conservatives agreed, supporting the ideas of Caspar Weinberger and Colin Powell that the U.S. military should only be used when important national interests were at stake, when the military objectives were clear, the commitment closed ended, and when force could be applied in an overwhelming fashion. There was tension between the political Right and Left, with liberals adopting a more expansive view of the American world role and what the armed forces could contribute to it. This was a new development. Conservatives and liberals had sometimes disagreed over the size of the U.S. armed forces but seldom on how American military power should be used.

In 1995, President Clinton ordered an interagency review of multinational peace keeping operations to clarify his policy and assuage critics. The result was a 1996 Presidential Decision Directive (PDD 25).[30] It stated that multinational peacekeeping was not a substitute for warfighting capability, but can be a "force multiplier," helping to decrease the chances that war would occur. "During the Cold War," the directive stated, "the United Nations could resort to multinational peace operations only in the few cases when the interests of the Soviet Union and the West did not conflict. In the new strategic environment such operations can serve more often as a cost-effective tool to advance American and collective interests in maintaining peace in key regions and create global burden-sharing for peace." The final phrase was important. The Clinton strategy viewed American activism as a temporary expedient—the United States would play a leading role in engineering regional security systems only until local capacity could be developed and assume the burden. American activism sought its own obsolescence.

Torn between its desire to manage regional conflicts and the reluctance of the U.S. military and Republican leaders to become mired in expensive, costly, and protracted peacekeeping, the Clinton administration constructed a strategic division of labor. In this, the United States, particularly the U.S. military, might, under certain circumstances, do what only America could do—provide rapid, large-scale stabilization and relief. The U.S. military would focus on what it did best: rapid, massive action within a finite time period. Washington would politically organize the stabilization and reconstruction efforts and provide logistics, transportation, and other support. But—and this was crucial—responsibility for long-term political reconciliation, economic reconstruction, and the maintenance of daily security would fall on someone else, whether the United Nations, regional organizations, other states, or nongovernmental organizations. This made good sense if other states and organizations had the capacity and willingness to play that role. They had to see the issue in basically the same way that the United States did.

There was one hidden flaw in this scheme: it assumed that the U.S. military, working with other advanced armed forces, could reestablish stability relatively quickly, thus paving the way for international organizations and nongovernmental organizations to undertake relief and reconstruction. The underlying assumption was that the U.S. military, because of its immense combat capability, could intimidate the array of militias, armed bands, and warlord armies who might oppose it. But American strategists often overestimate the extent to which the U.S. military can intimidate opponents coming from warrior cultures. On the division of labor, the Clinton strategy did not account for who would undertake protracted stabilization or counterinsurgency operations when the forces of disorder were not quickly cowed or overcome. Somalia (and Lebanon during the Reagan administration) suggested that in those instances, the United States would simply disengage and let the conflict burn itself out over time. This was feasible so long as the stakes were low. Ironically, then, the strategy worked best where American interests were minimal, but provided little guidance on stabilizing regions or nations of extensive concern.

While the U.S. military was not enthusiastic about greater involvement in multinational peacekeeping, once the administration moved in that direction, the services began a series of actions to become more adept at it. They refined their doctrine, concepts, and training for multinational peace operations and, in conjunction with the State Department, developed a number of programs to strengthen the capability of regional organizations and states. One good example was the African Crisis Response Initiative (ACRI). Africa was rife with internal conflicts and the type of conflict-induced humanitarian disasters that begged for peacekeeping. But it was also a region of limited tangible U.S. national interests. ACRI was designed to train African militaries in peacekeeping so that they, acting under the aegis of the United Nations or the Organization of African Unity, could preserve regional stability without a major American role.[31] This same idea—that active U.S. participation in peacekeeping was a temporary situation until regional capacity could emerge—applied to Europe, Asia, and the Americas as well.

But the problem was larger than simply peacekeeping. Peacekeeping implies the existence of a peace to keep. The more common challenge in the tumultuous time following the Cold War was *making* peace—using a combination of force and other means to stop what Leslie Gelb called the "teacup wars" that spawned humanitarian disasters and threatened to engulf entire regions.[32] This was contentious both within the American foreign policy elite and among scholars of U.S. statecraft. Opponents of peacekeeping deprecated the idea, calling it "foreign policy as social work" or disputing the notion that any intervention could be impartial (with the conclusion that taking sides in complex, internal struggles in cultures the U.S. poorly understood was a bad idea).[33] Many others warned of a growing gap between the multiple missions an activist policy required of the military and the resources it was given.[34] The defense budget and military force were adequate only if the use of force was rare. Protracted humanitarian interventions ran the risk of eating away at the military by complicating recruitment and retention (and thus increasing the cost of labor), and by forcing the military services to shift funds intended for research and development

or new acquisitions into operations and maintenance. The Clinton administration itself remained torn—its humanitarian instincts and desire to construct a seamless global peace were constrained by the costs and risks of a
long series of humanitarian interventions. The official policy allowed humanitarian intervention but only under strict conditions.

■ ■ ■

The United States knew how to use its high-tech, transforming military to reverse conventional aggression and support a friendly regime threatened by leftist insurgency. It was learning how to use military force as part of
a multinational coalition to restore order in a collapsed state and set the
stage for reconstruction by the United Nations or the coalition partners.
But this was not the problem set posed by Iraq from 1992 on. The challenge
was to use military power in a modulated form to support political and economic pressure, attempting to coerce a determined and skillful opponent
to do things it did not want to do.

Clinton kept the containment policy he had inherited from the Bush
administration: sanctions, U.N. inspections, diplomatic isolation, and prohi-
bitions on certain types of military activity, including "no-fly" zones in northern and southern Iraq.[35] There simply were no better options, particularly
ones with lower costs or risks. Clinton, as Kenneth Pollack notes, "disliked
the whole issue of Iraq" and "wanted to have as little to do with it as possible."[36] While some administration officials such as National Security Council official Martin Indyk pushed for a more aggressive stance based on covert
support to Iraqi opposition movements and more air strikes, Clinton's closest advisers were satisfied that the containment strategy kept Hussein at bay
without risking international support for the sanctions. Containment was,
in many ways, the least bad of a range of bad alternatives. Hussein was well
aware of this and crafted his own strategy to paint himself as a victim and
thus split off the less determined members of the international coalition.

Initially containment and the sanctions increased the pressure on
Hussein. By the end of 1993, his regime had gone through its stockpiles of
goods and money. Iraq faced mounting inflation and shortages. The regime
cut food rations. Dissatisfaction spread to Hussein's core constituency, Sunni
Arabs. An uprising among the al-'Ubayd tribe was suppressed and several
assassination attempts thwarted, but this did not portend well for the regime. In March 1994, the United States succeeded in having the sanctions

renewed despite opposition from France, Russia, and China. Frustrated, Hussein decided to up the ante in the way he knew best—threats of violence. In October 1994, he moved several Republican Guard divisions to Iraq's border with Kuwait. While it was not clear whether he actually intended to invade, the Clinton administration took no chances. In what became called Operation Vigilant Warrior, the United States reinforced its military in the Gulf, deploying additional Marines, Army mechanized forces, land-based aircraft, and a carrier battle group.[37] The United Nations Security Council passed Resolution 949, demanding that Iraq withdraw its forces. With this demonstration of American resolve, Hussein backed off.

Ironically, both the United States and Iraq failed to attain their political objectives through bluster and threat. Hussein then returned to chipping away at the international coalition and manipulating and publicizing the suffering of the Iraqi people, which he blamed on the sanctions. This resonated in the Arab world. It provoked other Muslims to the point of violence, serving as one of the inspirations for Osama bin Laden and his al-Qaeda colleagues to declare war on the United States.[38] Hussein's psychological operations also found sympathizers within the United States. Writers and organizations on the Far Left were particularly receptive—as seen most famously in Noam Chomsky's book *Iraq Under Siege* and the work of groups like the Peace Action Education Fund.[39] But Hussein's propaganda eventually resonated within mainstream publication like *Foreign Affairs*, on the editorial pages of national newspapers, and even among liberal members of Congress.[40]

In 1995, the United States began a diplomatic initiative to shore up support for the sanctions. In April the Clinton administration proposed U.N. Security Council Resolution 986—the "oil for food" resolution—which would allow Iraq to sell a certain amount of oil and buy food and medicine with part of the proceeds. In 1995 the defection of Hussein Kamel, Saddam Hussein's son-in-law and one of the managers of Iraq's weapons of mass destruction program, showed Washington the extent to which Iraq had misled and duped the U.N. weapons inspectors, particularly on biological weapons. This revived debate within the Clinton administration between the hard-liners advocating greater pressure for regime change and soft-liners who feared the Iraq issue would distract from settlement of the Palestinian conflict. Continued provocations from Hussein including periodic interference with U.N. inspectors and a military offensive into the Kurdish city of Irbil failed to blunt his political manipulation of the human impact of the sanctions or to stir senior Clinton administration officials into greater action than occasional air or cruise missile strikes or the extension of the no-fly zones. The Clinton strategy was truly one of "ignore it and hope it goes away."

Personnel changes in 1997 suggested a more aggressive turn in American policy. Samuel R. Berger replaced Anthony Lake as national security adviser, and Madeleine Albright followed Warren Christopher as secretary of state. Instead the pattern of the past years—challenges and threats from Hussein countered by equal threats or limited strikes by the United States— continued. In October 1997 Hussein announced that he was expelling the American members of the United Nations Special Commission (UNSCOM— the weapons inspectors) and would shoot down U.S. surveillance planes monitoring Iraq's compliance with the sanctions. Washington again sent additional military forces to the Gulf and threatened additional strikes. In what had become a ritual dance, Baghdad then rescinded its decision. In February 1998, the Clinton administration was again preparing military action when United Nations secretary general Kofi Annan negotiated a deal that made concessions to Hussein and weakened the inspections in return for an agreement to give the inspectors unhindered access. In August 1998, Hussein announced he was ending all cooperation with the inspectors and, in October, began blocking U.N. monitoring. As the United States prepared to strike, Hussein again backed off. The Clinton administration began planning a major attack. In December, UNSCOM chairman Richard Butler reported to the United Nations that Hussein had failed to cooperate with the inspections and imposed new restrictions on the inspectors. From Clinton's perspective, Iraq "abused its final chance."[41] In response, the United States and the United Kingdom undertook a sustained seventy-hour air offensive against ninety-seven targets in Iraq, including command centers, missile factories, and airfields. In what was called Operation Desert Fox, American and British forces launched around 600 aircraft sorties and 400 cruise missile strikes.

The escalation did not alter Saddam Hussein's behavior in any major way. As Daniel Byman and Matthew Waxman put it, "The Desert Fox air campaign was not so much a case of coercion as it was a recognition that past coercion efforts had failed and that any campaign should focus on future coercion efforts."[42] That only one partner nation actually contributed forces (the United Kingdom), that the Arab world condemned of the raids, and that Russia, France, and China called for swiftly lifting sanctions imme-

diately afterward showed that the use of force eroded rather than strength-
ened support for the sanctions. There was also little sign that the strikes had
any effect on Saddam Hussein's will or that of his key supporters. In a com-
bative press conference following the strikes, Iraqi deputy prime minister
Tariq Aziz labeled Clinton and British prime minister Tony Blair "criminal
aggressors" and stated that Iraq would not allow the U.N. inspectors to return until the sanctions were lifted.[43]

With the sanctions in trouble and little sign that Hussein planned to
comply with the 1991 settlement, Clinton revisited the idea of regime change
in Iraq. While this had been part of American policy since the end of the
Gulf War, the administration had put little energy into it. Senior officials
had even stopped CIA programs designed to strengthen armed resistance
to Hussein.[44] But some mid-level officials continued to push it. Pressure
mounted from outside the administration, particularly among Republicans.
In February 1998 an open letter to President Clinton signed by forty prominent former officials including Richard Allen, Frank Carlucci, Robert
McFarlane, Donald Rumsfeld, and Caspar Weinberger stated, "Only a determined program to change the regime in Baghdad will bring the Iraqi crisis
to a satisfactory conclusion." A letter to Clinton from the Project for the
New American Century stated that American strategy "should aim, above
all, at the removal of Saddam Hussein's regime from power." Changing the
Iraqi regime had become a "leading alternative" to Clinton's containment
policy.[45] In October, Congress passed H.R. 4655, the "Iraq Liberation Act of
1998," which made support for Hussein's opponents official U.S. policy. It
called for assistance to Iraqi democratic opposition organizations and for
the United States to push the United Nations to create a war crimes tribunal
to prosecute Saddam Hussein and other senior Iraqi officials, but stated,
"nothing in this Act shall be construed to authorize or otherwise speak to
the use of the United States Armed Forces . . . in carrying out this Act" other
than providing equipment, education, and training to opposition groups.[46]
In signing it, Clinton indicated that his administration would follow the law.[47]
The revised approach was called "containment plus regime change."

As with the use of military force, though, the Clinton policy on regime change in Iraq was inconsistent and tentative. In early December 1998,
National Security Adviser Berger stated that the Clinton administration was
committed to a "new government" in Baghdad.[48] A few weeks later he said
that it was "neither the purpose nor the effect" of the Desert Fox military
strikes "to dislodge Saddam from power." Apparently rejecting regime change,

Berger said, "The only sure way for us to effect his departure now would be to commit hundreds of thousands of American troops to fight on the ground inside Iraq. I do not believe that the costs of such a campaign would be sustainable at home or abroad. And the reward of success would be an American military occupation of Iraq that could last years. The strategy we can and will pursue is to contain Saddam in the short and medium term, by force if necessary, and to work toward a new government over the long term." In December, influential senators Trent Lott, Jesse Helms, Richard Shelby, John Kyl, Richard Lugar, and Sam Brownback expressed their frustration in a public letter to Clinton: "Your decision to sign and fully implement the Iraq Liberation Act (P.L.105-338) appeared to be the change of course many of us had urged. . . . Unfortunately, it appears that your commitment to support the political opposition to Saddam Hussein has not trickled down through the Administration."

The Clinton administration's unwillingness to embrace regime change was initially based on the desire to focus on other issues and the fear that a post-Hussein Iraq would fragment, to the advantage of Iran. Once the Clinton team did reluctantly move in this direction, it did not know how to remove Hussein without a full-scale invasion (which the administration considered politically unsupportable). Two methods were considered and, to some extent, tried. One was to provoke a military coup. But this was unappealing since any Iraqi military leader powerful enough to overthrow Hussein would have been little better. Moreover, Hussein had, through the expansion of his security apparatus and brutal repression, virtually "coup proofed" his regime by the mid-1990s.[49] The alternative was cultivating and strengthening the Iraqi resistance. While this had emotional appeal—one analyst likened it to the "Reagan doctrine" of the 1980s, which helped expel the Soviets from Afghanistan—most Iraq experts were skeptical.[50] The resistance was too weak and divided and Hussein too entrenched for success without massive and direct U.S. involvement.[51] Even Gen. Anthony Zinni, commander of the U.S. Central Command, expressed open skepticism of supporting Iraqi resistance movements.[52] Having backed off support for the Iraq resistance a few years earlier, the administration did not expend much effort resuscitating the relationship even after the 1998 congressional act.[53]

Devoid of other options, the Clinton administration preserved the sanctions and launched limited air strikes when Hussein provided a reason. After Operation Desert Fox, Hussein ordered his air defense system to a more aggressive stance, regularly "painting" coalition aircraft enforcing the no-fly zones with radar and firing antiair missiles. The United States and United Kingdom respond by attacking air defense and other targets. Coalition air raids became a daily occurrence—by August 1999, U.S. and British aircraft had flown around 10,000 sorties and launched 1,000 bombs and missiles against more than 400 targets. In December 1999, the United Nations created a new but less intrusive inspection system. According to Daniel Byman, this had the opposite of its intended effect—it stood little chance of actually revealing or stopping Hussein's weapons of mass destruction programs but gave the Iraqi more ammunition for his psychological campaign, creating the illusion of compliance.[54]

As the Clinton administration wound down, critics such as Andrew Bacevich warned that Hussein was on the verge of reversing the results of the 1991 Gulf War.[55] Few administration officials seemed convinced that the air strikes were likely to either change the Iraqi dictator's behavior or lead to his overthrow. Clinton's unenthusiastic relationship with the weak and fractured Iraqi resistance was similarly devoid of promise. There was, in Daniel Byman's words, "a yawning gap between the administration's ambitious rhetoric and its halfhearted actions."[56] The sanctions and inspections were crumbling. Ultimately, the Clinton strategy of "containment plus regime change" was simply the least bad approach designed to delay any sort of resolution of the conflict in either direction. The Iraq problem (or, as it was seen at the time, the Hussein problem) was left for Clinton's successor.

■   ■   ■

While the George H. W. Bush administration had to temper the change in American strategy while there was still a breath of life in the Soviet Union, the Clinton administration was free from this constraint. It could have engineered a profoundly new strategy but did not. Much, even most, remained constant. Iraq was a major reason. Clinton did increase U.S. involvement in regional security, including areas with little history of such activity. He continued Bush's revival of collective security, involving the United States in U.N. peacekeeping missions and expanding programs to build defense capacity in local states. He began to shift from deterring aggression to preempting both aggression and proliferation. Iraq, though, was a brake on change. Saddam Hussein kept Southwest Asia the top priority in American strategy, and his large, conventional military allowed the U.S. military to retain its focus on conventional combat against "rogue states." Had the Iraq threat dissipated, the U.S. military and its supporters would have had a much more difficult time convincing American political leaders to sustain and even improve the ability to defeat conventional, cross-border aggression. But the lingering Iraqi threat increased the deference that administration policymakers accorded the military, allowing it to chart its own future (and that of the nation).

The core strategic dilemma for the Clinton administration was limiting the costs and risks of managing regional security. Only by doing this, senior officials believed, would the American public and Congress support an activist strategy in what was perceived as a relatively benign global security environment. Most of the Clinton strategy—the transformation of conventional military capabilities, capacity building in partners, involvement in multinational peacekeeping—was designed specifically to mitigate costs and risks. But Iraq also demonstrated the enduring problems the United States faced when using force as an integral element of diplomacy. As Henry Kissinger and Richard Nixon had found when attempting to use armed force to signal and coerce North Vietnam during peace negotiations, the American public and Congress have little understanding of or patience for this. The idea that force should be used only in war, and then used for total victory, lingered. Like Kissinger and Nixon, Clinton discovered that force only supports diplomacy when the United States is able and willing to surpass the pain tolerance of its opponent. It worked against Slobodan Milosevic but did not work against the more determined, ruthless, and psychologically savvy Saddam Hussein. Clinton left office with the Iraq problem no closer to resolution than when he entered.

4

TERRORISM AND FORCE

Thou shalt not be afraid for the terror by night
nor for the arrow that flieth by the day.
—PSALMS 91-5

After a decade of looming large over American strategy, Iraq receded during the 2000 presidential campaign. It seldom came up in speeches and debates, even those dealing with international affairs or national security. When the Republican platform mentioned Iraq, it offered no new ideas but only insisted that existing policies be enforced. "A new Republican administration," it stated, "will patiently rebuild an international coalition opposed to Saddam Hussein and committed to joint action." The Democratic platform said even less, promising to continue the Clinton policy, which, it contended, had Saddam Hussein "boxed in." Neither Texas governor George W. Bush nor Vice President Al Gore considered foreign policy in general and Iraq in particular major concerns. Both focused on domestic policy and economic issues. But events have a way of derailing intentions.

Like Clinton in 1992, Bush was a successful Southern governor with no track record in foreign policy or national security. Unlike Clinton, though, he had a deep and talented pool of potential advisers to draw from, most of whom had held senior or mid-level positions in the Reagan or George H. W. Bush administrations. While not obvious at the time, this was both a blessing and a burden. He had talented advisers, but their past success made it more difficult to jettison old ideas even when circumstances changed.

As Bush's foreign policy and national security ideas coalesced, there was strident opposition to any program or idea associated with Clinton. As Ivo Daalder and James Lindsay noted, the statements of Bush and his core foreign policy advisers "dripped with disdain for the forty-second president."[1] This reflected the general tenor of the campaign, which, under the guidance of Karl Rove, sought to make the distinctions between Bush and Clinton on policy and personal ethics as stark as possible. But it also grew from deeper trends in American politics. With the end of the Cold War, partisanship exploded in debates over foreign and national security policy. The demise of the Soviet threat removed the incentive for bipartisanship and ended the idea that politics "stop at the water's edge." The discord characterizing many domestic issues seeped into international ones.

The emergence of new media, particularly twenty-four-hour cable news, talk radio, and the Internet, amplified partisanship. Media pundits rather than elected leaders shaped the public's political positions. Elected leaders often had an instinct for moderation. To accomplish anything, they had to work not only with like-thinking colleagues but also with the opposing party. Media pundits, most of whom had never held elected office, felt less compunction for moderation. In fact, their quest for audience share drove them toward the poles of the political spectrum. As talk shows, blogs, and other information sources proliferated, only an extreme position stood out from the crowd. Combat discourse became the norm; entertainment merged with political discussion. The segment of the public that drew its political cues from the new media was dragged along. Savvy elected leaders picked up on the trend and gravitated to the political poles.

As he defined himself as the "anti-Clinton" (and, by association, the "anti-Gore"), Bush hammered the Clinton administration for failing to set priorities in foreign and security policy, allowing the U.S. military to atrophy, and shackling the United States with multilateralism. In a key 1999 speech at the Citadel—a historic military college in South Carolina, one of the most strongly Republican states in the nation—Governor Bush blamed Clinton for "sending our military on vague, aimless, and endless deployments. . . ."[2] As president, he pledged to "replace uncertain missions with well-defined objectives" and "begin creating the military of the next century."

Bush's thinking on foreign and national security policy included a strong dose of the political realism that dominated his father's administration. Its defining features were a focus on great power interactions and the belief that the United States should maintain a balance among the great powers. Its clearest expression was in an article for the journal *Foreign Affairs* by Condoleezza Rice, a National Security Council official in the administration of the senior Bush who had also become one of the closest foreign policy advisers to candidate George W. Bush.[3] Rather than setting clear priorities based on American national interests, Rice argued, Clinton approached every issue serendipitously, never attempting to see them in a larger perspective. To gain the approval of other nations, Clinton pursued multilateral solutions even when doing so was not in America's interest. Rice advocated a clear focus on the few "big powers" that could disrupt international peace, stability, and prosperity. And, mirroring the central theme of Bush's Citadel speech, she advocated "building the military of the twenty-first century rather than continuing to build on the structure of the Cold War." She felt that U.S. technological advantages "should be leveraged to build forces that are lighter and more lethal, more mobile and agile, and capable of firing accurately from long distances."

Rice did not spell out exactly what the transformed U.S. military was to do. Presumably it would dissuade competitive great powers, especially Russia and China, from challenging the status quo through military means and deter or defeat "rogue regimes and hostile powers" such as North Korea, Iraq, and Iran (although it was not immediately evident why this required lighter, more lethal, mobile, and agile forces). She was clear, though, on what the U.S. military should *not* do:

> The president must remember that the military is a special instrument. It is lethal, and it is meant to be. It is not a civilian police force. It is not a political referee. And it most certainly is not designed to build a civilian society. Military force is best used to support clear political goals, whether limited, such as expelling Saddam from Kuwait, or comprehensive, such as demanding the unconditional surrender of Japan and Germany during World War II. It is one thing to have a limited political goal and to fight decisively for it; it is quite another to apply military force incrementally, hoping to find a political solution somewhere along the way. A president entering these situations must ask whether decisive force is possible and is likely to be effective and must know how and when to get out.[4]

Rice was describing the Weinberger and Powell principles—the idea that military force should only to be used for clear and close-ended objectives. Against the backdrop of Bosnia or Somalia, where the stakes were low and the United States could have resisted military involvement at a minimal cost, this made sense. What Dr. Rice and other realists had not explained at that point was what they would do when the stakes were high yet the mission was ambiguous and complex. How should the United States act when the world needed a "political referee" or to "build a civilian society"? During the course of the 2000 election, though, such dilemmas seemed unlikely and Governor Bush was able to portray himself as the candidate who would resist embroiling the U.S. military in stabilization, peacekeeping, or nation-building operations.

While Rice and other realists claimed to define the Republican foreign policy, they had competitors. This group was widely known as "neoconservatives" (although this was a misuse of the term coined to refer to liberals who, in the 1970s, moved to the Right out of frustration with what they considered the Democrats' weakness toward communism).[5] Opposed to what they saw as the amoral and misguided realism that had originated with Henry Kissinger and continued through the administration of the senior Bush, they sought to revive the conservative idealism of the Reagan foreign policy. Idealism is that the belief that the domestic political organization of states plays a major, even a determining, role in their statecraft, and that morality should shape foreign and national security policy. While realists believed that all states, from totalitarian dictatorships to liberal democracies, behave more or less similarly, pursuing their national interests within the framework of power balances, idealists felt that democracies were different. The greater the number of democracies there were in the world, the more stable and less conflict-prone regional and global relations. From this viewpoint, promoting democracy and opposing evil should be central elements of American foreign and national security policy. What distinguished *conservative* idealists from their liberal counterparts was the idea that the major tool for promoting democracy and opposing evil was American power, not international institutions and law.

As it evolved in the 1990s, the neo-Reaganism of the conservative idealists diverged from the original. Most obviously, it took an expansive view of the ability of the United States to reengineer the world. The new breed of conservative idealists believed that American power was so great and its cause so just that no task was impossible. Equally important, Reagan's heirs began to stress American military power to a much greater extent than their hero did. Certainly Reagan had recognized the importance of military power and was the architect of one of the largest peacetime increases in the defense budget. But for him, military strength was a means to allow political strength—the appeal of democracy and economic freedom—to change the world. During the course of the Cold War, American strategy had been based on the idea that communist principles were inferior to those of the West. So while the Soviet Union could have prevailed militarily, if prevented from attaining military victory it would falter in the face of inherently superior Western political and economic ideas. Hence American military power was essentially defensive. The new generation of conservative idealists turned this on its head, seeing military power as the fulcrum of American strategy. Military power, they thought, could allow the United States to accelerate the growth of freedom. Like Lenin, they believed they could speed the pace of history.

Why this change? In part it stemmed from the predominance of the American military. Since the chances of regional war escalating to the thermonuclear level were minimal (with the possible exception of a conflict with China over Taiwan), the use of military power was considered less risky than it was during the height of the Cold War. The U.S. armed forces were virtually undefeatable by any conceivable enemy or hostile coalition. The major remaining constraint on the exercise of American power was a self-imposed lack of confidence and will. "In a world in which peace and American security depend on American power and the will to use it," William Kristol (son of Irving Kristol, an original neo-conservative) and Robert Kagan wrote, "the main threat the United States faces now and in the future is its own weakness."[6] Impatience was also a factor. As students of history, the conservative idealists knew that unipolarity was a rare thing. Charles Krauthammer—the high priest of unipolarity—described the gap between American power and that of other states as "unprecedented."[7] Eventually it would end. The conservative idealists thus sought to reengineer the global security system while they could. Military power was the quickest way to do that and thus the preferred method. The use of the armed forces to restore democracy in Panama during the George H. W. Bush administration had, to the conservative idealists, demonstrated the viability of advancing freedom at the point of the bayonet. This was a precedent they hoped to replicate on a larger scale.

One of the key lessons conservatives had learned during their reemergence in the 1970s and 1980s was that ideas mattered. Their ascent came from both Ronald Reagan's charisma and vision and the strengthening of a conservative network of policy research institutes (most important the American Enterprise Institute [AEI] and the Heritage Foundation), publications such as *Commentary* and *The National Interest*, and other organizations such as the Committee on the Present Danger. These provided the intellectual fuel for the Reagan revolution. During their exile from power in the Clinton years, conservative idealists became convinced that their basic ideas and policy prescriptions remained as valid as ever, but the institutional framework of their movement and its ability to undertake (and win) political combat had weakened, in large part because the centrist administration of the senior Bush blurred the distinction between liberals and conservatives. The conservative idealists planned to change that. They were revivalists seeking to reignite the faithful to reclaim power.

Kristol and Kagan—both former Reagan administration officials—led the effort. One of the most important steps was the creation of an organization called the Project for the New American Century (PNAC) to provide a conservative forum on security issues that could challenge Clintonism. The name was intended to evoke publisher Henry Luce's 1941 essay claiming that historians would one day see the twentieth century as the American one. So too, the conservative idealists believed, could the twenty-first century be an American one. PNAC's 1997 statement of principles noted that conservatives had not provided an alternative strategic vision during the Clinton administration. The organization sought to do that, insisting that if the United States revived the strength of its military and its confidence to exercise power, it could recapture the Reagan spirit. The signatories included a number of future officials in the George W. Bush administration, most important Vice President Dick Cheney; Secretary of Defense Donald Rumsfeld; I. Lewis Libby, a key Cheney adviser; and Paul Wolfowitz, deputy secretary of defense. Not content to rely on collective efforts, Kristol and Kagan also coauthored a seminal 1996 article in *Foreign Affairs*, the most important journal of the foreign policy establishment, which touted America's "benevolent hegemony" and called for an increased defense budget.[8] They later expanded their thinking into an edited book that included contributions from conservative policy luminaries such as Richard Perle, Paul Wolfowitz, and Elliott Abrams.[9] The title of the book—*Present Dangers*—was a direct allusion to the Committee on the Present Danger, the hawkish lobbying group that had included many of the original neo-conservatives. Kristol became editor and publisher of *The Weekly Standard*, a journal of ideas and opinion that played the same catalytic role *Commentary* had during the earlier conservative revival.

The distinction between conservative realism and conservative idealism was always as much about the purpose of strategy as about specific policy options. Sometimes strategy is simply a patterned way of dealing with individual issues, challenges, or threats. The grand strategies of most of history's great empires—whether the Roman, the British, or some other—fell into this category. There was no identified end state. Each generation of leaders only sought to leave a strong and stable empire—perhaps an enlarged one— to their heirs. The other type of strategy is teleological. It does, in fact, have an identified end state. Broadly speaking, the strategy of conservative realists was of the first type—a patterned way of dealing with individual issues, challenges, or threats. The strategy of conservative idealists was of the latter type. However far in the future or difficult to attain, they saw an end state: a world composed of free market democracies. In 2000, this difference seemed unimportant. Republicans joined in their quest to reclaim the White House, pushing any conceptual tension into the background. Bush himself was able to unify the realists and the idealists within his party, using the desire to retake the White House from the Democrats as inspiration. Eventually, though, the conservative coalition developed fissures.

As the new administration took shape, realism appeared to dominate. Rice became national security adviser. Colin Powell, a realist, was secretary of state. Secretary of Defense Donald Rumsfeld and Vice President Dick Cheney, while they had signed the PNAC statement of principles, were not idealists. Both had entered government service under Richard Nixon, the consummate realist. They were assertive nationalists little inclined to use the American military for democratization or to cast their policy positions in grand moralism. Only Deputy Secretary of Defense Paul Wolfowitz was a card-carrying member of the idealist faction. The initial Bush strategy thus looked more like that of his father than like Reagan's. There may have been Reaganite thinking—the potential for revolution—in Republican commentators and a few of the administration's associated advisers, but it was sublimated. Then came the epiphany.

■　■　■

No event in American history sparked a greater shift in strategy than the attack of September 11, 2001. Pearl Harbor, the invasion of South Korea, and the attack on the *Lusitania* were monumental, but they simply propelled the United States faster and further down a road it had already taken. They were bursts of clarity rather than a change of course. September 11 not only gave the Bush strategy the focus that it had been missing, but also drove it in a direction it would not have taken had the attacks not occurred.

In the weeks after September 11, it was clear to President Bush, his advisers, and the nation that conservative realism was inadequate for confronting al-Qaeda. A power imbalance did not cause the attacks on the United States, and the great powers alone could not counter the new threat. In fact, the global security system based on sovereign nation-states was an additional (and intended) victim of al-Qaeda. How, then, was Bush to respond? Some commentators contended that the new threat, being seamlessly transnational, interspersed within global financial and information networks, and consummately non-state, could only be defeated by increased multinational cooperation, weaving together various national intelligence and law enforcement communities. Had Al Gore won the 2000 presidential election, the United States might have taken this path. But there is little evidence that George Bush seriously considered it. His epiphany led elsewhere.

When faced with a new threat or challenge, it is human nature to look for some preexisting solution or explanation to adapt and use. Conservative idealism filled this role, providing a coherent, alternative conceptual framework. It was predicated on the idea that existing policy options, whether the conservative realism of George H. W. Bush or the liberal multilateralism of Clinton, failed to protect the United States. Conservative idealism held intrinsic appeal to President Bush. Take, for instance, its neo-Reaganism. There is no doubt that he sought to solidify his place in history, so emulating a popular predecessor made sense. Conservative idealism fit Bush's personality and philosophy. It was imbued with the sense of moral clarity that seemed to have slipped away with the end of the Cold War. George H. W. Bush and Bill Clinton seldom spoke of evil. American statecraft was no longer a crusade but simply a workaday quest to promote the national interest. This changed in a matter of hours on September 11. The world once again pitted good against evil. A great moral crusade—that most American of quests—began.

Bush's receptivity to crusading moralism was a reflection of his inexperience. Ideological struggle pitting good against evil appeals even to someone not deeply versed in statecraft and strategy. It makes common sense. Only long experience and rigorous study can create a realist; it is not an intuitively obvious position. An idealist, by contrast, can be developed quickly, perhaps even in a matter of minutes. Moreover, the notion of confronting evil reflected deep currents in the American strategic culture. Because the public and most members of Congress know little about world affairs and the complexities of strategy, realism, with its emphasis on maintaining power balances, is a difficult sell. It is much easier to mobilize support for a morally unambiguous cause. Defeating evil the American public understands; maintaining anamoral power balance it does not.

The problem was—and always has been—that focusing on evil drives the United States into a reactive posture, responding to threats rather than preventing them. Since it takes extant and obvious evil to inspire the American public, the United States could confront Saddam Hussein in the 1990s after the invasion of Kuwait had revealed his true colors, but probably could not have in the late 1980s, when his evil was masked and overshadowed by the Iranian threat. It would have been easier to have dealt with al-Qaeda in the early 1990s than after September 11, but doing so would have been a difficult sell to the American public, particularly if it involved bloodshed. Unfortunately, it takes moral clarity to inspire great American exertions, and this is a rare commodity in statecraft.

After September 11, this was not a problem. By portraying American strategy as a crusade against evil, Bush mobilized massive public and congressional support (at least for a while). His approval ratings were some of the highest ever recorded for an American president. But launching a crusade is easier than leading one to a successful conclusion. Much remained to be done in order to turn America's moment of moral clarity into an effective strategy. The first requirement was a basic conceptualization of the enemy and the conflict. This had immense implications for the future direction of American strategy. Ironically, President Bush's decisions were similar to ones made in the initial years of the Cold War. As that conflict took shape in the late 1940s, some policymakers and national security experts argued that the Soviet Union simply wanted a security buffer. The solution was to help Moscow feel secure. The other camp in Washington saw the conflict as one of ideology rather than policy. The Soviet Union did want secure borders; it also wanted to rule the world. Communism was its vehicle to do so. Clearly, those who took the ideological perspective assumed a basic incompatibility between liberal democracy and communism. The two could not coexist forever. One had to triumph.

In reality, the Soviet Union was simultaneously an insecure nation seeking security and the architect of an aggressive, evil ideology with global ambitions. Both positions were correct. Ironically, what made American strategy effective was that it vacillated between the two. During the 1950s and 1960s, U.S. policymakers treated the Cold War as a purely ideological structure. In the 1970s with détente, they treated it as a policy conflict. Then, with Reagan, the United States returned to an ideological approach. This shifting conceptualization worked. As Edward Luttwak noted in his assessment of the paradoxical logic of strategy, what works today is unlikely to do so tomorrow as the opponent adjusts. America's strategic shifts during the Cold War inadvertently capitalized on this, changing the nature of the conflict every time that the Soviets adjusted.

The initial task was developing clarity and focus. When the "global war on terror" took shape in the late summer and early autumn of 2001, President Bush adopted a decidedly ideological perspective, defining the conflict with Islamic militants as a war of incompatible ideas akin to the Cold War. His explanation of the conflict was remarkably similar to those developed in the early years of the Cold War. As Douglas Feith, Bush's under secretary of defense for policy, pointed out, al-Qaeda, unlike previous terrorist groups, sought absolute victory over the United States, not simply concessions.[10] The group's objective, according to President Bush, "is remaking the world and imposing its radical beliefs on people everywhere."[11] The attack on the United States was not because of anything America *did*, according the President Bush, but because of what it *is*. "They hate . . . democratically elected government. Their leaders are self-appointed. They hate our freedoms—our freedom of religion, our freedom of speech, our freedom to vote and assemble and disagree with each other."[12]

Linking the conflict with Islamic militants to the Cold War helped Americans understand it. They could easily call up old mental images. But the analogy was imperfect. While the Cold War was, to a large extent, an ideological "war of ideas," it was a symmetric one. Both sides offered different political and economic prescriptions, but they ultimately were talking about the same thing—the organization of daily life. The peoples of the world had to decide whether they wanted to live in a political system built on free enterprise and democracy or on communism. The Cold War was a *civil* war within Western culture (albeit one that also played out in non-Western cultures).[13] The emerging ideological conflict with Islamic militants was asymmetric and cross-cultural. The United States talked about the structures of political and economic life; al-Qaeda and other militant groups talked about spiritualism and fealty to God. While not yet evident in

2001, countering spiritual and religious arguments with political and economic ones was difficult, perhaps even impossible. Americans knew how to conduct a symmetric, intracultural war of ideas, but they were novices at asymmetric, cross-cultural ideological warfare, particularly when it involves spirituality. The separation of politics and religion hamstrung them in this strange, new conflict.

As Bush developed his new strategy, he initially elected to define the enemy using a tactic—terrorism—rather than ideology, political objective, ethnicity, religion, nationality, or any other normal means. This had no historical precedent. While the "war on terror" began with al-Qaeda, it would not end, according to the president, "until every terrorist group of global reach has been found, stopped and defeated." Since the U.S. Department of State and private organizations such as the Search for International Terrorist Entities (SITE) Institute identified more than forty transnational terrorist organizations, this was a monumental undertaking. In addition, it complicated the psychological dimension of the strategy. Terrorist entities did not share a unified ideology or strategy, only a tactic. Ideas that might weaken or undercut some of them would have no effect on others. As the Bush strategy evolved, it became more tightly focused, concentrating on Islamic extremists. But even this was unclear. Were Islamic militants who sought to impose their ideology on the world but which did *not* use terrorism acceptable? Would a group that used terrorism to overthrow a dictatorship and replace it with a democracy be acceptable?

Ultimately, the way that the Bush administration conceptualized the conflict was best suited for a domestic audience. Few Americans were bothered by the idea that not all Islamic militants were terrorists or that terrorism could be used to promote democracy. President Bush's explanation made perfect sense to them. The problem was that the administration correctly noted that the conflict was essentially a war of ideas. Simply killing militants would not end the threat so long as the conditions that gave rise to them— especially the ideology legitimizing terrorist violence—persisted. But the problem was that President Bush's explanation of the conflict and his identification of the threat did not resonate nearly as well in Islamic cultures as in the United States. What played in Peoria did not in Islamabad. It would prove impossibly difficult to de-legitimize the terrorism of Islamic militants when American bombs and American-backed Israeli security forces also killed civilians. While the United States saw itself as the beacon of freedom, to many in the Islamic world it was the architect of injustice.

■   ■   ■

During the 2000 campaign and the first few months of the administration, President Bush talked little of promoting democracy. But after September 11, President Bush concluded that the long-term solution to Islamic
extremism was ameliorating what he saw as its causes: the absence of political and economic freedom. This reflected a long-standing, consummately
American perspective on the nature of human society and conflict. America's
enemies, according to this position, consist of the *evil* and the *misguided*. Evil
people seek to dominate others; they oppose democracy and freedom. When
people are free to choose their leaders, they do not choose evil aggressors.
Evil leaders must convince others to support them through lies, fear, repression, and force. Those who follow dictators and militants do so, in other
words, because they have no choice.

The administration's strategy for defeating terrorism sought to undercut the factors that allowed the evil to misguide others into supporting
them. In a free market of political ideas Bush and his supporters assumed
that most people would opt for peaceful solutions and moderate policies,
not violence and extremism. Terrorism emerged from dysfunctional markets—
from the absence of political freedom. Of course imparting political freedom would not, in itself, end the threat from terrorism. Evil people would
still use it. But political freedom would limit the ability of evil people, stripped
of their support, to undertake violence. For Bush, America's role as a promoter of freedom legitimizes its exercise of power. After September 11, his
America was unbound.

While Reaganism as interpreted by the conservative idealists provided
a template for a new strategy, President Bush and his advisers did not simply
cut and paste from any preexisting body of ideas. Clearly September 11 demanded new concepts and policies. One of the most important innovations
in the Bush strategy was the melding of terrorism and the proliferation of
weapons of mass destruction (WMD). Since the collapse of Soviet military
power in the early 1990s, national security experts had considered proliferation and terrorism the most pressing threats to American security.[14] The
nightmare scenario was a marriage of the two. But while there was agreement on the challenge this would pose, little was done to prevent it. Richard
Clarke, who headed counterterrorism efforts for the Clinton National Security Council, had formed an interagency working group on terrorism and

weapons of mass destruction in the early 1990s, but it had not been terribly active.[15] At Clarke's urging, a 1995 Presidential Decision Directive on terrorism stated that preventing terrorists from gaining such a capacity was a top national priority.[16] Tom Clancy's 1991 novel *The Sum of All Fears* brought the issue of nuclear terrorism into popular culture and consciousness. In American strategy, though, things happen when resources, talent, and high-level attention are applied to an issue. By this standard, the interface of terrorism and WMDs did not top the list of strategic priorities.

While the September 11 attacks relied on conventional technology (albeit used in a new way), as the president and his advisers developed their strategy in the autumn of 2001, they defined the combination of terrorism and WMDs as the most important threat. This was inspired by a series of intelligence warnings in September and October 2001 that suggested al-Qaeda was planning another spectacular attack using even more powerful weapons, and by information collected in Afghanistan that showed al-Qaeda's interest in obtaining WMD.[17] But groups like al-Qaeda, the administration concluded, could not attain WMD without help. This probably meant a state. Before September 11 both terrorism experts and popular culture treated criminal organizations from the former Soviet Union as the most likely source of WMD for terrorists. The most common image was of a corrupt and renegade former KBG official, perhaps from one of Russia's restive ethnic minorities, selling nuclear weapons to terrorists. Now attention turned to hostile states acting not for money but as a policy decision.

Just as the Soviet Union had sponsored Third World insurgents during the Cold War, the Bush strategy assumed that the rogue states of the world would use transnational terrorism as an asymmetric counterweight to America's military strength. This was a frightening prospect. American power—and the American-engineered world order—relied on military strength. If weapons of mass destruction could deter the United States, whether in the hands of hostile dictators or terrorists, the strategy unraveled. American power could be rendered irrelevant. This was the asymmetric threat that defense experts had warned of since the 1990s, except now it seemed imminent rather than conceptual. Reflecting this concern, President Bush stated that he would make no distinction between terrorists and states that "knowingly harbor or provide aid to them."

State sponsorship of terrorism was not the only problem. Terrorist organizations like al-Qaeda exploited the world's "ungoverned spaces" to organize and train. Hence state *weakness* contributed to the terrorist threat.

Afghanistan was the classic example. There was little evidence that the Taliban regime was directly involved in September 11, but it was unwilling or unable to control the regions where al-Qaeda was based. The Islamic world had many other ungoverned spaces, including Pakistan's North-West Frontier Province; parts of its large cities, particularly Karachi; sections of most Central Asian states; all of Somalia; and much of Africa's Sahel region. This had profound implications: to address ungoverned spaces, the United States had to embrace nation building, which then-Governor Bush had dismissed in the 2000 campaign. The eventual goal was a strengthening of state capacity until there were no ungoverned spaces.

In an even broader sense, Bush altered the basic calculus of strategy following September 11. Strategy entails assessing the magnitude of a threat and its probability, then crafting a response or preventative that balances expected costs and risks with magnitude and probability. The key is proportionality. A threat with a high magnitude and probability—say, a Soviet conventional incursion into Western Europe—inspired extensive (and costly) preparation. A less plausible threat such as a "bolt out of the blue" Soviet nuclear attack received less attention. That, at least, is the concept.

As President Bush focused on the possibility that hostile states might sell or provide weapons of mass destruction to terrorists, the magnitude of such a threat appeared to be his sole concern.[18] Plausibility—or the lack thereof—became unimportant. In his 2002 State of the Union address, for instance, President Bush said that regimes *could* provide weapons of mass destruction to terrorists. In the 2003 State of the Union address, he repeated, "The gravest danger facing America and the world, is outlaw regimes that seek and possess nuclear, chemical, and biological weapons. These regimes *could* use such weapons for blackmail, terror, and mass murder. They *could* also give or sell those weapons to terrorist allies, who would use them without the least hesitation." In his 2002 graduation speech at West Point, President Bush stated, "Unbalanced dictators with weapons of mass destruction *can* deliver those weapons on missiles or secretly provide them to terrorist allies."[19] Secretary of Defense Rumsfeld told Congress that hostile states "have discovered a new means of delivering" weapons of mass destruction—terrorist networks. They "*might* transfer WMD to terrorist groups. . . ."[20] Vice President Cheney made similar assertions with even fewer qualifications. In a 2002 speech he treated transnational terrorists and hostile states as identical, saying, "In the days of the Cold War, we were able to manage the threat with strategies of deterrence and containment. But it's a lot tougher to deter enemies who have no country to defend. And containment is not possible when dictators obtain weapons of mass destruction, and *are prepared* to share them with terrorists who intend to inflict catastrophic casualties on the United States."[21] A year later he commented, "There is no containing a terror state that secretly passes along deadly weapons to a terrorist network."[22]

Neither Bush nor his top advisers explained why a hostile regime would provide weapons of mass destruction to terrorists given the extraordinarily high risk and low strategic benefits of doing so. Nor did they offer any evidence that a hostile regime had considered this. Possibility rather than plausibility was enough. The key to the administration's thinking may lie with the phrase "unbalanced dictators," which the president often used. American strategy had always been based on the assumption that even enemies were rational, at least to the extent they were not suicidal. Enemies might miscalculate and, in the end, destroy themselves. But they did not *seek* destruction. In the post–September 11 security environment, Bush and his advisers concluded that not only did al-Qaeda welcome what it called "martyrdom," but so too did regimes that supported it. In normal times, Congress, national security experts, the media, or the public might have questioned such assertions. But the period just after September 11 was not a normal time. The perniciousness of America's enemies was considered boundless. And this applied to *all* enemies (or at least all Muslim ones).

Assuming the irrationality of hostile regimes changed the toolbox of American strategy. During the Cold War, deterrence and containment had formed its foundation. Washington sought to prevent decisive outcomes in the military realm, confident that it could then persevere in the political and economic ones. But, of course, deterrence and containment cannot work when the enemy is irrationally suicidal. Rather than considering that part of the enemy—al-Qaeda—might be irrational but other parts, particularly hostile regimes, might be rational, the administration conflated them. This justified the preemptive use of force against hostile regimes. If they could not be contained or deterred, prudence held that they must be removed. Again, this was never debated or explained—only asserted. This rejection of containment and deterrence and embrace of military preemption became, in the minds of many, the defining feature of the Bush strategy. The administration seemed to assume that if it acted boldly, the American public, Congress, and allies would willingly follow without questioning the underlying logic of the action.

■   ■   ■

In the first year after September 11, the Bush administration under-took four interrelated steps to implement its new strategy: a massive effort to reorganize and augment homeland security, a global offensive against al-Qaeda and its supporters (heavily relying on law enforcement and intelli-gence), removal of the Taliban regime and destruction of the al-Qaeda fa-cilities in Afghanistan, and a reenergizing of defense transformation. The Afghan campaign and transformation were closely linked. While the "Joint Vision" model of transformation sought greater effectiveness at conventional, state-on-state war—the 1991 Gulf War writ large—when the U.S. military was told to overthrow the Taliban, it proved exquisitely adaptable. The De-partment of Defense concluded that even though transformation had been designed for a conventional opponent with relatively advanced weaponry, it had produced capabilities applicable to other types of warfare.

From the day he entered the Pentagon for his second stint as defense secretary, Rumsfeld had his own ideas about warfighting and, unlike his Clinton administration predecessors, was disinclined to defer to the uni-formed military. Given the inherent conservatism of the military, he believed such deference slowed or even derailed transformation. Rumsfeld was con-vinced that speed, agility, and jointness determined battlefield success. Any-thing that did not augment these was not "transformational." Anything not transformational would not be funded. But September 11 came with his intended revolution incomplete. The first major statement of the Rumsfeld transformation plans came in the September 2001 Quadrennial Defense Review report. This intermixed ideas on transformation, which had clearly gestated over several months, with sections on terrorism and homeland se-curity added after the attacks. It was, though, the clearest expression of the Bush-Rumsfeld approach to transformation seen to that point, building on a number of themes, each with cascading effects across the military and the defense establishment.

Anticipated missions or enemies had always shaped the trajectory of transformation. Until September 11, the U.S. military had focused on de-feating the armed forces of other states, be they "rogue nations" with some advanced technology, such as Iraq and Iran, or a "near peer competitor" such as China or a revived Russia. Non-state opponents, low-intensity con-flict, and irregular challenges were peripheral despite warnings of a growing threat from that quarter. The 2001 QDR did not fully abandon this idea, but the war on terror amplified the importance of "challenges and threats emanating from the territories of weak and failing states" and began to push state enemies from the center of American military strategy.[23] A second important theme was a shift from a "threat-based" model of defense planning to a "capabilities-based" one. This "reflects the fact that the United States cannot know with confidence which nation, combination of nations, or non-state actors will pose threats to vital U.S. interests or those of U.S. allies and friends decades from now."[24] Rather than using extant enemies or likely enemies to shape the force, the Pentagon would pursue a series of capabilities considered applicable to all missions and opponents. A capabilities-based planning approach, the QDR said, "requires the United States to focus on emerging opportunities that certain capabilities, including advanced remote sensing, long-range precision strike, transformed maneuver and expeditionary forces and systems, to overcome anti-access and area denial threats, can confer on the U.S. military over time."[25] This shift was motivated by the fact that focusing on extant or likely enemies was a brake on transformation. After all, if the U.S. military could defeat existing or likely enemies, there was little need for deep change. Theoretical enemies, on the other hand, demanded innovation, change, and new spending.

The months after the release of the 2001 QDR provided an opportunity to test changes that had taken place in the U.S. military during the previous decade, as well as Secretary Rumsfeld's approach to military strategy. The first order of business was destroying al-Qaeda's sanctuary in Afghanistan. The campaign there broke markedly from the past. The most important contribution from the U.S. military came from precision air strikes directed by Special Forces on the ground. The marriage of Special Forces and aerospace power—a combination of the low tech and the high tech— extended the ability of the U.S. military to find targets that might have been overlooked by other means. American firepower thus allowed the Northern Alliance and other anti-Taliban forces to quickly defeat the regime and its al-Qaeda allies. Almost immediately some defense analysts advocated elevating the "Afghan model" with its combination of aerospace power, Special Forces, and local allies to a general paradigm for warfighting.[26] This found a receptive audience among the Pentagon's senior leadership. Special Forces and long-range precision strike were both considered "transformational" by Secretary Rumsfeld; Afghanistan illustrated that they made a valuable team. This was not a total divergence from the ongoing trajectory of transformation—long-range precision strike had been a core capability since the beginning—but the inclusion of Special Forces added a new twist. This was a logical response as the threat shifted from rogue and near peer states to the "nexus" of terrorists, states supporting them, and weapons of mass destruction. Still, it was not clear exactly what the transformed military was to do under the new strategy. Clearly it did not take a networked, transformed armed force to break up al-Qaeda cells and facilities. Speed and precision—the benchmarks of the transformed force—had little to do with controlling ungoverned spaces. That left only one major task in the "war on terror" that required a high-tech, transformed military: compelling state supporters of terrorism to change their behavior or removing them if they did not.

■   ■   ■

With its basic ideas forged in the autumn of 2001, the Bush strategy was gradually solidified and fleshed out in the 2002 State of the Union address, the president's June 2002 West Point commencement address, and finally, in its most polished form, in the September 2002 *National Security Strategy of the United States of America*. The rhetoric and the core ideas were pure Reagan, illustrating the extent to which the conservative idealists, as the bearers of Reaganism, influenced the president's thinking:

> The great struggles of the twentieth century between liberty and totalitarianism ended with a decisive victory for the forces of freedom—and a single sustainable model for national success: freedom, democracy, and free enterprise. . . . Today, the United States enjoys a position of unparalleled military strength and great economic and political influence. In keeping with our heritage and principles, we do not use our strength to press for unilateral advantage. We seek instead to create a balance of power that favors human freedom.[27]

What all of this helped hide were the fragile assumptions of the new strategy.

Karl Marx contended that every social system contains the seeds of its own destruction. Marx was wrong about many things but probably got this one right. Every new strategy is based on assumptions. They are both necessary and a source of weakness. If the assumptions of a strategy do not hold, the strategy itself may fail or, at least, need significant revision. They are the seeds of its destruction. Generally, the longer a strategy is applied, the more information becomes available about what works and doesn't work. Hence assumptions become less important. But in the revolutionary strategy developed by President Bush and his advisers in 2001 and 2002, assumptions were crucial and, as time has shown, questionable.

Take, for instance, the decision to portray the conflict as "war." Certainly September 11 required bold action. But it did not have to be a "war" on terrorists of global reach. Casting it as such was a vital decision. Admittedly al-Qaeda claimed to be at war with the United States, but so have a range of other motley groups, bands, and organizations throughout history. This alone did not compel the United States to treat the conflict as war. For a war to exist, both sides have to agree that it does. And "all terrorists of global reach" certainly did not consider themselves at war with the United States. Ultimately the decision to cast the conflict as war probably had more to do with politics—with symbolism—than with an assessment that declaring war was the most effective approach to the threat. It demonstrated seriousness. And leading the nation in war is more appealing, more glorious than leading it in irregular conflict, global counterinsurgency, or transnational law enforcement. More broadly, portraying the conflict as war gave the Bush administration "operating space" both internationally and domestically, allowing it to undertake actions that it never could during peacetime. Other nations initially muted reservations they might have had about American actions. Domestic opposition and partisanship were dampened (at least until the extent of the fiasco in Iraq became clear). There is, after all, a powerful tendency to "rally 'round the flag" in time of war.

Portraying the conflict with Islamic militants as war was immensely popular among some segments of the American polity, particularly evangelical Christians convinced that September 11 was the cataclysmic beginning of a biblical, end-of-the-world struggle between Christianity and Islam, and individuals like Norman Podhoretz—one of the original neo-conservatives—David Frum, Richard Perle, and others with an inclination for ideological crusades.[28] The Committee on the Present Danger was revived to promote the idea that the conflict with militant Islam was "World War IV" (the Cold War being World War III). It included such luminaries as R. James Woolsey, a former director of Central Intelligence; George Shultz, former secretary of state; Senators Joseph Lieberman and Jon Kyl; Newt Gingrich; Steven Forbes; Jack Kemp; and Edwin Meese.

Portraying the conflict as war, however much it helped galvanize the American public, also involved tensions, contradictions, disadvantages, limitations, and adverse second-order effects. To take one example, it created an expectation that there would be demonstrable progress and, ultimately, victory. The American public expects to win wars. Despite the efforts of President Bush and his advisers to warn the public that this conflict could last for decades (sometimes with little progress), more than 200 years of American history said otherwise. History told Americans that war is abnormal and episodic. It has a beginning and an end. In the early stages the United States might experience setbacks, but eventually the momentum shifts and America marches inexorably toward victory. When the Bush administration explained to the public that "this" war was different than all past ones, it was not always persuasive. Expectations accreted over 200 years are hard to change.

When the nation is at war, everything else is shoved to the background. U.S. concern for a country, region, issue, or conflict is determined by the presence (or absence) of transnational terrorism. In the "war on terror" this had led some states to overemphasize their own potential for terrorism, seeking to sustain American interest and support. And it led the United States to ignore security problems unrelated to Islamic militancy, such as social strife in Latin America, ecological decay, trade imbalances, immigration, domestic extremism, and technology proliferation. Moreover, the war on terror led the Bush administration to cultivate repressive security partners who were useful in the conflict with al-Qaeda. Similarly, the constriction of legal rights that followed September 11, particularly those related to personal privacy, had the potential to provoke opposition. The assumption was that the public and Congress would defer to the executive and accept whatever actions it deemed necessary. By portraying the conflict as war, the Bush administration indicated that it could constrict personal privacy rights. But by describing a war with no end point, it broke with the tradition of approaching such constrictions as temporary expedients. This plus the treatment of terrorists or terrorist suspects have complicated attempts to portray the United States as a promoter of freedom.

Logically, portraying the conflict as war militarized it. While the American public is accustomed to metaphorical uses of the word "war"—the "war on poverty," the "war on drugs"—the "war on terror" was not presented that way. It was portrayed as a *real* war. By definition, real wars are primarily resolved by military force. If state support was not vital to transnational terrorism, then the utility of military force was limited. But the idea of a *real* war where military force had limited utility was counterintuitive. The only way to reconcile this logical discontinuity was to emphasize state support even though there was little evidence that al-Qaeda depended on it. To make the case for war with Islamic militants, the Bush administration began describing them as potential states. Hence the frequent mention of al-Qaeda's quest for a "new caliphate." Political commentators and administration officials applied the term "Islamofascism" to al-Qaeda and its allies. But fascism is defined by hyper-nationalism, corporatist economics, the militarization of society, and the concentration of political power in the hands of a single dictator. The Islamic extremists, however vile and evil they may be, are not fascists. This inappropriate word may have resonated with some segments of the American public, but it gave foreign audiences—including the Islamic populations that the administration sought to influence in its "war of ideas"—the impression that the United States did not truly understand the conflict. The Bush strategy, in other words, undertook a "war of ideas" with concepts that made sense in the American heartland but not in the primary ideological battleground.

The Bush administration's decision to portray the conflict with al-Qaeda as war never played as well abroad as it did at home. Many of America's partners, particularly the Europeans, did not consider war the appropriate or most effective response to Islamic extremism. As Michael Howard put it, "The United States considers itself to be 'at war', but, with the obvious exception of Israel, no one else does."[29] Most European states simply did not believe terrorism is an enemy that can be defeated in war or is amenable to military force. The decision to portray the conflict as war was based on the assumption that other nations would "bandwagon"—cooperate with the United States or at least not oppose it. Administration officials seemed to believe that after a few military victories, protests against American assertiveness would diminish, particularly in the Arab world. President Bush himself indicated that if the United States developed an effective plan for dealing with transnational terrorism, the world "will rally to our side."[30] This was contingent on another fragile assumption: that other states would consider American power, even when exercised aggressively and with extensive reliance on military power, benign.

During the Cold War, other nations accepted American power less because they considered it benign than because it was less threatening than communism or regional instability. When the Soviet Union collapsed,

American power became a greater concern. While the George H. W. Bush and Clinton administrations muted this anxiety by stressing multilateralism, they simultaneously embraced the revolution in military affairs. Many foreigners concluded that the only reason the United States would undertake defense transformation while already preponderant was because it intended to impose its will on others. The post–September 11 assertiveness of the United States, President Bush's bluntness and inexperience at diplomacy, the administration's tendency to lump any nation it opposed with terrorism, and Secretary Rumsfeld's drive to turbocharge defense transformation stoked anxiety abroad. Many nations willing to tolerate the exercise of American power to adjust or maintain regional power balances were less sanguine about a policy that called for changing the internal political system of states, perhaps even unilaterally. In a prescient comment, Robert W. Tucker wrote in 2002, "The world's loss of confidence in the benign purview of American power might well turn out to be the principle legacy of the war on terror."[31]

Even the exportability of liberal democracy was subject to question. This idea was inspired by the wave of democratization in the 1980s and 1990s but did not consider that this took place in nations that were part of Western culture or, at least, Western influenced. Most important, liberal democracy took root in cultures that separated religion and politics. Sustaining a liberal, tolerant democracy in cultures integrating the spiritual and the political may not be impossible, but its feasibility remained unproven. The Bush strategy simply assumed this was not a problem. And it assumed that once a liberal democracy existed in the Arab world, other states would emulate the experiment.

President Bush concluded that "poverty, deprivation, social disenfranchisement, and unresolved political and regional disputes" allowed militants to misguide others.[32] Corrupt and militaristic dictators who pursued ineffective, statist economic models had beguiled Muslims. The militants redirected the ensuing anger and frustration toward scapegoats—most especially the United States and Israel. Hence the Bush policy sought to focus attention on the "real" culprit—the absence of political freedom and economic opportunity. The long-term solution, according to the 2006 *National Strategy for Combating Terrorism*, "is the advancement of freedom and human dignity through effective democracy."[33] This idea pivoted on several additional assumptions. One was the notion that liberal democracy was culture-neutral. The second was that the source of the anger and frustration that al-Qaeda and other military groups exploited had been properly identified and, more important, could be addressed. It was not what militants said (American involvement in the Islamic world, particularly the support for regional despots and Israel), but something entirely different (which American policymakers had accurately identified). The third was that the existing elites in the Islamic world could either be convinced to join in the revolutionary transformation of their nations or be replaced with other elites who would.

President Bush often explained his quest for liberal democracy in the Islamic world by contending that the desire for freedom was universal. That is undoubtedly true: no one desires bondage. But democracy requires more than a desire for personal freedom. Democratic citizens must also tolerate the freedom of others even when it is not in their immediate benefit to do so. It was not clear that this degree of toleration existed in the Islamic world. In fact, the militants were able to construct a theological argument against democracy. Democracy, they contended, is based on man-made laws. But God had provided a complete set of laws. For men to make laws, even through democratic means, was to arrogate God's role—a sin of the first magnitude. Men could interpret and apply God's laws, but not alter, improve, or expand them. While this interpretation was not universally accepted in the Islamic world, it did resonate in parts of it, creating an environment hostile to the type of liberal democracy envisioned by the Bush strategy. The potential was for Islamic parties that did not accept the idea of man-made laws to win political power and subvert the democratic process (just as totalitarian parties had in Europe between the world wars), thus undercutting the idea that democratization would invariably lead to moderation. The Bush strategy did not account for what Fareed Zakaria calls "illiberal democracy."[34]

The Bush strategy also assumed that the absence of democracy was the source of the anger and frustration exploited by al-Qaeda and other military groups. One problem with this lay with the phrase "unresolved political and regional disputes." This was, of course, code for the Palestinian conflict, which, as much as any single issue, motivated Islamic militants and their supporters. But the Bush administration faced a Gordian knot in Palestine. Resolution seemed to require compromise by both the Palestinians and Israel. But compromise on the part of Israel would be a concession to terrorism and send the terrible message that it worked. The best the Bush administration could do was to strengthen its support for Israel, hoping that the Palestinians would conclude that terrorism did not work and abandon it. This angered Muslims even more, further stoking militancy. Bush's approach to the Palestinian conflict also overlooked two other important factors. First, many Palestinians (and other Arabs) believed that terrorism worked. They assumed that without it, Israel would never have made the concessions it did. Second, the Bush strategy underestimated the important role that *justice* plays in Arab culture. Actions were not solely to attain a desired political objective (in this case, a Palestinian state), but also to promote justice by punishing Israel for its transgressions. So even if terrorism was not the most effective political tool, it still promoted justice.

Unable to resolve these shortcomings in its policy, the administration responded with sophistry. The 2006 *National Strategy for Combating Terrorism,* for instance, attempted to rebut the militants' claim that their actions were motivated by the Palestinian conflict by stating, "Terrorism is not simply a result of Israeli-Palestinian issues. Al-Qaida plotting for the September 11 attacks began in the 1990s, during an active period in the peace process."[35] Since no one—including al-Qaeda—ever argued that terrorism was "simply a result" of the Palestinian conflict, this was a red herring. And since al-Qaeda was fundamentally opposed to the *existence* of Israel, it had no faith in the peace process. So the fact that bin Laden and his cronies plotted the September 11 attacks during "an active period in the peace process" did not mean that terrorism and the Palestinian conflict were unrelated. In this particular battle in the "war of ideas," the administration's explanations that made perfect sense to an American audience did not resonate in the Islamic world.

Then there was the question of whether the Bush strategy accurately identified the causes of anger and frustration that the militants exploited. Democratic nations such as the United Kingdom, Spain, and the United States itself produced Islamic terrorists (some successful, some not). The Bush administration had no explanation for this, weakly suggesting that "in some democracies, some ethnic or religious groups are unable or unwilling to grasp the benefits of freedom otherwise available in the society."[36] It did not explain how, if robust Western democracy did not undercut the anger and frustration fueling terrorism, new, fragile, and probably "illiberal" democracies in the Islamic world could.

The Bush strategy assumed that the existing elites in the Islamic world could either be convinced to join in the revolutionary transformation of their nations or be replaced with other elites who would. This reflected a long-standing problem in American strategy. Although the word was not used until a few years after September 11, the Bush approach to transnational terrorism took the form of counterinsurgency.[37] As in counterinsurgency, the strategy for combating terrorism included parallel tracks to defeat existing enemies and undercut the conditions that gave rise to them. Like counterinsurgency, much of the effort was *indirect*. The United States acted through partner regimes, increasing their security capabilities and encouraging them to undertake reform. But this meant that the counterterrorism strategy faced a persistent dilemma that the United States stumbled on in counterinsurgency: the elite in partner states have a vested interest in preserving the existing political and economic system. Even though this system generates conflict, it also rewards the elite, often immensely so. Unless the elite is facing outright defeat, it will obstruct deep reform. In the "war on terror," the Bush strategy asked regimes like Mubarak's in Egypt, the Saudi royal family, and Pervez Musharraf's military dictatorship in Pakistan to change the system that makes them rich and powerful. Equally, the strategy also did not deal with the risks of pushing ossified dictatorships like Saudi Arabia and Egypt toward reform. Revolutions are notoriously easier to start than to control once instigated. History is full of revolutions—the Protestant Reformation, the French Revolution, and the Russian Revolution to name just a few—that spiraled uncontrollably in directions that their architects never intended. Given the history and social dynamics of the Islamic world, it was possible that democratization in Egypt, Saudi Arabia, Pakistan, or elsewhere could lead to Islamic states actually more amenable to militancy than opposed to it, thus *increasing* terrorism.

Ultimately, then, the Bush strategy placed great stress on democratization but never fully explained how the spread of freedom would decrease militancy and hostility toward the United States. An old adage says that when all one has is a hammer, every problem looks like a nail. Promoting democracy was a long-standing tradition for Americans and a central part of the Reagan strategy. The Bush administration, with its great admiration for Reagan and desire to emulate his success, thus adopted democracy promotion for a different strategic problem than the one the United States faced in the last decade of the Cold War.

Based on the wave of democratic transitions in the 1980s and 1990s, the Bush strategy underestimated the effort and time democratization required. It appeared to believe that democratic roots existed in most societies; once the totalitarian surface was removed, democracy would grow and blossom. This may have been a misreading of the Latin American or Eastern European experience. In those places, democracy had existed in the past but had been subverted. Then when the dictatorships were removed, democracy could be rebuilt relatively quickly (albeit with mixed results). The

Bush strategy seemed to overlook the fact that no Arab state had experience with liberal democracy (or at least it seemed to consider this fact unimportant). It also was unclear on who would fund and support democratization. During the last half of the twentieth century, an impressive system of democracy-building institutions grew up around the world. Some were part of governmental structures, some associated with international organizations, some non-state. The Bush strategy appeared to assume that once the U. S. military removed a dictator, this system would kick into gear and undertake the difficult, protracted work of building a functioning, open political system. The administration confused the process of *starting* democratization (which is relatively easy for a nation as influential as the United States) with *consolidating and sustaining* democracy.

With these assumptions, the Bush strategy saw the primary purpose of the American military as the removal of hostile regimes. Hence for the first few years of the Bush administration, defense transformation continued to focus on augmenting the capabilities needed for regime removal —precision firepower, global force projection, networked military organizations, and so forth. Ironically, the United States gave little thought to the type of conflict most similar to the "war on terror": counterinsurgency. Military and security experts knew that the military (and nonmilitary capabilities) demanded by counterinsurgency were not those that the Rumsfeld revolution was pursuing. The strategy also assumed that the threat of regime change by force would remain realistic. Once hostile states— proliferators and supporters of terrorism—knew that the United States would intervene militarily, they would change their behavior. This was contingent on the United States having both the ability and the willingness to undertake regime change by force. If other states did not believe that Washington had the will and the ability to do this, then the first time the United States undertook regime change, other dictators would simply search for a way to deter the United States. This suggested the pursuit of WMDs. The policy of removing hostile regimes was likely to fuel proliferation rather than stop it.

The Bush strategy assumed that state sponsorship was crucial to transnational terrorist movements like al-Qaeda. If it was not, then changing hostile regimes would simply draw off efforts and resources that could otherwise have been used directly against terrorists. It is possible, though, that the Bush administration never really believed that state support was so vital to al-Qaeda and its ilk that taking such support away would harm or destroy them. Administration officials may have simply concluded that while the American public was mobilized and much of the world community was deferential because of terrorism, they would be able to address other lingering security problems that were only tangentially related to terrorism. The "war on terror" was more to alter the strategic zeitgeist than to defeat a specific enemy. If so, this too was risky since a public mobilized by a purported connection between hostile states and transnational terrorism could turn oppositional if this connection proved false.

■ ■ ■

Still, as 2002 drew to a close, any potential problems with the new strategy were latent. All seemed manageable. The anger and fear generated by the September 11 attacks had made it easy for President Bush to mobilize public support for his new strategy. The fact that the political Right was much better organized to mobilize public opinion than the Left also helped. This included both "inside the Beltway" opinion shaped by policy experts in think tanks and conservative publications, and mass opinion influenced by conservative talk radio and websites and the immensely popular Fox News Network. Conservative opinion shapers simply overwhelmed and delegitimized opposition to the new strategy. Questioning the Bush strategy while the nation was "at war" was seen as unpatriotic, even treasonous.

In practical terms, the Bush administration made great strides in the sixteen months after September 11, reorganizing homeland security, removing the Taliban regime, striking massive blows against al-Qaeda, and engineering the most radical strategic shift in American history. To some security experts, this seemed to be only the first step of a much deeper revolution that would shift American strategy from a state-centric to non-state-centric approach to strategy. But the administration's emphasis on state supporters of terrorism and on the linkage of proliferation and terrorism inexorably led back to more familiar terrain. Hostile states were a better-known and hence more comfortable enemy than shadowy, networked non-state opponents, at least for the U.S. military. What the administration needed was a test bed for its new strategy, a demonstration to intimidate supporters of terrorism and proliferators, and, hopefully, one that would light the fuel of democratic reform, which, administration officials believed, existed around the world. What they did not know was that such a demonstration would illustrate not only the power of the new strategy, but its fissures and shortcomings as well.

5

DECISION AND TRIUMPH

The weight of this sad time we must obey;
Speak what we feel, not what we ought to say.
—SHAKESPEARE
KING LEAR

By 2002 Saddam Hussein had been the towering master of Iraqi politics for nearly three decades. His domination came through raw brutality and also by the clever use of patronage, dividing his opponents, bravado, and a talent for what Americans called "strategic communications," or sending well-honed political messages to internal and external audiences. While much of his personality cult seemed ludicrous to outsiders—across Iraq there were murals, statues, and busts with Hussein as the reincarnation of Saladin, Hammurabi, and Nebuchadnezzar (none of whom were Arabs)— it helped sustain a working combination of fear and awe among his subjects. Having come to power via the proto-fascism of Ba'athism, Hussein periodically recast his image to solidify his grasp on power and reflect his changing goals. After September 11 he recognized the growing appeal of Islamic extremism as practiced by al-Qaeda and similar groups. He thus undertook some tentative and wary steps to associate himself with it in image if not in practice. This might have bolstered his popularity in a few parts of the Arab world, but it had disastrous results elsewhere.

Ever inept at reading Americans, Saddam Hussein did not understand how deeply they and their president were angered by September 11. Nor did he understand how determined they were to punish their enemies, real and imagined. Unlike other Islamic leaders (including the Iranians) who had condemned September 11, Saddam Hussein attributed the terrorist attacks to the "evil policy" of the United States.[1] He had a mural painted with a smiling, cigar-smoking image of him standing beside the World Trade Towers as one burned and the other was struck. While the Iraqi dictator was simply embracing an action he almost certainly had nothing to do with, some in Washington, including Bush administration officials, were inclined to make the connection. It was a bad moment for Hussein to appear even more threatening than he had been before. This time his miscalculation would prove fatal, both politically and literally.

In its first eight months, the Bush administration had "more of an attitude than a plan" for Iraq.[2] The major concern was developing "smart sanctions" that would pressure Hussein with less harm to the Iraqi people (thus lessening criticism from the Arab world). A meeting of the National Security Council in June 2001 considered options but reached no decision. Other security issues were more important at the time. Then September 11 provided both the incentive and the opportunity to clean up a wide slate of unfinished business.

Attention quickly turned to Iraq. Immediately after the attacks, President Bush wondered if Saddam Hussein might have played a part.[3] He asked Richard Clarke, the counterterrorism director on the National Security Council, to look into it.[4] During post–September 11 strategy sessions, a cleft emerged in the administration between the expansive idealists and the constrained realists. Secretary of State Colin Powell—ever the cautious realist—advocated a narrow counterterrorism campaign focused primarily on al-Qaeda.[5] He believed it would maximize international support and follow the guidelines for the use of force that he had developed a decade earlier. Deputy Secretary of Defense Paul Wolfowitz—the administration official most closely linked to conservative idealism—and I. Lewis Libby, chief of staff for Vice President Cheney, proposed a broader effort designed not only to break up al-Qaeda's sanctuary in Afghanistan but also to clean out other terrorist bases in Lebanon's Bekaa Valley, Iraq, or wherever else they might be. Their war was against all enemies, great and small. In the broadest sense, the Bush administration was torn between addressing existing threats and altering the basic architecture of the global security system. This reflected profound strategic and philosophical differences over the utility of military force. Was it, as Powell contended, a tool of last resort applied for limited objectives or was it, as Wolfowitz and other conservative idealists believed, an implement for systemic reengineering? The president rejected the idea of attacking Iraq at the time but indicated that he would deal with Saddam Hussein at a later date. He also instructed the Defense Department to prepare plans for seizing Iraq's southern oil fields should Hussein attempt to take advantage of American distraction as it confronted al-Qaeda.[6]

Outside the administration, conservative writers, intellectuals, and former policymakers began promoting war against Saddam Hussein, using September 11 to support their case. The October 1, 2001, cover of *The Weekly Standard* had a "wanted" poster with side-by-side pictures of Osama bin Laden and Saddam Hussein, suggesting their equal importance in transnational terrorism. William Kristol became one of the most persistent promoters of removing Saddam Hussein by force. Laurie Mylroie, with a Harvard doctorate, had spent a number of years arguing that Saddam Hussein orchestrated the 1993 World Trade Center bombing and many other attacks and provided additional intellectual fuel.[7] James Woolsey contended, "There are substantial and growing indications that a state may, behind the scene, be involved in the attacks (of September 11)."[8] Being a past director of the CIA added credibility to his claim. Richard Perle, a former Reagan official who headed Rumsfeld's Defense Policy Board, opined, "The war against terrorism cannot be won if Saddam Hussein continues to rule Iraq."[9] Charles Krauthammer, the most consistently brilliant of the conservative idealist pundits and one of the first to link September 11 and weapons of mass destruction, argued that after overthrowing the Taliban in Afghanistan, Syria should be "stage two" and Iraq "stage three."[10] Conservative icon William Buckley, in his obtuse way, also sketched the connection between Hussein and bin Laden.[11]

Writing in Buckley's *National Review*, the bastion of mainstream conservative thinking, Richard Lowry claimed, "Early indications are that Iraq had a hand in the September 11 attacks. But firm evidence should be unnecessary for the U.S. to act. It doesn't take careful detective work to know that Saddam Hussein is a perpetual enemy of the United States."[12] This phrasing presaged what would become the Bush administration's key argument: even without evidence of a functional connection between Hussein and al-Qaeda, there was enough surface similarity—particularly hatred of the United States—that America must act as if a connection existed. And even without such a connection, Hussein posed an enduring threat that could be eliminated in the post–September 11 political climate. In all likelihood, though, the chorus of advocacy for attacking Saddam Hussein did not make up the president's mind. There is little indication that he drew ideas from *National Review* or *The Weekly Standard.* But the pundits and writers did assist the administration by preparing the public and Congress for the idea. From September 11 to the beginning of the war, they worked in parallel with administration hawks, building support for military intervention.

While the military operation in Afghanistan was under way, the administration seemed content to keep discussion of Iraq simmering but not boiling. In mid-October, National Security Adviser Rice told an Arab satellite television network that "we worry about Saddam Hussein. We worry about his weapons of mass destruction."[13] A few weeks later she added, "The world would clearly be better and the Iraqi people would be better off if Saddam Hussein were not in power." But she also cautioned, "I think it's a little early to start talking about the next phases of this war."[14] As usual, Rice was the best gauge of the president's own thinking. In the months after September 11, he too was convinced that the Hussein problem had to be solved but had not yet decided how to do so.

During the autumn of 2001 Cheney joined Wolfowitz in the hawk camp. Given the vice president's influence in the administration, this shifted the overall balance of power. Cheney was, in Bob Woodward's words, "a powerful, steamrolling force."[15] George Tenet and others have suggested that while Powell, Rice, Rumsfeld, and retired U.S. Marine Corps Gen. Anthony Zinni, the administration's special envoy to the Middle East, had not fully made up their minds at this point, Cheney, Wolfowitz, Libby, and Douglas Feith formed an informal lobby for war within the administration.[16] Their effect was quickly noticeable as President Bush also began taking a harder line. In a November 26 press conference, he stated, "Mr. Saddam Hussein, he needs to let inspectors back in his country, to show us that is not developing weapons of mass destruction."[17] When asked what the consequences would be if Hussein did not readmit weapons inspectors, Bush said, "He'll find out."

Ironically, much of the initial resistance to attacking Iraq came not from the Democratic Party or the political Left, but from conservative realists. L. Paul Bremer, who had been President Reagan's ambassador at large for counterterrorism and an assistant to Henry Kissinger, argued that other potential targets were more integral to al-Qaeda and hence should have priority.[18] Brent Scowcroft—the dean of conservative realists—warned that the war on terrorism would require a broad and effective coalition.[19] Military action against Iraq could endanger international cooperation and thus was a bad idea. But emotional arguments resonated with a still-angry public. To quell the need for vengeance, someone had to pay for September 11 and who it was seemed unimportant. This provided the opening that conservative idealists needed in their quest to change the world.

■　■　■

George Tenet wrote, "One of the great mysteries to me is exactly when the war in Iraq became inevitable."[20] While it may some day turn out that there was a discrete point—a meeting or a day—when President Bush decided to remove Saddam Hussein by force, it is equally possible that the choice was made in incremental steps, each small and none decisive on its own—a strategic decision-making process more like that leading to the Vietnam War than to the Gulf War. It is certainly true that by the spring of 2002, Bush and other senior officials stopped indicating that *if* Hussein did not take certain actions he would be removed from power and began stating he *would* be removed from power. Initially, the administration seemed to hope that this could be done covertly—the same idea that had appealed to Clinton. President Bush signed a new intelligence order that greatly expanded CIA covert operations to oust Hussein, allocating $100 million to the plan.[21] There was little sign, though, that this would have any greater effect in 2002 than it had in the 1990s. To again quote Tenet: "Our analysis concluded that Saddam was too deeply entrenched and had too many layers of security around him for there to be an easy way to remove him."[22] Yet rather that being dissuaded from attempting regime change, as Clinton had been, Bush pushed on. The costs and complications did not deter him.

The central question is why after a decade had Saddam Hussein become so intolerable that he had to go? Even the most hawkish hawks inside and outside the administration did not argue, at that point, that Hussein had nuclear weapons. Nearly everyone believed that he had stockpiles of chemical and biological weapons or, at least, the ability to make them. But policymakers, strategists, and defense experts understood the limited utility of such devices. Properly trained and equipped military forces can overcome chemical and biological attacks; they would not deter the United States. As the Japanese experience with Aum Shinriko showed, chemical and biological weapons are of marginal use in terms of attaining political objectives.

They can cause fear and turmoil but cannot bring strategic success. It was not, then, that Saddam Hussein stepped across some discernible threshold that demanded his removal, but that President Bush was convinced that trends were adverse and there was a closing window of opportunity during which he could resolve the problem. Iraq was a "gathering storm." This idea grew from the continuing erosion of the sanctions that had been in place for a decade. Hussein had chipped away at them, withholding food and medicine from his own people to convince other Muslims and the political Left in the West that the sanctions themselves rather than his policy were responsible for the suffering. Russia and other European nations, to which Hussein owed huge amounts of money, were convinced that they would only be repaid when the sanctions were lifted. Without sanctions, the Bush administration believed, Hussein would revive his WMD programs, including the nuclear one.

Why would that matter? According to the Bush administration, it would allow Saddam Hussein to deter the United States and thus free him to renew the conventional aggression he had undertaken in 1980 and 1990. In hindsight, this is a peculiar argument. Hussein had missiles and chemical and biological weapons in 1991 and that had not deterred the U.S. military. Certainly Iraqi nuclear weapons would have been a greater concern, but again the administration did not explain why the combination of pressure on suppliers of nuclear technology, the threat to retaliate in kind for any use of nuclear weapons, and, if necessary, strikes on Iraqi nuclear facilities would not suffice. Ultimately the administration's case was built on potential and intent rather than capability. President Bush insisted that Hussein with WMDs *could* "dominate the Middle East and intimidate the civilized world."[23] Yet, history suggests that possession of nuclear weapons does not automatically give a nation the ability to dominate a region or intimidate the world. Neither President Bush nor his advisers explained why an Iraq with such weapons could. As so often during the buildup to war with Iraq, the administration's position was based on an assumption of historical discontinuity— what held in the past would not in the future.

According to the Bush administration, Hussein's WMD programs also mattered because he "could" give them to terrorists. But, again, policymakers never explained why Hussein would do something potentially suicidal. He had WMDs for more than two decades, and there was no evidence that he considered offering them to terrorists. Nothing in his background suggested that he would act in a way that endangered his grip on power or control over the implements of power that he had accumulated. Again the administration claimed a historical discontinuity: Hussein's behavior would be markedly and dangerously different in the future than in the past. It did this without evidence or explanation. In the post–September 11 climate of fear and anger, none was demanded.

While the notion of the "gathering storm" may have been the Bush administration's primary motive as it moved toward war with Iraq, the idea of opportunity—that there was a closing window of opportunity—also mattered. Saddam Hussein was so despicable, administration policymakers believed, that most of the world would accept his removal even if not openly welcoming it. This, in turn, would allow the United States to reengineer the security balance in Southwest Asia. A festering sore could be healed and one of the world's major petroleum-producing regions stabilized. Bush's critics abroad and on the American left would later claim that the intervention was "about" oil. It was in the sense that the world needs petroleum from Southwest Asia so instability in that region affects the economy of all nations. It was not in the sense of the United States attempting to control petroleum production.

The opportunity President Bush saw was symbolic as well as tangible: with Hussein gone, Iraq could demonstrate the viability and advantages of free market democracy in a part of the world that had seen little of it. Paul Wolfowitz was the most passionate advocate of this idea. Iraq, he said, could become "the first Arab democracy" if "properly managed."[24] President Bush, naturally comfortable with moralism in foreign policy and eager to inherit Reagan's role as the promoter of democracy, adopted Wolfowitz's position. "A new regime in Iraq," he stated weeks before the military campaign to overthrow Saddam Hussein, "would serve as a dramatic and inspiring example of freedom for other nations in the region."[25] The thinking was that Iraq's wealth and modernity (compared to its neighbors) would allow it to become a stable, free market democracy—and, importantly, an *Islamic* free market democracy. Iraq would then spark regional reform, playing much the same catalytic role that Lech Walesa's Solidarity movement had in the Soviet bloc. In an even broader sense, removing Saddam Hussein would demonstrate America's willingness to deal with proliferators and supporters of terrorism. Other hostile regimes pursuing weapons of mass destruction or supporting terrorism would get the message and change their behavior.

In reality, both the "gathering threat" and the idea of opportunity probably influenced the president. The rationale for military intervention against Iraq evolved; it was always a polyglot of ideas and themes, none entirely persuasive in isolation but together making a convincing case. The problem was that such a complex rationale was difficult to sell to the American public. Hence the administration elected to emphasize the theme likely to find the most receptive audience in the post–September 11 political environment: weapons of mass destruction.

■   ■   ■

As the campaign in Afghanistan wound down in early 2002, President Bush contemplated his next move in the war on terror. In one of the most memorable phrases of his presidency, he included Iraq in what he called an "axis of evil" which posed "a grave and growing danger" to American security.[26] Time, he dramatically stated, "is not on our side . . . as peril draws closer and closer." The members of the axis of evil "could attack our allies or attempt to blackmail the United States." If the word "could" was intended to mean "have the potential," then it was true. That applied to any nuclear power and possibly any of the dozens of nations that had or could manufacture chemical or biological weapons. But, as intended, much of the American public interpreted "could" as meaning "is likely to" or "will." Bush and his advisers were gradually acclimating the public to the idea of intervention by carefully escalated rhetoric and the creation of connections and implications that were never openly stated. During a press conference a few weeks later Bush said, "I will not allow a nation such as Iraq to threaten our very future by developing weapons of mass destruction."[27] He did not explain how an Iraqi nuclear weapon would "threaten our very future."[28] It was not necessary. In the hypercharged post–September 11 political climate, such statements had the desired psychological effect and went unchallenged.

While President Bush had not yet committed the United States to military action, war was on the table. This sparked growing concern abroad, particularly in Europe and the Arab world. In March 2002, Vice President Cheney began a ten-day trip to allay concerns.[29] "We are going to consult," President Bush said when asked about the Cheney visit, but he did not indicate that the desires of other states would shape his decisions. Reflecting the conservative idealist themes that had come to dominate the administration's strategy, senior officials suggested that Arab states would protest the removal of Saddam Hussein but accept it once success was evident. Boldness would overcome paralysis. Aware of the growing anxiety in Europe, Bush told a German reporter, "There are no war plans on my desk."[30] That was technically true but military planning was already well under way.

The president walked a fine line. If he signaled that he had decided on war, opposition would explode from those who felt that diplomacy had not been given a full chance to work. But to be ready for war required extensive planning and preparation. While Pentagon hawks, particularly Wolfowitz and Feith, continued to push for action, the uniformed military favored a slower approach, stressing the risks of war. There were reports that senior military leaders were skeptical of armed regime change in general, arguing that Hussein did not pose a "gathering threat" and that containment was working.[31] To administration officials, this was simply more evidence of hidebound and overly cautious thinking by those in uniform. As a senior administration official noted, "The military has limited influence in this administration."[32]

Bush had instructed Rumsfeld to initiate planning for military action against Iraq in November 2001. The secretary then met with Gen. Tommy Franks, the commander of Central Command, to review the existing plan for Iraq.[33] The regional combatant commands normally have plans prepared for possible contingencies in their areas. CENTCOM's existing plan for intervention in Iraq (OPLAN 1003-98) was developed in the 1990s. It was based on a massive stabilization effort following the collapse of the Hussein regime. The plan called for three corps—around 380,000 troops. For Rumsfeld, with his intense belief that the United States should be heavily involved in peacekeeping or stabilization and that the U.S. military was overly conservative and thus inclined to allocate more troops to missions than necessary, this was unacceptable. He wanted the smallest and fastest force possible, believing that the Hussein regime and its military were so fragile that they would collapse when attacked.

While addressing Rumsfeld's instruction, Franks resisted proposals that he considered infeasible or overly risky. One that was floated was called the "Afghan model," which combined American airpower and Special Operations Forces with local fighters but involved few conventional U.S. ground forces.[34] This was also known as the "Downing plan" since retired Army Gen. Wayne Downing had proposed a variant of it to the Clinton administration in 1998. While Deputy Secretary Wolfowitz backed the idea, the State Department, the Central Intelligence Agency, and the uniformed military all opposed it.[35] Franks convinced Rumsfeld that the Iraq and

Afghan situations were fundamentally different. Hussein's Army was nearly twenty times the size of the Taliban force and had ten times as many tanks. More important, despite American funding for Iraqi resistance movements, none were militarily effective. There was no equivalent of the Afghan Northern Alliance. Another idea—again floated by Wolfowitz—assumed that one heavy American division plus airpower could create an enclave in southern Iraq, allowing resistance groups to then overthrow Hussein. "This line of thinking," according to General Franks, "was absurd, and I wanted to terminate it as quickly as possible."[36]

Within a few weeks, General Franks presented Rumsfeld with a "commander's estimate"—a broad outline of an anticipated mission and alternative courses of action along with an assessment of the combat power of both sides.[37] In late December, Franks traveled to Bush's ranch in Texas to brief the president. He presented what he called "robust," "reduced," and "unilateral" options based on the amount of support the United States received from other nations, particularly those in the region.[38] To organize his thinking and the staff planning process, Franks divided the mission into "lines of operation" (operational fires, Special Forces operations, operational maneuver, information operations, unconventional warfare or support to Iraqi resistance groups, political-military activities, and civil-military operations).[39] He cross-checked these with what he called "slices"—things necessary to destroy or control in order to remove the Hussein regime. These included leadership, internal security and intelligence, WMD infrastructure, elite forces (Republican Guards and Special Republican Guards), selected regular Army forces, territory, infrastructure, the civilian population, and commercial and diplomatic leverage.

This was an important divergence from Desert Storm. In the 1991 war, coalition forces concentrated on Iraq's infrastructure and its frontline military forces. This time, they would strike directly at the foundation of Hussein's power. As Thomas Ricks put it, Franks intended "an attack on a government, not a country."[40] "Our interest is to get there very quickly," a military planner explained, "decapitate the regime, and open the place up, demonstrating that we're there to liberate the country."[41] This was predicated on the belief that most Iraqis did not actively support the Hussein regime and that the United States needed to minimize collateral damage from the war to avoid provoking political opposition, particularly in the Arab world. Operational and technological advancements—a decade of defense transformation—made decapitation feasible. What Franks sought was a military strategy appropriate for a world saturated by twenty-four-hour news feeds, satellite television, the Internet, and globalization. A successful war needed to be over before opposition to it gained strength.

Franks and his subordinate commanders made several crucial assumptions. One was that regular Iraqi Army units, composed largely of Shiite conscripts and being poorly led, trained, and equipped, would offer little resistance. CENTCOM developed an extensive psychological campaign to erode their morale and ensure they would give up easily. However, Hussein's elite units, particularly the Republican Guard and Special Republican Guard, were expected to fight and use chemical or biological weapons. CENTCOM believed that the Special Republican Guard was trained for urban operations, and thus would be the primary forces Americans would face in and around Baghdad.[42] Franks also recognized the problem that Iraqi Scud missiles posed in the 1991 war. To prevent a new Scud problem, he assigned Special Forces to the areas of western Iraq suitable for launching mobile missiles, believing this would be more effective than trying to find and destroy actual launch systems.

The actual war plan developed in stages, shaped by extensive staff work, war gaming, input from Rumsfeld and Bush, and additional intelligence. It initially was based on what Franks called a "generated start" with 275,000 troops in the theater at the start of the conflict. In a sense, this was Desert Storm II. Rumsfeld asked for a leaner and faster option. By April 2002 Franks had what he called a "running start" plan, which would begin the war with 180,000 troops and eventually involve 250,000. Rather than using airpower to soften up Iraqi forces before a ground attack, the "running start" relied on "virtually simultaneous" air and ground operations.[43] By the summer of 2002, Franks combined the generated and running start concepts. President Bush approved the hybrid idea at Camp David in September. At that point, the administration had an executable military plan. But the revision process did not end. With subordinate commanders requesting a larger force, Franks eventually settled on a plan called COBRA II, or OPLAN 1003v, which relied on air attacks and an assault by two ground corps.

This represented a compromise between Rumsfeld and the uniformed military. Because things always go wrong in warfighting, the military commanders sought the strongest possible force as an insurance policy. Civilian leaders, particularly Rumsfeld, believed that military transformation based on the revolution in military affairs had dramatically decreased fog and friction. This allowed greater risk taking with potentially greater payoffs.

Two major political considerations influenced the war plan. First was the concern that Hussein would be able to inflict extensive casualties on the invading force, whether by the use of chemical or biological weapons, by urban warfare in Baghdad, or a combination of the two. A protracted, bloody conflict could endanger public support, provoke international opposition, and embolden other hostile states. Therefore, the president and secretary of defense pushed for a military plan that minimized the number of American forces on the ground and maximized the speed of the campaign. This, they thought, would limit the vulnerability of U.S. troops to WMDs and the chances of becoming embroiled in urban operations. Such a tight integration of political and military concerns was unusual for Americans. More often, they put political considerations in abeyance during conventional wars, shaping campaigns and operations strictly by military considerations. The defeat of Nazi Germany in World War II was typical: rather than doing so in a way that optimized America's postwar political position in Europe, Eisenhower designed a campaign to limit military risk and casualties. But Rumsfeld was more Churchill than Eisenhower or George Marshall, refusing to fully sublimate political objectives to military concerns.

The second consideration was the need to keep diplomatic options open while military planning and preparation moved forward. Bush had to convince Hussein that he was fully prepared to use force and convince the American public and other nations that he was not committed to a military solution. For this reason, debates and discussions on the military strategy were limited to a small circle in CENTCOM, the Pentagon, and the White House. Unfortunately, this excluded many regional experts both inside and outside the government. In fact, there is little evidence that anyone who would be considered an Iraqi or Middle Eastern political expert played a major role in the shaping of the military plan. While this may not have hindered combat operations, it had a decided effect on the post-conflict situation. It was not that Rumsfeld was unaware that the way a war is fought shapes the peace that follows, but that he thought that *this* peace would best be shaped by sending the message that it was a war of liberation solely targeting the regime. The absence of Middle East expertise hindered Rumsfeld's ability to gauge whether that message would resonate with Iraqis.

■ ■ ■

By the summer of 2002 British officials were convinced that President Bush "had made up his mind to take military action, even if the timing was not yet decided."[44] CENTCOM planners had the same impression. If so, the administration still had to sell the notion to the American public, Congress, and allied states. Thus began a concerted and coordinated program of persuasion interweaving multiple themes: Hussein's support for terrorism, pursuit of weapons of mass destruction, human rights abuses, and refusal to implement U.N. Security Council resolutions calling for disarmament.

With the memory of September 11 still fresh, Saddam Hussein's ties to terrorism had the greatest emotional impact with the American public. But it was also the most fragile and least substantiated. Still, administration officials hammered it relentlessly. During his September 2002 address to the United Nations General Assembly, Bush said, "Iraq continues to shelter and support terrorist organizations that direct violence against Iran, Israel, and Western governments."[45] He did not spell out who these groups were and did not explain the strange claim that Iraq supported terrorism against Iran, which was, by nearly all assessments, the foremost state supporter of terrorism. Bush later amplified this point, stating that Saddam Hussein and al-Qaeda "work in concert." "The danger," he said, "is that al-Qaeda becomes an extension of Saddam's madness and his hatred and his capacity to extend weapons of mass destruction around the world."[46] The president did not explain or substantiate this point.

Vice President Cheney was the most persistent and rhetorically skilled at linking Hussein and al-Qaeda. In a September 2002 interview, he first stated that "I'm not here today to make a specific allegation that Iraq was somehow responsible for 9/11" and then went on to list purported ties between Iraq and al-Qaeda.[47] These included the later-disproved claim that Mohamed Atta, the lead September 11 hijacker, had met senior Iraqi intelligence officials in Prague. Cheney also professed that Iraq and al-Qaeda had "a pattern of relationships going back many years." And, he stated, "we've seen al-Qaeda members operating physically in Iraq and off the territory of Iraq." National Security Adviser Rice followed along: "No one is trying to make an argument at this point that Saddam Hussein somehow had operational control of what happened on September 11," but al-Qaeda personnel "found refuge in Baghdad" after they were expelled from Afghanistan.[48]

As military action became more likely, the administration continued to escalate its rhetoric. In a February 2003 radio address, President Bush said:

> Saddam Hussein has longstanding, direct and continuing ties to
> terrorist networks. Senior members of Iraqi intelligence and al

Qaeda have met at least eight times since the early 1990s. Iraq has sent bomb-making and document forgery experts to work with al Qaeda. Iraq has also provided al Qaeda with chemical and biological weapons training. And an al Qaeda operative was sent to Iraq several times in the late 1990s for help in acquiring poisons and gases.[49]

A month later Bush added that Saddam Hussein "provides funding and training and safe haven to terrorists who would willingly deliver weapons of mass destruction against America and other peace-loving countries."[50] Saddam Hussein, Bush said, "has trained and financed al Qaeda—type organizations before, and al Qaeda, and other terrorist organizations."[51] In his speech to the United Nations a few weeks before the onset of war, Colin Powell described a "sinister nexus" between Iraq and al-Qaeda, mentioning the presence of Abu Musab al-Zarqawi and the al-Qaeda–affiliated organization Ansar al-Islam in Iraq, meetings between al-Qaeda and Iraqi intelligence agents (some supposedly including Osama bin Laden himself), and reports that Iraq had sent trainers to al-Qaeda camps in Afghanistan.[52]

Even while saying that it did not hold Saddam Hussein responsible for the September 11 attacks, administration officials structured speech after speech so that the two became linked in the minds of much of the American public. Often this was done simply by discussing September 11 and Saddam Hussein in sequence. To take one example, in President Bush's October 7, 2002, speech in Cincinnati, the second paragraph discusses Iraq's violations of U.N. resolutions, the third paragraph is an emotional reminder of September 11, and the fourth paragraph returns to a discussion of Saddam Hussein. While no explicit connection was made, a psychological one was.

Few in the public parsed or analyzed statements like Rumsfeld's contention that "after September 11, they [terrorist states] have discovered a new means of delivering these weapons [of mass destruction]—terrorist networks."[53] What evidence, one might ask Secretary Rumsfeld, was there that Iraq or Iran "discovered" the utility of giving weapons of mass destruction to terrorists "after September 11"? If it made no strategic sense for them to do so prior to September 11, why would they afterward? But in 2002 and 2003, simply linking a threat to September 11 was enough. The attacks on the World Trade Center and the Pentagon dulled critical inclinations on the part of Congress and much of the American public.[54] No elected official was willing to pay the political costs of opposing what the administration skillfully portrayed as defense against terrorism. In simple terms, the Bush administration made use of a false syllogism: the leaders were comprised of al-Qaeda were Arabs who hated the United States and would do anything to harm it. Saddam Hussein was an Arab who hated the United States; therefore, he would do anything to harm it.

As it later turned out, much of the information that senior administration officials used to connect Saddam Hussein and al-Qaeda was incorrect or, at least, not supported by the intelligence community. Douglas Feith's Pentagon policy shop supplied much of it. In a 2007 report, the Pentagon's Inspector General found that this organization "developed, produced, and then disseminated alternative intelligence assessment on the Iraq and al-Qaida relationship, which including some conclusions that were inconsistent with the consensus of the Intelligence Community, to senior decision-makers."[55] This was, in the Inspector General's assessment, "inappropriate."

Despite the efforts of Feith, Cheney, and Wolfowitz on the inside, and Mylroie and journalist Stephen Hayes (who pressed the Hussein–al-Qaeda connection the hardest) on the outside, the terrorism connection was weak.[56] It was hard to convince the public and Congress that a few meetings or the provision of sanctuary to old, retired terrorists like Abu Nidal, justified war. In fact, Hussein had him killed in 2002, possibly to avoid provoking the United States any further. This led the administration to stress something that seemed more persuasive: Saddam Hussein's WMD programs. To President Bush, Hussein's failure to demonstrate compliance with the U.N. resolutions demanding the dissolution of his WMD program suggested that he had not done so. Claims that Iraq sought additional fissile material and had purchased high-grade aluminum tubes added to the point. In early 2003, CIA director Tenet told Congress, "Iraq has established a pattern of clandestine procurements designed to constitute its nuclear weapons program. These procurements include—but also go well beyond—the aluminum tubes that you have heard so much about."[57] As usual, Vice President Cheney pushed the point the furthest, stating that he believed "Saddam will acquire nuclear weapons fairly soon" and "we believe he has, in fact, reconstituted nuclear weapons."[58] In a February 2003 address to the United Nations Security Council, Colin Powell detailed "an accumulation of facts and disturbing patterns of behavior" that, he felt, demonstrated that Hussein had WMDs and was pursuing more. He summarized by saying, "We know that Saddam Hussein is determined to keep his weapons of mass destruction; he's determined to make more."[59] Powell's personal credibility added gravitas to the case for war and convinced many skeptics that the administration was correct.

Why did the administration push so hard beyond what the intelligence on Hussein's WMD capabilities suggested? In part, this reflected an enduring tension in the American strategic culture. In the United States, the public and its elected leaders in Congress have a say in national security policy but often lack a sophisticated understanding of the strategic environment. This means that strategy must be marketed. Once President Bush opted for war against Iraq, he had to convince Congress and the public. But his case was not self-evident to those not schooled in national security affairs. It was based on conjecture and potential—what Saddam Hussein *could* do rather than what he was doing. To convince the public and Congress with an inherently weak body of evidence, the Bush administration approached it like a courtroom lawyer, never lying but carefully selecting information that bolstered its position and ignoring information that weakened it. Rather than developing an explanation best fitting the information, it selectively used information to support an explanation it had already developed.

While this might not have been possible in normal times, it was in the post–September 11 political climate. Fear and anger can be liberating, making the impossible or implausible suddenly seem feasible, even necessary. The United States was experiencing a collective and sustained adrenaline rush. Aggression aroused enthusiastic support. Doubters remained mute or ineffective. The administration convinced many in Congress and the public that September 11 de-legitimized deterrence, and they skillfully used intelligence to further their case. On the one hand, they discounted intelligence that did not support their preconceptions. The thinking was that the failure to prevent the September 11 attacks demonstrated the inherent flaws and weaknesses of the intelligence community, particularly at "connecting the dots" without clear information. Like the uniformed military, the intelligence community was seen as too slow, cautious, uncreative, and hidebound for the new security environment. Just as Secretary Rumsfeld filled the perceived vacuum in military creativity with his own strategic ideas, Douglas Feith's office sought to "connect the dots" in ways that the intelligence community could not or would not. But while ignoring or discounting the intelligence community, the administration also used intelligence as cover, relying on the time-tested method of suggesting that if the public knew what administration officials knew, it would agree with the official position.

As it developed the case for intervention, the administration exploited the American public's propensity to believe any claim of Saddam Hussein's intended perfidy, no matter how illogical or even bizarre. Bush officials asserted that there were no limits to Hussein's evil other than capability shortfalls. If he had nuclear weapons, he *would* use them against the United States or give them to terrorists because he was a pathologically evil tyrant. But Hussein had a penchant for miscalculation, not for suicide. He was willing to use chemical weapons against the Iranians or his own people, but had not used them against coalition forces in 1991 specifically because he knew that to do so would risk his own grasp on power and survival. Despite the claims to the administration, nothing, not even September 11, had changed Hussein's desire for survival and for retention of power. When an opponent is prone to miscalculation, the logical solution is clear communication of intent.

Making the WMD case also required clever rhetorical devices. One technique was to conflate the types of WMDs. Experts usually hold that chemical weapons have limited strategic utility and nuclear weapons some utility (at least as deterrents). The strategic utility of biological weapons is unknown. Clearly the acquisition of nuclear weapons by Saddam Hussein would have been the worst outcome. But most of the public was not able to make that distinction. Possession of *any* WMD by Saddam Hussein was equated to the possession of the *worst* type of WMD—deliverable nuclear weapons. The way the administration created this impression was to say that "we know" that he has WMDs (meaning chemical and biological weapons) and then to describe the dangers of nuclear weapons. Take, for instance, Rumsfeld's Senate testimony: "We know that the Iraqi regime has chemical and biological weapons of mass destruction and is pursuing nuclear weapons; that they have a proven willingness to use the weapons at their disposal." In reality, the Iraq regime had a proven willingness to use chemical weapons when the risks of doing so was modest. To leap from that to the assumption that if Hussein had nuclear weapons, he would use them against the United States or its allies was simply unsupportable by evidence or logic. But the crux of the administration's position was that Saddam Hussein's record of behavior made evidence unnecessary. As President Bush explained, "The first time we may be completely certain he has a nuclear weapon is when, God forbid, he uses one."[60]

Administration officials also had no qualms about the use of red herrings to further their argument. Secretary Rumsfeld's September 2002 Senate testimony, for instance, addressed the evidence necessary for the use of force against Iraq. He then spent some time arguing that in the post–September 11 security environment, it was impossible to obtain "evidence that would prove guilt 'beyond a reasonable doubt' in a court of law." Having rejected that idea, he then went on to justify preemptive action against Saddam Hussein. The "beyond a reasonable doubt" explanation was, of course, a red herring since no one ever held security strategy to that standard. But the method of presentation gave the impression that only two alternatives existed: demanding evidence "beyond a reasonable doubt" or trusting the administration to act appropriately in the absence of evidence.

Ironically, the Bush administration gave the least emphasis to the strongest component of its case: Saddam Hussein's human rights record. His ties to terrorism were tenuous and relatively unimportant to al-Qaeda. His pursuit of weapons of mass destruction was uncertain. But his genocidal behavior and repression were indisputable. The administration did use this but for a specific purpose. In his September 2002 speech to the U.N. General Assembly, President Bush discussed Hussein's human rights abuses even before addressing terrorism or WMD. But he made little mention of it in speeches aimed at domestic audiences, whether his 2002 and 2003 State of the Union addresses or other important ones such as the October 2002 speech in Cincinnati. Clearly the administration believed that the human rights argument could sway other nations and foreign audiences but not Americans.

The way the Bush administration elected to portray Hussein's human rights record offers important insights into its thinking. Rather than treating it as a rationale for removing Hussein, the administration linked repression to terrorism and weapons of mass destruction. Anyone evil enough to gas his own people, they argued, would certainly use WMD against other nations or give them to terrorists. By doing this, the administration took an ironclad argument and weakened it. The idea that anyone who would gas his own people would provide biological or nuclear weapons to terrorists for use against the United States was an illogical assertion. Gassing Kurdish villages or Iranian troops carried little additional risk for Hussein. Arming terrorists always entailed at least a chance that the action could be traced back to Baghdad. There was no evidence that Hussein's hatred for the United States transcended his desire to survive and retain power. In all likelihood, the Bush administration tied Hussein's human rights record to terrorism and WMD rather than letting it stand on its own because military intervention based largely or solely on human rights considerations smacked of Clintonism. It was too "liberal" for an administration that defined itself by opposition to liberalism.

Ultimately, then the Bush administration's case combined both known facts and assumptions:

Known Facts

* Hussein had stockpiles of chemical and biological weapons and ballistic missiles in the 1990s.
* Hussein had a program to acquire a nuclear weapons that was within a few years of fruition in the 1990s.
* Iraq retained the expertise to develop nuclear weapons
* For a decade, Hussein had failed to demonstrate that he had complied with resolutions demanding that he destroy his WMD stockpiles, ballistic missiles of a certain range, and programs to develop additional WMDs or ballistic missiles.
* For a decade, Hussein had obstructed U.N. efforts to verify his compliance with resolutions.
* Hussein had an extensive track record of aggression against and coercion of neighboring states. He wanted to dominate his region.

Assumptions

* Hussein's refusal to verify compliance with U.N. resolutions and obstruction of weapons inspectors attempting to verify his compliance indicated that he had not complied.
* Hussein would not comply until forced to do so.
* The sanctions against Iraq would soon collapse. Russia and France sought economic opportunities in Iraq and debt repayment; the Arab world was duped by Hussein's propaganda about the human costs of sanctions (costs that he intentionally created and manipulated).
* If the sanctions were lifted, Hussein would resuscitate his WMD and missile programs. Given that Iraq still had the expertise to produce nuclear weapons, it would, according to an October 2002 National Intelligence Estimate (NIE), be able to build one "within several months to a year" if it acquired sufficient fissile material from abroad.
* If the sanctions were lifted, Hussein would rebuild his conventional military.
* Once Hussein rebuilt his military and had a nuclear weapon to deter American involvement, he would return to his long-standing pattern of aggression against his neighbors. This might take the form of invasion or simply coercion.
* The only assured resolution of the threat was the removal of Hussein and development of a democratic government.

■ ■ ■

To persuade the public and Congress with such an assumption-based case, the Bush administration (and its supporters) had to downplay or ignore the potential risks and costs of removing Saddam Hussein by force. One of the most famous exchanges was in February 2003 when Gen. Eric Shinseki, the Army chief of staff, told Congress that "several hundred thousand" troops would be needed for occupation duty in Iraq after an American intervention. Soon afterward Deputy Secretary Wolfowitz disputed Shinseki's assessment, telling Congress that other nations would provide money and forces for the reconstruction of Iraq.[61] And, he continued, "I am reasonably certain that [the Iraqi people] will greet us as liberators, and that will help us to keep requirements down . . . we can say with reasonable confidence that the notion of hundreds of thousands of American troops is way off the mark." Secretary Rumsfeld piled on, stating in a press conference, "The idea that it would take several hundred thousand U.S. forces I think is far from the mark. The reality is that we already have a number of countries that have offered to participate with their forces in stabilization activities, in the event force has to be used."[62] "I really do believe that we will be greeted as liberators . . . to suggest that we need several hundred thousand troops there after military operations cease, after the conflict ends, I don't think is accurate. I think that's an overstatement."[63]

When pressed on the financial costs of military intervention, administration officials refused to provide any estimates even in the face of angry questioning from Congress. They argued that *not* removing Hussein might be more expensive than leaving him in power.[64] Cheney proposed that the costs of regime change would only increase over time (implying that it was more economical to do it sooner rather than later).[65] Rumsfeld, in an unusual leap of logic, listed the costs of the September 11 attacks as justification for any expenses involved with military intervention in Iraq, again associating Saddam Hussein and September 11 without explicitly claiming a direct connection.[66]

President Bush and his top advisers probably were convinced that the costs of removing Hussein would be limited because that was what Iraqi opposition figures told them. The paucity of American intelligence sources inside Iraq limited the administration's ability to cross-check this. And the administration's reading of history led it to believe that others would share the burden in Iraq once the United States removed Saddam Hussein. In the past, key allies often opposed American actions but then went along once the deed was done. Bush's hero Ronald Reagan, for instance, ignored European protests and deployed intermediate-range ballistic missiles to Europe in the 1980s. NATO allies complained and then acceded. President Bush likely thought this would happen again if he intervened in Iraq—both Europe and the Arab world would step in and help with the stabilization process. This reflected one of the most basic elements of George Bush's personal political philosophy: the belief that others instinctively follow bold leaders. This obviated the need to build consensus among "stakeholders" before acting—a process that destroyed boldness and led to "lowest common denominator" solutions. President Bush assumed that this action-oriented style of leadership that had served him well throughout his political career would continue to do so, both internationally and domestically.

Within the administration, only Secretary of State Powell appeared to encourage the president to weigh the political and economic costs of occupying Iraq. In a private meeting with Bush, Powell argued that if the United States invaded, Iraq would define the president's first term and be the central issue in the 2004 election.[67] It would tie down significant parts of the military and make them unavailable for counterterrorism activities elsewhere. It would alienate partners necessary for the war on terror. The secretary did not press the point or openly advise against military action in Iraq, concluding that he had fulfilled his responsibility by bringing these points to the president's attention. Powell did influence Bush in one other important way: even though his instincts were those of a realist, he alone among senior policymakers couched his advice in moral terms, convincing the president that following intervention, the United States bore a responsibility for remaining engaged in Iraq to help rebuild and reformulate it.[68] This later influenced the president's decision to reject a quick in-and-out intervention.

Military leaders, including members of the Joint Chiefs of Staff, also expressed concern about the costs and risks of intervention.[69] Like Powell, once they had their say and were overruled by the president and secretary of defense, they remained quiet. Even Shinseki did not openly oppose intervention. This was eerily reminiscent of the public silence of the Joint Chiefs as the United States became more heavily involved in Vietnam in the 1960s.[70] Like that earlier time, the service chiefs seemed to conclude that the danger the United States faced—that the nation was "at war"—meant that they should err on the side of subservience to their civilian superiors even if they had misgivings.

Democrats in Congress attempted to explore the potential costs and risks of war. In July and August of 2002 Senator Joseph Biden (D-DE), chairman of the Senate Foreign Relations Committee, convened hearings involving a wide range of experts to, his words, open "a national dialog on Iraq that sheds more light than heat and helps inform the American people so that we can have a more informed basis on which they can draw their own conclusions."[71] Reflecting the tenor of the time—the bipartisanship that had blossomed in the year after September 11—Biden noted that the hearings "are not intended to short-circuit the debate taking place within the administration" and were closely coordinated with the White House. The hearings included testimony from a wide range of experts. Some supported the administration's position, some did not. Richard Butler, former executive director of the United Nations Special Commission, stated, "There is now evidence that Saddam has reinvigorated his nuclear weapons program in the inspection-free years. And over two years ago, the IAEA (International Atomic Energy Agency) estimate was that if he started work again on a nuclear weapon, he could build one in about two years."[72] Butler's comments added weight to the Bush position, making note of Hussein's "apparently cataclysmic mentality." Former Iraqi nuclear physicist Dr. Khidhir Hamza stated that Hussein had more than enough fissile material to build atomic weapons and connected Saddam Hussein to al-Qaeda.[73] Some prescient comments at the hearings drew little attention at the time. Morton Halperin of the Council on Foreign Relations noted, "We cannot assume that it is possible to have a short and immaculate war with few casualties which then miraculously puts in place a democratic regime which effectively runs the country and consolidates power without a continued massive American military presence."[74] He also pointed out the opportunity costs of intervening in Iraq, contending that the United States should, instead, be focused on other security issues more closely tied to the war on terror.

The hearings also raised another issue that later would increase in importance. When asked about the receptivity of the Iraqi public to democracy, none of the expert witnesses had more than vague feelings or anecdotal evidence. Some, like retired Air Force Lt. Gen. Thomas McInerney, expressed what had become a common theme among war advocates: democratization "will be a lot easier than people realize."[75] Professor Fouad Ajami opined, "We shall be mobbed when we go there by people who are eager for deliverance from the tyranny and the great big prison of Saddam Hussein."[76] This reflected what would become a glaring problem: no one really knew how the Iraqis would react to any given American action. Those insisting that democratization would come easily—Iraqi exiles, scholars such as Ajami and Bernard Lewis, conservative pundits, and, for that matter, administration officials—had either been out of Iraq for a long time or never been there at all.

While the witnesses in the July–August hearings and additional ones held by the same Senate committee in September noted that regime change would be difficult, no one openly contended that the costs and risks of military intervention outweighed the benefits of removing Saddam Hussein. Many did not subscribe to the rosy picture being painted by the administration and its outside supporters, but none anticipated what eventually happened. This held for Democrats, including former Clinton officials, as much as Republicans. Samuel Berger, who had been Clinton's second national security adviser, warned that if the United States removed Hussein by force, it should do it "right."[77] But he did not rule it out. Richard Holbrooke, Clinton's U.N. representative, said, "Collective action against Saddam is, in my view, justified by the situation and the record of the last decade."[78] Even former Secretary of State Madeleine Albright admitted that "if Saddam continues to behave like Saddam, we have legitimate grounds for acting on behalf of the Security Council to bring Iraq into compliance."[79] Clearly, then, there was no serious or insurmountable opposition to military intervention in Iraq even from Democratic policy experts. The inability to understand Iraq was bipartisan and pervasive within America's policy community.

■　■　■

Conservative commentators did their part to support the Bush administration's case, adopting and expanding its core theme. They advocated war with Hussein in both "old" media like print journals and newspaper op-ed pages, and in "new" media such as talk radio, cable news networks, and the Internet. Persuasion "inside the Beltway" was led by writers such as Kristol, Perle, Krauthammer, and Kenneth Adelman (another former Reagan official). Like the administration, these opinion shapers stressed the evil of Saddam Hussein and the ease with which he could be removed while giving little or no attention to the post-Hussein situation. In a *Washington Post* essay early in 2002, for instance, Adelman wrote, "I believe demolishing Hussein's military power and liberating Iraq would be a cakewalk."[80] Two important books added detail to the case against Hussein: Kristol and Kaplan's

The War Over Iraq and Kenneth Pollack's *The Threatening Storm* (which expanded on a *Foreign Affairs* article).[81] Pollack's conversion to the war camp was particularly noteworthy, as he had served in the Central Intelligence Agency, on the National Security Council, and at the National Defense University during the Clinton administration. The depth of his knowledge and understanding of Iraq added credibility to his call for action. Pollack's article and book, as Joshua Micah Marshall, put it, "played a key role in making a military solution to the Iraq problem respectable within the nation's foreign policy establishment."[82] Outside the Beltway, conservative talk radio hosts, most important Rush Limbaugh, and the Fox News Network trumpeted the need to remove Saddam Hussein from power, ridiculing anyone who opposed the idea. The Iraq issue had taken on a larger symbolism: to oppose the war was to be soft on terrorism and even anti-American. It had become an ideological litmus test.

The administration itself opened a "meticulously planned" campaign to make the case for action against Iraq in the summer of 2002.[83] President Bush and his advisers recognized the importance of swaying the two organizations that had the potential to derail the war: the United Nations and the U.S. Congress. On September 12, 2002, the president addressed the U.N. General Assembly. Even his critics admitted that it was "well-argued and well-received . . . the best speech of his presidency."[84] Stressing the collective threat from Saddam Hussein he said, "Above all, our principles and our security are challenged by outlaw groups and regimes that accept no law of morality and have no limit on their violent ambitions." This phrasing reflected the growing chasm between the American view of global security and that held by much of the rest of the world. While President Bush insisted that there was no distinction between transnational terrorists and states that supported them, many other nations did not equate the two. Nor did they consider the fight against terrorism to be war. But because Bush's instincts were to push on his elected course and assume others would follow, he did not seek a compromise that might have narrowed this perceptual gap. Instead, he and his top advisers simply hammered their position, hoping to wear down or convince skeptical foreign audiences. While calling on the United Nations to act, Bush made it clear that "if the United Nations Security Council won't deal with the problem, the United States and some of our friends will."[85] Colin Powell followed, stressing that "Saddam Hussein is not just offending the United States. Saddam Hussein and the Iraqi regime, by their inaction, by their violation of these resolutions of these many years, is affronting the international community, is violating the will of the international community, violating the will of a multilateral United Nations."[86]

The combination of Bush's U.N. address, the release of a new National Security Strategy integrating "proactive counter-proliferation efforts" into the Bush strategy, and public announcement of CENTCOM's war plan for Iraq got Saddam Hussein's attention. Iraq's foreign minister, Naji Sabri, advised U.N. secretary general Kofi Annan that international weapons inspectors could return "without conditions." The Bush administration was unenthusiastic, concluding that Hussein was simply making minimal and grudging political concessions to ameliorate the mounting pressure. "Iraqis did not suddenly see the error of their ways," Secretary Powell told Congress. "They were responding to the heat and pressure generated by the international community after President Bush's speech at the U.N."[87] In the secretary's words it was "a familiar, tactical ploy."

Bush's decision to reengage the United Nations had little effect abroad. The governments of Russia, France, China, and the Arab nations considered the return of the weapons inspectors adequate, at least for the time being. In Germany, Chancellor Gerhard Schroeder won a narrow reelection victory by declaring his opposition to what he portrayed as Bush's insistence on war with Iraq. This was a shocking development in one of the world's most steadfast international partnerships. Public opposition in the Arab world was even more strident. Within the United States, though, the administration's sales pitch took root. Polls showed significant public support for military action against Iraq, at least within a multinational context. A CNN/USA Today/Gallup poll on September 20–21, 2002, indicated that 79 percent of Americans would back an invasion of Iraq if the United Nations approved. Sixty-seven percent favored removing Saddam Hussein from power by military force in an October 3–5 CBS News/New York Times poll. America and the world were barreling in different directions.

A few days after the U.N. speech, Bush proposed a congressional resolution to authorize the use of force against Iraq. "If you want to keep the peace," he said to reporters, "you've got to have the authorization to use force."[88] With the encouragement of key lawmakers, Bush's resolution stressed that the United States would only do this if diplomacy failed, action would be limited to Iraq, and Congress would be consulted as soon as troops were engaged. As the legislature considered the measure, the administration sent its most articulate spokesman—Colin Powell—to the Senate Foreign Relations Committee. Powell's prepared testimony and response to questions emphasized that the administration was not committed to war but felt that the threat of force was necessary to make diplomacy work. "The United States has determined that Iraq's obstruction of UN Security Council resolutions and its gross violation of its obligations cannot continue," Powell said, so "we are discussing now the best way to proceed with the other members of the Security Council and with close friends. We are trying to find a solution."[89] He repeated the notion that regime change in Iraq could spark wider change in the Arab world: creating a democracy "in a part of the world where it's almost unknown . . . could be a model for other nations in the region. . . ." Powell also echoed the "liberation" idea, contending that Saddam Hussein's removal "would be greeted warmly by the people."

With the vote on the resolution approaching, the Senate Select Committee on Intelligence pressed the CIA for a National Intelligence Estimate on Iraq's WMD programs.[90] Surprisingly, there had not been one for several years. NIEs require extensive analysis and coordination within the intelligence community and normally take six to ten months to prepare. To meet the congressional deadline, this one was done in a few weeks. The result was what George Tenet later called "flawed analysis." But it did support the administration's case. An unclassified version of the NIE's "key judgments" stated, "Since inspections ended in 1998, Iraq has maintained its chemical weapons effort, energized its missile program, and invested more heavily in biological weapons; in the view of most agencies, Baghdad is reconstituting its nuclear weapons program."[91] If Iraq acquired fissile material from abroad, it "could make a nuclear weapon within several months to a year." If it had to enrich its own uranium, it would be ready to make a bomb some time between 2007 and 2009. Ultimately the NIE helped convince some members of Congress who might otherwise have been inclined to oppose the resolution. It did suggest a "grave and gathering danger." Even so, few members read the entire document and thus were unaware that the intelligence community was not nearly so certain as the "key judgments" section suggested.[92]

While Senator Edward Kennedy (D-MA) and a few others insisted that the administration had not made an adequate case for the use of force, the resolution had significant support, including that of Tom Daschle (D-SD), the Senate Democratic leader. Both Daschle and the White House sought bipartisan backing lest Saddam Hussein believe that the United States would not act against him. The resolution passed the House on October 10 by a vote of 296–133 and the Senate on October 11 by a vote of 77–23. In the House, eighty-one Democrats voted in favor of the motion and 126 against it; in the Senate, twenty-nine Democrats favored it and twenty-one were opposed. Only six House Republicans and one GOP senator voted against.

The resolution stated, "Whereas members of al Qaida, an organization bearing responsibility for attacks on the United States, its citizens, and interests, including the attacks that occurred on September 11, 2001, are known to be in Iraq. Whereas Iraq continues to aid and harbor other international terrorist organizations, including organizations that threaten the lives and safety of United States citizens . . . the President is authorized to use the Armed Forces of the United States as he determines to be necessary and appropriate in order to defend the national security of the United States against the continuing threat posed by Iraq; and enforce all relevant United Nations Security Council resolutions regarding Iraq." It did require the President to attest that diplomacy has failed if he opted to use force, and to continue to take "necessary actions against international terrorist and terrorist organizations." All in all, though, it was a great political victory for President Bush.

Given what was at stake, passage of the resolution was relatively easy. Since only a year had passed since September 11, few Democrats, particularly those with presidential ambitions in 2004, were willing to be painted as soft on defense. Being strident and vociferous toward America's enemies had limited political costs but being seen as soft was risky. September 11 had created a mob psychology among America's leaders. Even liberals like Richard Gephardt (D-MO), who opposed Bush on most issues, backed the Iraq resolution. It probably helped that on the issue of democracy promotion, there was a meeting of the minds between liberal Democrats and Republican conservative idealists. Democrats were loath to oppose an action portrayed as liberating the Iraqi people and bringing them democracy. Philosophically they could not take issue with the contention that democracy was culture-neutral and thus that it would easily and speedily grow roots in Iraq. Only a traditional conservative could oppose this idea, and most of them had been captured by the administration's argument that the threat from Saddam Hussein justified his removal. In effect, the administration's multipronged approach—its stress on both the "gathering storm" and "democracy promotion" narratives—had outflanked potential opponents on both the Left and the Right. It also helped that the Bush administration spoke with one voice, making the same arguments and emphasizing the same themes with immense skill. By contrast, the Democrats were fractured. Those who did oppose the resolution such as Edward Kennedy and Paul Sarbanes

(D-MD) could only pick at the administration's points. They did not suggest an alternative.

With Congress on board, the administration again turned to the United Nations. The goal was a Security Council resolution explicitly stating that Iraq was violating past resolutions and, hopefully, authorizing the use of force. The world body, stung by Bush's accusation in his September speech that it was becoming irrelevant on the Iraq problem, was receptive to an aggressive new inspections program suggested by the United States and the United Kingdom. The Bush administration itself seemed divided. Vice President Cheney and Secretary of Defense Rumsfeld scoffed at the idea that the United Nations could force Hussein to disarm while Powell and Bush appeared modestly optimistic. On November 8 the Security Council unanimously approved Resolution 1441, which declared that Iraq "has been and remains in material breach of its obligations under relevant resolutions."[93] It demanded that Saddam Hussein provide the United Nations Monitoring, Verification, and Inspection Commission (UNMOVIC), the successor to UNSCOM, and the International Atomic Energy Agency "immediate, unimpeded, unconditional, and unrestricted access." It also reminded Iraq that "it will face serious consequences as a result of its continued violations of its obligations." This was strong language, but even Russia and Syria went along. Both of these—along with other Security Council members—believed that the United States would attack Iraq if they failed to approve the measure. The resolution seemed a lesser evil. China, France, and Russia did indicate that they did not consider the resolution an authorization for the use of force without a second, explicit resolution. U.N. weapons inspectors soon returned to Baghdad after a five-year absence. The diplomatic track appeared to be moving ahead even if only slowly.

■   ■   ■

Rumsfeld and Franks continued honing their military plan even as U.N. inspections resumed. From the beginning, Bush made it clear that he did not want the force deployment to limit his diplomatic options. There would be no repeat of the summer of 1914 when military mobilization by the European powers throttled diplomacy and made war inevitable. Rumsfeld thus "took the deployment process and disaggregated it to support diplomacy."[94] The idea was that incremental increases in military activity, readiness, and force presence would draw less attention and not send the message that the United States was committed to war. Beginning in 2002, Franks upgraded key CENTCOM facilities in the Gulf, particularly ones dealing with logistics and command and control.[95] This had been planned for some time and drew little attention. He moved weapons and equipment from Qatar to Kuwait. Again, this was seen as a routine adjustment by a theater commander, not a prelude to war. American and British air forces patrolling the southern "no fly" zone began responding more aggressively to the daily Iraqi provocations, enabling them to further erode Hussein's air defense capabilities. When the press asked about it, Rumsfeld indicated that he was simply tired of Iraq acting "with impunity."[96] It was nothing major.

By December CENTCOM's deployment was far enough along that the Pentagon needed a major call-up of Reserves and National Guard forces. Such mobilizations are always difficult since they pull reservists away from their families and jobs. This one was particularly sensitive, coming during the holiday season. Rumsfeld had kept reserve mobilizations to a minimum during the long buildup, constantly prodding military planners to use active units whenever possible. But an operation as large as the one Franks was planning required extensive use of reservists. This meant that Rumsfeld's ability to keep the deployment below the threshold of public and world attention was ending. If the Rubicon had not yet been crossed, it was drawing near. Other adjustments and movements continued as well. In January, CENTCOM moved nearly 1,000 planners and other staff members from its headquarters in Tampa to a new command center in Qatar. The Army and Air Force sent an additional 27,000 troops to the Gulf. This brought the total to more than 120,000—an adequate number, according to Franks, to begin the war. By the beginning of March, everything except an execute order from the president was "essentially in place."[97] Bush knew he was approaching the point of decision—soon he would either have to go to war or begin withdrawal.

CENTCOM had been considering the question of post-Hussein governance from the inception of war planning in November 2001. Staff members had advised General Franks that there were three options: military governance, a government of Iraqi exiles, or civilian governance by an American. Clearly that decision would lie with the president and the secretary of defense rather than CENTCOM, but no firm decision was made at that point. While Rumsfeld did rule out military governance, the issue was unresolved as attention turned to how to remove Hussein rather than what would be done after he was removed. Throughout the process CENTCOM and the Pentagon devoted the bulk of their attention to combat operations rather than post-combat activities—"Phase IV" in military parlance. This did not reflect the strategic importance of the functions. Phase IV solidifies battlefield success and translates it into strategic victory. To Franks, though, Phase IV seemed more of an afterthought than a central concern. And, unfortunately, no other agency would or could fill this void. CENTCOM assumed that the State Department would lead post-conflict governance and therefore that agency would do the bulk of the planning. CENTCOM would simply provide support. Its planners believed that at some point they would meld their war plan with the State Department's post-hostilities plan. Unfortunately, the State Department did not have a fully developed, executable plan.

Given that the Bush administration's objectives were not only to remove Saddam Hussein, but to remake Iraq and the Arab world into something less threatening, it appears strange that so little time and effort was devoted to post-hostilities planning. But there are explanations. First, to gain public and congressional support for military intervention, the administration insisted that the stabilization of Iraq would be relatively easy. Iraqi exiles would form the core of a new, democratic government and Iraq's own military and police would ensure the nation's security. The administration, in other words, combined dark assumptions about the threat from Hussein with rosy optimistic assumptions about what would happen once he was removed. In all likelihood this was not deception but reflected the president's fundamental political philosophy—that liberal democracy is the "natural" state of affairs and flowers when a repressive regime is sliced off. This was one more instance of the profound influence that the Reagan experience had on Bush and his advisers. In Deputy Secretary of Defense Wolfowitz's words, "We're seeing today how much the people of Poland and Central and Eastern Europe appreciate what the United States did to help liberate them from the tyranny of the Soviet Union . . . I think you're going to see even more of that sentiment in Iraq. There's not going to be . . . hostility . . . There simply won't be."[98] Girded with this belief, senior administration officials fiercely resisted any effort within the government to evaluate what might go wrong after Hussein was gone—or to prepare for it.[99]

The second reason for the inadequate preparation for post-conflict Iraq was the flawed organization of the U.S. government. It simply was not equipped for a massive, protracted nation-building operation. There was a gap between the Bush administration's strategy and the resources available to implement it. Administration officials hoped that the United Nations would step in to address this capability shortfall. But they were unwilling to give the United Nations or any other nation (except the United Kingdom) a major say in post-Hussein Iraq. The administration wanted to make all major political decisions itself and have others help them. The United Nations and other governments wanted no part of this deal.

Still, some planning did take place. On January 20, 2002, President Bush directed all relevant agencies of the U.S. government to begin looking at post-war planning for Iraq.[100] The State Department had begun a few months earlier: in October 2001 Thomas S. Warrick, then special adviser to the department's Office of Northern Gulf Affairs, was instructed to created what was called the Future of Iraq Project.[101] He had developed a range of working groups combining regional and functional experts with Iraqi exiles.[102] The project held thirty-three meetings in Washington between July 2002 and April 2003 and eventually produced a 1,200-page, thirteen-volume report with extensive facts, recommendations, and warnings. Meanwhile, the National Security Council formed several interagency working groups to coordinate policy.[103]

Nothing had been decided, though, on the structure of the American administration of Iraq. As intervention became more and more likely in the opening months of 2003, President Bush decided the Department of Defense rather than the State Department would lead the stabilization and reconstruction effort. On January 20, 2003, National Security Presidential Directive 24 created the Office of Reconstruction and Humanitarian Assistance (ORHA) within the Department of Defense to do this. This shift in authority was less because the Pentagon was organized and trained for nation building than because it seemed the least ill prepared. Internal administration politics also played a role. Since the American victory in Afghanistan, Secretary of Defense Rumsfeld had been on the ascent. The quick, low-cost military campaign there and success at putting together a post-Taliban government seemed to validate Rumsfeld's ideas and leadership. Brimming with confidence, he convinced the president that he could replicate Afghanistan in Iraq. With its policymaking team of Rumsfeld, Wolfowitz, and Feith, the Defense Department was more attuned to the conservative idealism that President Bush had by then embraced. The State Department's senior leadership—Colin Powell and Deputy Secretary Richard Armitage—and its career professionals were less enthusiastic than Rumsfeld's staff about using Iraq as an experiment in social, political, and economic reengineering. It was, then, to be a Pentagon-managed mission. The idealists had trumped the realists.

ORHA was hamstrung from its inception. It was understaffed and short on necessary expertise. It had inadequate resources and policy guidance. But even if it had gotten everything it wanted, it might not have mattered. That the administration waited until a few weeks before the war to cobble together a new organization intended to manage the most monumental nation-building operation the United States had faced since the end of World II showed that President Bush and his top advisers continued to believe that post-conflict Iraq would be a "cakewalk." Rumsfeld tapped retired Army Lt. Gen. Jay Garner to head ORHA. He was a talented and energetic leader who had commanded humanitarian relief efforts in Northern Iraq after the Gulf War. But he had little other experience in the Middle East or in post-conflict stabilization. As Garner attempted to pull together his organization, Rumsfeld rejected a number of the State Department's experts including Thomas Warrick, the government official with the most experience assessing post-Hussein Iraq. The State Department turned over the reports compiled by the Future of Iraq Project, but did not constitute a plan that Garner could implement.

Because the Bush administration believed that Iraq would be a functioning state ready to move toward democracy after the war, ORHA's precise mission was never clear. As Douglas Feith described it, General Garner's "main role is fitting the pieces together and allowing this operation to deploy and connect effectively with CENTCOM."[104] ORHA was also charged with "establishing links with United Nations specialized agencies and with nongovernmental organizations that will play a role in post-war Iraq. It will reach out also to counterpart offices in the governments of coalition countries and to the various free Iraqi groups."[105] General Garner assumed his authority would be more extensive.[106]

While there was no detailed post-conflict plan, the administration did have ideas. When intervention was first contemplated, officials discussed a "MacArthur" model, with an American viceroy, probably a serving or retired general officer, ruling Iraq while democracy was built and the economy fixed. The alternative was the "Karzai" model—quickly pulling together a transitional government of pro-American Iraqis. Given the apparent success of Afghanistan and the Bush administration's dislike of nation building, the "Karzai" approach was more appealing. As in Afghanistan, administration policymakers assumed that with Hussein gone, Iraqis would quickly identify new rulers. Nonpolitical administration could be turned over immediately to existing agencies of the Iraqi government. The Bush administration assumed that Iraq was much like Eastern Europe's communist states in the dying days of the Soviet Union: a functioning society with a pathological and parasitic regime perched on top. In reality, Iraq was a deeply wounded nation held together and kept alive by the pathological regime. As Kanan Makiya, an Iraqi émigré and author of the 1989 book *Republic of Fear*, warned the Future of Iraq Project, "the extent of the Iraqi totalitarian state, its absolute power and control exercised from Baghdad, not to mention the terror used to enforce compliance, cannot be overestimated in their impact on the Iraqi psyche and the attendant feeling of fear, weakness, and shame."[107] Similarly, the Democratic Principles Working Group of the Future of Iraq Project noted, "There are no recognized domestic political institutions, groups or individuals that can step forward, invoke national legitimacy and assume power. A political vacuum will arise during the period of disintegration and following the downfall of the regime."[108] The gap between the administration's expectations and reality would soon grow to immense proportions.

■   ■   ■

Garner did what he could in the few weeks he had. In February, he pulled together 100 officials from across the government for a rehearsal at the National Defense University in Washington. Many of the participants left deeply worried about the status of planning, ORHA's lack of resources, and the scarcity of requisite expertise. As ORHA's "Unified Mission Plan for Post Hostilities Iraq" showed, Garner's focus was on a potential humanitarian problem—his specialty. The ORHA plan stated that "maintaining law and order will be necessary from Day 1. Existing police/security forces lack any legitimacy with the Iraqi people and are seen as oppressors. Extent of public voluntary compliance with law will be low. 200,000 security personnel in three ministries require vetting, supervision and reform." If the existing security forces had no legitimacy and compliance with the law was expected to be low, who exactly would maintain law and order during the complex process of vetting and reforming 200,000 security personnel? The ORHA plan also noted, "A security environment sufficiently stable for the provision of relief and humanitarian assistance will be established, using military resources as necessary." In other words, ORHA assumed that adequate U.S.

forces would be available for stabilization activities and would be devoted to that mission. Administration policymakers never said otherwise.

As the clock ticked down on the Hussein regime, the Bush administration seemed intent on developing a new approach to nation building and allowing ORHA to field-test it. Rather than relying on the United Nations and nongovernmental organizations (the 1990s model) or the U.S. government (the 1960s model), the Bush administration concluded that private contractors—particularly American firms—would do most of the work.[109] Nation building, in other words, would be "outsourced." This reflected a broader trend within the U.S. government (particularly the Pentagon) that had been under way for over a decade. Relying on contractors added efficiency and flexibility, giving the government access to specialized capabilities when it needed them without having to sustain the capabilities when they were not needed. Nation building was exactly the type of capability that the government needed on occasion but did want to pay for when it was not needed. In Iraq, huge engineering and construction corporations like Bechtel and Halliburton (especially its subsidiary, Kellogg Brown and Root) would be expected to perform much of the reconstruction.[110] Other tasks like social and political development and even many security functions would also be contracted. This not only reflected the pro-business and efficiency-focused philosophy shared by President Bush, Secretary Rumsfeld, and other Pentagon officials but, thinking went, would also contribute to the psychological dimension of the campaign by demonstrating to Iraqis "that the United States is a 'liberator' bringing economic prosperity and democratic institutions to their nation."[111] It was, from the perspective of the administration, a "win-win" solution. The problem with maximizing efficiency is that there is little extra capacity or adaptability when things go awry and plans collapse.

From the beginning, both ORHA and CENTCOM overestimated the role the other would play. CENTCOM, especially the Coalition Forces Land Component Commander (CFLCC)—the subordinate organization that would execute the land campaign—had worked on Phase IV of the campaign for months.[112] Eventually Army Lt. Gen. David McKiernan, the CFLCC commander, recognized that Phase IV planning had become too complex to remain an annex of COBRA II, the warfighting plan.[113] His staff developed a separate Phase IV plan called ECLIPSE II. CFLCC believed that its mission would be limited and of short duration and focused on humanitarian relief, basic security, and support for civil authorities. It expected to hand over responsibility to ORHA and a different CENTCOM organization fairly quickly. But CFLCC's planners saw upcoming problems. Since Iraq had about the same population as California, they concluded, it would need the same number of police and other security forces as California. This meant that it would take twenty brigades—nearly seven divisions—to execute the ECLIPSE II plan. Nothing close to that was expected to be available. This ominous analysis never reached the senior levels of CENTCOM or the Office of the Secretary of Defense.[114]

■ ■ ■

As the invasion grew nearer in the first few months of 2003, the administration continued to hammer the case it had carefully developed over the preceding year. Policymakers, particularly Wolfowitz and Feith, tirelessly reiterated key points to the press and placated lingering congressional reservations. Ultimately the administration succeeded in building and sustaining support among the American public, Congress, and some foreign leaders, but not the public (or the leadership) of major traditional allies. This had less to do with Hussein's venality than with what Iraq had come to symbolize. In 1991, Iraq represented the illegitimacy of cross-border aggression in the emerging post–Cold War world. It demonstrated that a concert of nations could enforce the rules of the international system as intended by the architects of the United Nations. By 2003 President Bush had decided that Iraq symbolized what he identified as the major threat to global security: the combination of weapons of mass destruction and a willingness to support terrorism. Other nations saw it differently. America's conflict in Iraq reflected the danger from a United States unconstrained by the opinion of others or the procedures of statecraft. "For a growing number of observers outside the United States," journalists Tyler Marshall and David Lamb noted, "the central issue in the crisis is no longer Iraq or Hussein. It is America and how to deal with its disproportionate strength as a world power."[115] Polls found that attitudes toward the United States had soured around the world. Eighty-four percent of Turks, 71 percent of Germans, 68 percent of Russians, 67 percent of French, 87 percent of Egyptians, and 94 percent of Jordanians and Moroccans held a negative view of the United States.[116] In mid-February 2003, 1.5 million Europeans demonstrated against the impending war. For most of them the question was not whether Saddam Hussein should be removed from power but whether the United States or, more specifically, George Bush, had the right to decide if or when it should happen. The Iraq issue had become a global mandate on the new American strategy.

It was never clear, though, whether foreign opposition truly represented fundamental disagreement over the way the global security system should function or simply a dislike of George Bush. The president's bluntness, his tendency to cast some political decisions in religious terms, his belief that boldness rather than consensus-building defined strong leadership, and even his Texas accent grated on many Europeans. Bush's unflagging support for Israel's Likud party made him unpopular in the Arab world. Even Colin Powell's smooth style and diplomatic skills could not compensate for the loathing of President Bush and of his acerbically blunt secretary of defense. While this melding of personality and strategy did not fully explain foreign hostility toward the removal of Saddam Hussein, it certainly added to it. The personality traits that helped Bush win over Americans hindered his ability to persuade foreign audiences.

In the United States, the foreign policy establishment remained divided. Key figures like former CENTCOM commander Anthony Zinni and leading Democrats like Senator John Kerry (D-MA) accepted the idea that Saddam Hussein might need to be removed by force, but they felt that the time was not yet right.[117] Senator Bill Bradley (D-NJ) wrote in the *Washington Post* that President Bush had not made a case for immediate military action.[118] The administration's argument always included two ideas: Saddam Hussein must go, and there is a rapidly closing window of opportunity to make this happen. Bradley and others accepted the first but not the second.

Within academic circles, John Mearsheimer of the University of Chicago and Stephen Walt of Harvard, both widely respected realist scholars of world affairs, offered a powerful argument that war was unnecessary.[119] They based this on the belief that Hussein was "eminently deterrable." By this point, though, not even the best logic could revive that idea. Most of the public and the policy-shaping elite had accepted the administration's repeated assertions that Hussein was irrational and hence undeterrable. Attitudes were set—Mearsheimer and Walt's essay came a year too late. Almost nothing could have altered the course of policy by 2003. Major studies from the influential Council on Foreign Relations and the Center for Strategic and International Studies advising that post-conflict preparation was inadequate had little effect.[120] Anthony Cordesman of the Center for Strategic and International Studies, one of the most experienced and astute observers of security in the Middle East, warned that because of its overly optimistic assumptions, the administration was "planning for a self-inflicted wound."[121] Again, there is no sign that this influenced administration policymakers.

There was, however, an emerging antiwar movement. In October 2002, 100,000 marched in Washington. It was the capital's largest demonstration since the Vietnam era. In February 2003—the same time as the mass demonstrations in Europe—200,000 rallied in San Francisco. In early March, tens of thousands demonstrated in Washington, San Francisco, Portland, Oregon, and Los Angeles. Iraq had become a symbolic battleground in the growing polarization of the American public. It was the galvanizing issue for everyone opposed to George Bush and less a question of national security than a mandate for (or against) the president. Opposition was most intense in "blue" areas—urban centers on the coasts that were strongly Democratic—but muted in the Republican "red" areas of the South, Midwest, and Rocky Mountain regions. This schism reflected the ability of both sides to exploit the new media. For those advocating the use of force, conservative talk radio and the increasingly popular Fox News Network were powerful tools. War opponents relied heavily on the Internet. Email lists, online discussion boards, and blogs provided methods unavailable to earlier generations of activists. But despite the public cacophony, Congress and the foreign policy elite remained divided or mute. With war looming, the Senate focused on confirming a federal judge while the House fought over a tax bill and passed a resolution mourning the death of Fred Rogers, the children's entertainer.[122] At most, public protests may have reinforced President Bush's conviction that his window of opportunity for overthrowing Hussein was limited. Certainly the administration wanted the war to be over before the 2004 presidential election.

While CENTCOM finished its preparations, President Bush and Secretary Powell sought U.N. approval for the use of force. Since Hussein was convinced that Washington would not act without U.N. approval, a Security Council resolution explicitly authorizing the use of force might convince him to comply. President Bush believed that Resolutions 1441 and 678 (the 1990 resolution that authorized member states "to use all necessary means to . . . restore international peace and security") authorized the use of force. But the French and Russians had explicitly said that 1441 did not do so when they voted in favor of it.

Bush's inclination may have been to abandon diplomacy, but British prime minister Tony Blair, America's key ally, warned that without a second resolution (or, at least, a serious effort to obtain one), his government could fall.[123] Secretary of State Powell also advocated pursuit of a second resolution while Vice President Cheney opposed the idea, scoffing that Saddam

Hussein would not change his behavior at that late date. To help Blair, Bush grudgingly went along. But Saddam Hussein had complied with the U.N. weapons inspections just enough to spark a tiny glimmer of optimism from Hans Blix, the lead inspector. For France, Germany, Russia, China, and the leaders of the European Union, this was enough to postpone armed action. Rather than allow the resolution to be defeated in a Security Council vote, the Bush administration withdrew it. He later told Irish prime minister Bernie Ahern that by opposing the second resolution and giving Saddam Hussein the impression that he was off the hook, France and Germany made war the only viable option.[124] It had been, as Steven Weisman of the *New York Times* put it, "a long, winding road to a diplomatic dead end."[125]

■   ■   ■

With the U.S. military coiled and ready to strike on Iraq's borders and after failure on the diplomatic front, President Bush addressed the American public in a televised address on March 17. "Intelligence gathered by this and other governments," he stated, "leaves no doubt that the Iraq regime continues to possess and conceal some of the most lethal weapons ever devised . . .The danger is clear: using chemical, biological or, one day, nuclear weapons, obtained with the help of Iraq, the terrorists could fulfill their stated ambitions and kill thousands or hundreds of thousands of innocent people in our country, or any other . . . All the decades of deceit and cruelty have now reached an end. Saddam Hussein and his sons must leave Iraq within forty-eight hours. Their refusal to do so will result in military conflict, commenced at a time of our choosing."

Bush's words resonated like a gunshot around the world. Saddam Hussein responded with defiance and bluster, warning that invading troops would face "holy war" and certain defeat. As usual, he was patently incapable of reading Washington's intent. Even though 72 percent of Americans had opposed the war in December 2002, an equal number favored it after Bush's speech.[126] In Great Britain, Tony Blair faced a mutiny within his Labor Party as three government ministers resigned. He was, though, able to retain power despite the fact that 138 of the 410 Labor parliamentarians voted against him and a significant portion of the British public opposed the war. Having failed in his attempts to rein in the United States, French president Jacques Chirac blasted Bush's decision but could do little else. Australian prime minister John Howard found his official residence blockaded by Greenpeace activists angered over the prospect of war with Iraq. This did not stop him from supporting the coalition. The Russian Duma shelved an arms control agreement that had been signed by Bush and President Vladimir Putin, thus beginning a downward spiral in U.S.-Russian relations. Remembering Hussein's missile strikes in 1991, Israelis braced for attacks. Plastic sheeting and duct tape sold rapidly. Public anger and gloom exploded in the Middle East, but many Arabs blamed their own governments for failing to head off the conflict. Moderate Muslims warned of an impending increase in extremism and terrorism. Saudi Arabia announced that it would not participate in a war against Iraq. In Yemen, a gunman killed an American, a Canadian, and a fellow Yemeni before shooting himself. Hans Blix, the chief U.N. weapons inspector, stated that he "would have welcomed more time."

CENTCOM headquarters and the various staging bases in the Kuwaiti desert buzzed with activity as the forty-eight hours that Bush had given Hussein ticked away. For Tommy Franks, though, things began going wrong before the war even started. While the armored thrust from Kuwait by American and British forces had always been the main effort of his campaign, Franks had also counted on an advance from the north of Iraq by the U.S. Army's 4th Infantry Division (ID)—its most technologically advanced. At the last minute, the Turkish Parliament denied transit rights for American forces despite a massive foreign assistance offer. Although it later turned out that Saddam Hussein believed this was a ruse and left some of his best divisions north of Baghdad to blunt the expected assault from Turkey, the 4th ID, which had been on ships in the eastern Mediterranean awaiting permission to land, had to sail to Kuwait.[127] Thus General Franks and Lieutenant General McKiernan would not have one of their best units in the opening weeks of the attack.

The timing of Franks's plan was also thrown off when the Central Intelligence Agency obtained intelligence on the location of Saddam Hussein and his sons. Killing the Husseins seemed to offer the possibility of a quick collapse of Iraqi resistance. But the Iraqi dictator had always been extraordinarily careful about his own security, moving to a different location every few hours, keeping his whereabouts a tightly held secret, and, it was rumored, using doubles to confuse his many enemies.[128] In this, instance, though, administration policymakers considered the intelligence sound enough to justify moving the beginning of hostilities up a day. On the night of March 20, cruise missiles and bombers pounded the Dora Farms complex on the southern edge of Baghdad.[129] Agents at the location reported—falsely as it turned out—that Saddam Hussein was badly injured and left in an ambulance. At that point, Operation Iraqi Freedom had begun. American and allied Special Forces were already on the Faw Peninsula, in the western desert, and in the north where they linked up with Kurdish rebels. During the night of March 21, large Marine and Army units crossed into Iraq while the Navy and Air Force began air operations. Targets considered important for Hussein's retention of power received special attention. This was, after all, a war against a regime, not against a country.

The Marines headed for the vital Rumaylah oil fields. Knowing the administration planned on using Iraq's oil revenues to fund reconstruction, Franks believed that the Iraqis would sabotage their production facilities rather than allow them to fall into American hands and badly wanted to prevent this.[130] Other Marine units took bridges across the Saddam Canal and Euphrates, which were crucial for the drive north. British units followed behind and hooked to the right toward Basra, Iraq's second largest city. Army units of the 3rd Infantry Division quickly captured Tallil Air Base and a vital highway bridge across the Euphrates at Nasiriyah. Lieutenant General McKiernan reported that initial Iraqi resistance, as expected, was sporadic and light.

CENTCOM knew that the Iraqi military was not configured and deployed to defend against an invasion, but to protect the regime from a domestic uprising. This was one more factor working against it. The Iraqis in the southern part of the country were regular Army units, which were poorly equipped, led, and trained.[131] Most simply melted away as coalition forces approached. By March 22 the 3rd ID and the Marines were 100 miles into Iraq; the Rumaylah oil fields (including the important petroleum separation plants and pumping station), the Faw Peninsula, the port facilities at Umm Qasr, and the river bridges were secured. In the western desert, Special Forces took two key airfields and controlled potential missile launch sites. None of the missiles that the Iraqis were able to fire at Kuwait did serious damage; most were intercepted by the Patriot air defense missiles, which had been much improved since the 1991 war. By March 23, U.S. forces were half way to Baghdad.

Even while the American forces raced toward Baghdad, protests exploded in the Arab world, Europe, and Asia. In the United States, though, rallies supporting U.S. troops were overwhelmingly more common than protests. By March 24, U.S. forces had reached the "red zone"—the area around Baghdad defended by Hussein's elite units, the Republican Guard and Special Republican Guard. At this point CENTCOM expected resistance to stiffen and braced for a chemical or biological attack. Ominously Iraqi irregular forces called "the Saddam Fedayeen" were becoming increasingly active in the areas that the lead American units had moved through. This surprised CENTCOM. According to General Franks, "We'd had no warning that Saddam had dispatched these paramilitary forces from Baghdad."[132] The Fedayeen threatened the vital supply line from Kuwait. They showed little tactical skill: created to intimidate the regime's domestic opponents rather than fight foreign militaries, the Fedayeen often undertook suicidal attacks against American tanks and armored personnel carriers that led to one-sided slaughter. But unlike the regular Army units, they did fight, often fanatically.

Problems then began to mount for Franks and McKiernan. On March 23, the 507th Maintenance Company, a Patriot support group, became lost; blundered into Nasiriyah, which was still full of Fedayeen and a few regular forces; and was ambushed. Eleven of its members were killed, nine wounded, and seven, including two women, were captured. Televised images of the dead and the captured appeared almost immediately on the popular, anti-American Arab satellite television network al Jazeera. While they were later rescued, the debacle forced Franks to devote additional combat units to protecting his long and precarious supply lines from Kuwait. Rather than bypass the southern cities during the push to Baghdad, Franks recognized that they needed to be cleared of Iraqi forces, regular or irregular. This drew off troops from other tasks, potentially including the assault on Baghdad. The battle for Nasiriyah became emblematic as Marines from Task Force Tarawa fought for twenty-four hours to secure the town.[133]

The Fedayeen's resistance, however futile and suicidal, was viewed with pride across the Arab world, even in nations allied with the United States. The Arab media further enflamed passions, falsely portraying the war as a killing field with extensive civilian casualties and damage. Prominent Arab clerics called for jihad. Inspired by this, a number of young Arab males began planning to travel to Iraq and join the fight. As irregulars in civilian clothes interspersed with actual civilians attacked American units, they fired back, sometimes hitting noncombatants. This was the tip of a large iceberg. On March 30 a suicide bomber killed four American soldiers manning a checkpoint. Taha Yassin Ramadan, the Iraqi vice president, promised that such attacks would become "routine military policy."[134] Ramadan also called on Arabs outside Iraq to help "turn every country in the world into a battlefield."[135] Then a nighttime raid on March 23 by the 11th Attack Helicopter Regiment, designed to strike Republican Guard units near Baghdad, was ambushed by massive ground fire using small arms, rockets, and antiaircraft artillery. Thirty-one out of thirty-two helicopters were struck; one was downed and its crew captured and paraded on Arab television. Soon after that, massive sandstorms slowed the American advance.

These setbacks led military commentators in the United States (including a number of retired officers) to question Franks' war plan. Some pointed out that the invading force was too small to fully protect its supply lines, thus allowing the Fedayeen and other irregulars to attack logistics units. The public's euphoria over the easy progress of the first few days began to fade to some degree. Even President Bush admitted, "This war is far from over."[136] Rumsfeld and his senior military leaders, however, remained optimistic. Air Force Gen. Richard B. Myers, chairman of the Joint Chiefs of Staff, called Franks's plan "brilliant."[137]

By March 27 the storms had subsided and American forces were again on the move. In one of the largest combat paratroop drops since World War II, the 173rd Airborne Brigade entered northern Iraq to help the Kurdish militias. Iraqi forces abandoned their positions and withdrew toward Kirkuk. Around Baghdad, Hussein's military was astounded by the speed of the American advance. His soldiers had expected their comrades in the south to fight for at least several weeks.[138] By that point, they hoped, world public opinion would rise against the United States. When Hussein did attempt to shift forces to meet American thrusts, they faced the risk of deadly air strikes. Most Iraqi troops believed that if they moved, communicated, or fired, death would invariably descend from above. Even though U.S. forces did not have the perfect view of the battlefield promised by the revolution in military affairs, the likelihood of air attack was so great that even elite Iraqi units deserted rather than move.[139] By the first week of April, McKiernan's advanced units were closing in on Baghdad. On April 1 the 3rd ID first encountered Republican Guard elements of the Nebuchadnezzar Division in the Euphrates River town of Hindiya and brushed them aside. Army units penetrated the Karbala gap to the southwest of the capital while the Marines pressed up the east bank of the Tigris River. As Army Brig. Gen. Vincent Brooks, CENTCOM's press spokesman, described it, "The dagger is clearly pointed at the heart of the regime right now."[140]

Franks's plan called for a pincer attack on Baghdad with the 3rd ID coming from the southwest and the Marines from the east.[141] Rather than engage in close urban conflict, U.S. ground forces were to create a loose cordon around Baghdad while airpower attacked defending military and sapped their morale.[142] As it turned out, this was unnecessary: CENTCOM and the Pentagon had overestimated the capabilities of the Iraqi armed forces and Hussein's strategic skills. Fearing his own military more than foreign invasion, Saddam Hussein had not trained his military for urban combat. Elite Iraqi forces crumbled under constant air attacks and artillery barrages and suffered heavily whenever they were able to engage American units in close combat. By April 5 CENTCOM estimated that two of the six Republican Guard divisions had been destroyed. As American ground forces approached, even these supposedly elite formations deserted in large numbers. Often the officers, who had entered combat with civilian clothes close at hand, fled before the enlisted soldiers did.[143]

The weak resistance during the fight for Saddam International Airport west of Baghdad convinced CFLCC that Hussein's military was on the verge of collapse.[144] On April 5 Maj. Gen. Buford Blount, commander of the 3rd ID, approved an armored probe into Baghdad by Col. David Perkins's 2d Brigade Combat Team.[145] In what became known as the first of two "thunder runs," Perkins accompanied a battalion of tanks and armored personnel carriers into the city, probing for weaknesses and gathering information on how the Iraqis intended to defend their capital. Despite intense but disorganized opposition, Perkins and his battalion penetrated into the heart of Baghdad and then returned to their base at the airport. The next day Perkins was ordered to undertake a second raid with his entire brigade. This time Blount authorized him to stay in the city if he felt that he could hold his position and be resupplied. Perkins was able to remain in Baghdad, fending off desperate counterattacks over the next two days. On April 9, Marines fighting their way into the city from the east linked with Perkins's units. For all practical purposes, organized resistance had ended. There was no "new Stalingrad." The Iraqi military, like the Hussein regime, proved pathologically weak, at least at conventional combat. But of the hundreds of thousands of Iraqi troops and other security forces in uniform before the war, only a few thousand had surrendered or been captured. Most had simply gone home.

On May 1, President Bush announced that major combat operations were over. The Department of Defense, journalists, and other commentators lauded the campaign as vindication of Rumsfeld's emphasis on operational speed and the smallest possible force. Reflecting the administration's belief that the post-Hussein stabilization of Iraq would be easier than removing the regime, the secretary of defense halted the deployment of some inbound units, most important of which was the 1st Cavalry Division.

There were a few signs that the Bush administration's assumptions about the condition of Iraq might not hold. But in the weeks after the conventional campaign, this seemed more of an annoyance than a crisis. The dominant image of President Bush was his famous thank-you address aboard a U.S. Navy aircraft carrier with a huge sign behind him stating Mission Accomplished." In those halcyon days, all signs were that America's long conflict with Iraq was nearing an end. In reality, the conflict *with* Iraq was simply becoming the conflict *in* Iraq.

6

★ الله ★ اكبر ★

COUNTERINSURGENCY

The world is grown so bad
That wrens make prey where eagles dare not perch.
—WILLIAM SHAKESPEARE
RICHARD II

When General Franks flew into Baghdad on April 16, 2003, he and the Bush administration were flush with victory. Their greatest concerns—that American forces would be attacked with chemical weapons or dragged into bloody urban combat—had not come to pass. For Franks, the worst was over. He ordered his generals to develop withdrawal plans. By September, he expected to have little more than a division of troops still in Iraq. Garner and his ORHA staff, which were in Kuwait preparing to move to Baghdad, would handle the reconstruction. Back in Washington, administration officials believed a transitional Iraqi government to be in place within weeks or, at most, months.

Unfortunately, events did not follow the script. Even before Franks began his victory lap, Iraq collapsed into a spasm of looting and street crime. The Iraqi security and police forces that the administration counted on to help the U.S. military with public order had disappeared. Anarchy sparked public anger, which gathered energy with each passing week. For a brief interlude, little violence was directed against Americans. But that did not last long. Trouble first broke out in the restive city of Fallujah, thirty-five miles west of Baghdad. Fallujah was insular, conservative, intensely religious, and fiercely resistant to outside control. It was a traditional hotbed of smuggling, where complex tribal connections mattered greatly, helping to define personal loyalty, obligation, and honor. Even Saddam Hussein largely left the place alone. The U.S. military had bypassed the city in its assault on Baghdad, but elements of the 82d Airborne Division arrived in late April. Fallujah did not take kindly to occupation and the 82d did not take kindly to occupation duty. Within a few days, a rally celebrating Saddam Hussein's birthday led to angry denunciations of the U.S. presence and heated demands for withdrawal. Shooting broke out, leaving at least thirteen Iraqis dead.[1] Two more died the next day in a second round of clashes. Attackers then tossed grenades into a U.S. Army compound. Without drawing a moral comparison, Fallujah was like Lexington and Concord—an inadvertent clash that began turning anger into organized resistance, taking on symbolic significance far beyond its real importance.

Among Iraqis, frustration grew, faster in some places than others. "Thank you for removing the tyrant," they said (or thought), "but now go home." At the same time—and contradictorily—they complained that a nation as powerful as the United States *could* restore order and public services if it desired. The failure to do so obviously was intended to punish or dishonor them. Even many who had opposed Hussein were convinced that the Americans sought only to control Iraq's oil and promote Israeli security. The mutual incomprehension that had shaped Saddam Hussein's relationship with three U.S. presidents now played out in daily contacts between Iraqis and Americans. Anger began turning violent. In early May, two American soldiers were killed in Baghdad. A few weeks later, two more died during a nighttime attack on an Army checkpoint near Fallujah. Iraq's south appeared quieter but was far from stable. U.K. forces, despite a June incident in the town of Majar al-Kabir that left six British military policemen dead, took a relaxed approach to their occupation duties, leaving local religious and militia leaders (and, as it turned out, criminal gangs) to compete for power. In the holy cities of Karbala and Najaf, clerics preserved a fragile order.

In the middle of May, several thousand Shiites marched in Baghdad, demanding an immediate transfer of power to an elected government. Grand Ayatollah Ali Hamid Maqsoon al-Sistani, Iraq's senior Shiite cleric, issued a *fatwa* condemning the idea of a constitutional council named by the American occupation authority, saying Iraqis should draft their own constitution.² But the most worrisome development in the Shiite areas was the emergence of Moqtada al-Sadr, son of an esteemed cleric who had been killed by Hussein. He was gaining fervent supporters, especially in Basra and the sprawling Shiite slum on the east side of Baghdad. He found that opposing the Americans increased his stature among the disgruntled Shiite lower classes. As often happens during political turmoil, extremism trumped moderation as leaders competed for public attention. Sadr was only one of many who grasped this.

Elsewhere violence against American forces spread, particularly in Baghdad and the region west and north of the capital known as the "Sunni triangle." The initial attacks were unsophisticated, but as experienced soldiers unemployed by the disbanding of the Iraqi Army joined in, they became more effective. Armed bands began to focus on isolated checkpoints and slow-moving convoys. They made greater use of rockets and mortars, allowing them to retreat and fight again rather than die en masse as the Saddam Fedayeen had in the March and April battles. Iraqis who worked for the Americans or were part of the new government and administrative structure became targets. Translators were among the favorites. Insurgents sabotaged the electrical grid, water system, and oil pipelines. Like their forebears in earlier insurgencies, Iraqi fighters understood that a country's rulers—the Americans in this case—were blamed for the lack of water, electricity, and fuel even when the insurgents themselves were responsible. The greater public anger and frustration, the insurgents knew, the better for them.

During the summer a group of Hussein loyalists calling itself *al-Awda* ("the return") made open overtures to Islamic militants linked to al-Qaeda while others sent feelers to leading Shiite clergy. There were reports of former regime officials recruiting foreign fighters. U.S. forces soon encountered Syrians, Saudis, Yemenis, Algerians, Lebanese, and Chechens, indicating that the international jihadist network, born in Afghanistan in the 1980s, was refocusing on Iraq. Capitalizing on the number of unemployed Iraqi men with military and police training and criminals released from prison earlier in the year, Hussein loyalists began paying for the killing of American troops.

As early as June, some strategic analysts warned that the fighting constituted an organized guerrilla war. But U.S. officials rejected this idea. Secretary of Defense Rumsfeld attributed the violence to "the remnants of the Ba'ath regime and Fedayeen death squads" and "foreign terrorists" who were "being dealt with in an orderly and forceful fashion by coalition forces."³

Maj. Gen. Raymond Odierno, commander of the Army's 4th Infantry Division, described his unit's operations as "daily contact with noncompliant forces, former regime members, and common criminals." He said, "This is not guerrilla warfare, it is not close to guerrilla warfare because it's not coordinated, it's not organized, and it's not led."[4] As summer wore on, though, it was increasingly difficult to sustain that position. Finally, on July 16, Gen. John Abizaid, who had replaced Franks as CENTCOM commander, admitted that the United States was facing "a classical guerrilla type campaign." He said, "It's low-intensity conflict in our doctrinal terms, but it's war, however you describe it."[5] The optimism of a month earlier, the hope of a quick and relatively painless transition to a post-Hussein Iraq, was gone. As journalist Thomas Ricks put it, the insurgency was in "deadly bloom."[6] The United States found itself thrust into a type of conflict it thought it had left behind with the end of the Cold War—counterinsurgency.

■　■　■

America's road to counterinsurgency in Iraq was long, winding, complex, and bloody. The first forays came when Harry Truman and Dwight Eisenhower provided support and advice to a handful of regimes threatened by leftist rebels. It then became a major component of American strategy when John Kennedy, concerned by Nikita Khrushchev's January 1961 speech endorsing "wars of national liberation," the eroding security situation in Laos and South Vietnam, the consolidation of Fidel Castro's regime in Cuba, the French defeat in Algeria, and the outbreak of communist insurgencies in Colombia and Venezuela, became convinced that the Soviet Union sought to weaken the West by stoking insurgency. Blocked from direct aggression in Western Europe, Moscow had devised an indirect strategy for global domination. Insurgency was a proxy war between the two ideological blocs. While any single communist-backed insurgency might not constitute a strategic risk, Kennedy was convinced that in combination they could. The result could be the proverbial "death by a thousand small cuts."

Americans instinctively respond to threats or strategic challenges by reorganizing, reforming, and funding new programs. Kennedy ordered a series of initiatives to improve the counterinsurgency capacity of the military and the government as a whole. Southeast Asia provided a laboratory. But by imbuing Vietnam with great symbolism, its perceived strategic significance was skewed far out of proportion to its real importance. This was to be an enduring problem in counterinsurgency: to mobilize and sustain support from Congress and the public, presidents had to portray a conflict as vitally important, the opponent as quintessentially evil. Once that perception was established, disengagement was politically difficult even if the effort was no longer worth its strategic costs. It was always easier to begin counterinsurgency than to end it.

In an even broader sense, Vietnam demonstrated how difficult counterinsurgency was for the United States. By historic tradition and strategic culture, Americans do well in conflicts with moral clarity—when there is unjustified or unprovoked aggression. This is particularly true when the aggressor can be personified as a Hitler or Hussein. Americans cannot believe that an entire people hates them but understand that tyrants can mislead their subject populations into evil or aggression. Americans do best in conflicts amenable to relatively quick, decisive resolution, preferably using technology and industrial production to minimize the blood costs. Americans accept some military setbacks early in a war but then expect steady, demonstrable progress until victory is attained. Unfortunately counterinsurgency is not like that. The psychological battlespace matters more than the military. It is not amenable to technological or industrial solutions. Counterinsurgency is imbued with ethical ambiguity. Both sides are good *and* evil. Counterinsurgency entails supporting a deeply flawed partner regime. If it were not, the insurgency would never have taken root in the first place. Counterinsurgency often takes place in cultures that are strange to Americans and difficult to understand. It is protracted, typically lasting at least a decade. And during the long, torturous process of defeating insurgents and altering the causes that gave rise to them, there is seldom steady, demonstrable progress. The norm is a frustrating mélange of progress and setback.

All of this led the United States to disaster in Vietnam. Still, the military and the strategic communities left there with a vastly improved understanding of insurgency, or, at least, of the most successful and threatening form of insurgency—Maoist "people's war." But Vietnam also left the public and the military with a deep distaste for counterinsurgency. Both would probably have preferred that the United States never again undertake it. But in strategy, the enemy "has a vote." Following Vietnam, a series of victories by insurgents backed to one degree or the other by the Soviets or Chinese— Angola, Mozambique, Zimbabwe, and Nicaragua—made the "death of a thousand small cuts" again seem plausible.

With renewed presidential concern and an active push from an important group of defense specialists in Congress, counterinsurgency experienced a resurgence throughout the 1980s, this time as part of a broader challenge named "low-intensity conflict." Again Washington responded with new organizations and programs. The military's Special Operations Forces grew. Congress created an assistant secretary of defense for special operations and low-intensity conflict as well as the United States Special Operations Command (USSOCOM). It urged the National Security Council to form a low-intensity conflict board. The Army's Special Warfare Center, the School of the Americas, and the Air Force's Special Operations School expanded their course offerings. USSOCOM created a program on low-intensity conflict at the Naval Postgraduate School in Monterey, California. The services developed low-intensity conflict "proponency offices" to coordinate thinking and education. The Army and Air Force established a Center for Low-Intensity Conflict at Langley Air Force Base near Hampton, Virginia. The Central Intelligence Agency augmented its covert action capability.

While Ronald Reagan was convinced of the need to confront the Soviets in its proxy war, he knew that the United States needed a different approach than the one it had taken in Vietnam. This time the small Central American nation of El Salvador became the laboratory. For the U.S. military, it was a chance to "get counterinsurgency right." Armed with lessons from Southeast Asia, American advisers urged the Salvadorans to stress pacification, civil defense, and population security rather than combat against guerrilla units. The military, American experts believed, should operate in small units with strict constraints on the use of firepower. Since support from the population was considered the crux of counterinsurgency, military activities were subordinate to economic, political, and psychological ones. The American footprint was kept small. By law, the United States was to have no more than fifty-five military personnel in El Salvador at any given time. All of this worked. By the end of the 1980s, El Salvador was a democracy—albeit a fragile one—its military was reasonably proficient and under civilian control, and the insurgents stood little chance of victory. A 1992 peace accord ended the conflict and integrated the insurgents back into Salvadoran life and its political system.

While the outcome in El Salvador may have been determined more by the end of Soviet sponsorship of the rebels than anything the United States did, the American military heralded it as the new model for counterinsurgency. There was, though, one problem: after the demise of the Soviet

Union, almost no one in the American military or government cared. Counterinsurgency became a lost art, remembered only by a few security experts and a handful of serving officers, most of those in the Special Forces.[7] Then Iraq changed everything.

■ ■ ■

A revolutionary slogan attributed to Vladimir Lenin states, "the worse, the better." When a weak organization like an insurgent movement attempts to overthrow a regime, anything that causes disorder undercuts public trust in the state. The Iraqi insurgents may not have studied Lenin, but they understood this concept. Their strategy was one of mayhem designed to make the country ungovernable by the majority Shiites and other U.S. supporters. Since Iraq teetered on the verge of chaos even without insurgent action, this was not difficult. In one twelve-hour stretch in August 2003, insurgents temporarily cut off Baghdad's water supply, fired mortar rounds into a prison holding Iraqi detainees, and set fire to a major oil pipeline. By August, Ramadi, west of Baghdad, saw a number of attacks on U.S. forces. Violence mounted in Mosul, Iraq's third-largest city and one with a mixed population of Arabs, Kurds, and other minorities.

Terrorism was integral to the strategy of mayhem. In August 2003, a car bomb destroyed the Jordanian embassy in Baghdad, causing nineteen deaths. Two weeks later, another massive car bomb exploded outside the Canal Hotel, which housed the U.N. headquarters, killing Sergio Vieira de Mello, the secretary-general's special representative, and nineteen others. These attacks—which were probably the work of foreign extremists—were intended to illustrate the inability of the United States to ensure security, and to deter international organizations and other nations that might have helped stabilize and rebuild Iraq. Remembering Reagan's 1983 withdrawal from Lebanon and Clinton's decision to remove U.S. peacekeepers from Somalia after a 1993 battle in Mogadishu, the insurgents concluded that American will could be shattered by terrorism. Again Iraqis did not understand that American resolve after September 11 was markedly different than in the past.

During the first year of the insurgency, many groups, most small and localized, competed for exposure, recognition, recruits, and financial support. Both Sunni Arab insurgents and the smaller number of Shiites believed an American exodus would benefit them or the constituency they claimed to represent.[8] They assumed that helping drive out the Americans would bolster their own power in whatever political order followed. At this stage insurgent attacks were uncoordinated but often followed by effective psychological actions such as the distribution of videos showing the operation (a technique pioneered by Chechen insurgents). Because Hussein had so tightly controlled all means of communication, few of the insurgents initially understood the power of the Internet and the global reach of the media, but they (and their supporters) learned quickly, developing a sophisticated Web presence and a penchant for exploiting outlets such as al Jazeera. Unlike the Americans, the insurgents understood that they were in a quintessentially psychological struggle in which culture-specific messages and themes had the greatest effect. (American "strategic communications" seemed to assume that what worked in Middle America would work in Iraq.) Gradually the insurgents settled on a four-part military strategy: attacks on Americans, sabotage, attacks on Iraqis who supported the new political order, and occasional spectacular terrorist acts.[9]

To coalesce, insurgencies require time and space when security forces either are not aware of them or unable to quash them. The Iraqi resistance gained such a respite because the United States had greatly underestimated the force size, money, and effort needed to stabilize and reconstruct Iraq. During the crucial spring and summer of 2003 the U.S. military and other elements of the government were unprepared for the magnitude of the task they faced. While expecting humanitarian challenges and perhaps a spate of sectarian score-settling, CENTCOM, ORHA, or administration policymakers did not anticipate (or prepare for) sustained, organized armed resistance. As Ambassador L. Paul Bremer, who replaced Jay Garner as head of the U.S. occupation effort, put it, "We planned for the *wrong* contingency."[10]

After a decade of transformation focused on small forces, precision, and speed, the U.S. military simply was unprepared for counterinsurgency. According to an operations officer from a task force of the 1st Infantry Division, "While we were very well trained for conventional warfare against a conventional enemy, we did not receive appreciable training in counterinsurgency operations."[11] Or as a brigade commander from the 1st Armored Division phrased it, unit "training focused on high-intensity combat and not on the type of operations in which the brigade found itself when it arrived in Baghdad."[12] The military's counterinsurgency doctrine was decades old and designed for a Cold War–style rural "people's war." It portrayed counterinsurgency as support for a threatened but functioning regime—a situation that characterized El Salvador in the 1980s but was different from Iraq in 2003. There were also too few forces, leaving important parts of Iraq without a U.S. presence, particularly Iraq's western Anbar Province, which included Fallujah and Ramadi. As Secretary Rumsfeld admitted, these areas were largely bypassed in the war.[13] His unstated assumption seemed to be that the combat prowess of the American military would intimidate any opponents of the occupation into submission. But as earlier U.S. experience in Lebanon and Somalia showed, this did not always work when American forces intervened in cultures based on a warrior tradition and resistance to outsiders, both reinforced by religious conviction. The U.S. military was configured to break the will of conventional opponents through rapid decisive operations, not to break the will of an irregular opponent through protracted psychological and political actions.

The civilian side of the government was equally ill prepared. It had failed to adapt to the new Bush strategy. ORHA remained under- and incorrectly staffed with little time to prepare for its mission.[14] Its relationship with the military was problematic.[15] "ORHA," according to a CFLCC staff officer, "is not treated seriously enough by the command (CENTCOM)."[16] A brigade commander from the 101st Airborne Division (Air Assault) noted "philosophical differences on everything from local governance to the selection and training of local security forces" between the military and ORHA/CPA.[17] Military officers complained that ORHA and the Coalitional Provisional Authority (CPA—the renamed and redesigned occupation authority under Ambassador Bremer) were ineffective and absent all together in parts of Iraq.[18] The military had resources and a widespread presence but no specific mandate for reconstruction or an overarching national strategic plan to indicate how to do so. ORHA had the mandate but not the resources. ORHA staff members could not even travel around Baghdad without transportation and escort from the military. The organization did not have the personnel and money it needed. Nor did it have a detailed, executable plan.[19] Bremer brought energy to the occupation, but the problems remained.

In the broadest sense, the United States made four major mistakes in the spring of 2003 (putting aside the question of whether it should have intervened in the first place). One was underestimating the human and economic resources—and the time—needed to stabilize Iraq and set it on the path to democracy. This, of course, was largely a result of downplaying the magnitude of the task to sustain public and congressional support for the war.

The second was assuming that partners—other states, international organizations like the United Nations, and nongovernmental organizations—would shoulder a large part of the burden of stabilizing and rebuilding Iraq. While several dozen states did send help, it was not as much as needed. The rest of the world seemed content to let the United States be punished even if the price was chaos in Iraq.

Third was using Iraq as a laboratory for social reengineering. This played out in several ways. The Bush administration and Ambassador Bremer implemented radical free market reforms. While this was necessary for Iraq to become competitive in the globalized economy, the shock of dragging a decrepit system based on socialism, patronage, and corruption into the free market was simply too much for Iraqis to bear. It was the right policy at the wrong time. The result was massive unemployment. This dishonored the men who were put out of work, stoking their anger and resentment. It also created a huge number of insurgents-for-hire. Many of the insurgent foot soldiers cared little about politics but found violence the best paying job available. The administration and Ambassador Bremer also ordered radical "de-Ba'athification" modeled after "de-Nazification" in post–World War II Germany.[20] While no one questioned the need to dissolve the Ba'ath Party and Hussein's apparatus for ruling Iraqi, critics contended that Bremer went too far, excluding many Iraqi professionals from participation in the political, administrative, and economic life of their country because they had been forced to join the Ba'ath Party. Finally (and, according to many security experts and military officers, most important), Ambassador Bremer (or Pentagon policymakers) decided to abolish the Iraqi armed forces.[21] Again, this dishonored and angered its members. They had been promised that if they did not fight against the Americans, they would be brought into the armed forces of the new, post-Hussein Iraq and could help stabilize their country. Instead, they found themselves unemployed. Many of them turned to the only skill they had—the use of violence. In their minds, this was to punish the United States for its deceit.

Fourth was the failure to shift to a full-fledged counterinsurgency strategy until the conflict was well under way. Rather than admit that a serious insurgency had taken root, Secretary Rumsfeld blamed "people who were the enforcers for the Saddam Hussein regime—the Fedayeen Saddam people and the Ba'ath Party members and undoubtedly some of his security guards" and "fifty to one hundred thousand prison inmates who were put back out in the street, criminals of various types."[22] General Myers explained that "we continue to root out residual pockets of resistance from paramilitary forces and Ba'ath Party personnel."[23] During a June press conference, Ambassador Bremer characterized the attacks on American forces as the work of "Fedayeen Saddam or former Republican Guard officers."[24] President Bush described the conflict as "hunting down the terrorists."[25] This led American leaders to conclude that there was no need for a comprehensive, integrated counterinsurgency strategy, only for continued vigilance and aggressive military action until the criminals and the former regime loyalists grew tired, were caught, or killed. To have developed and implemented a comprehensive counterinsurgency strategy, the Bush administration would have been forced to admit that its management of Iraq was fundamentally flawed. The strategy would then have simultaneously weakened the insurgents while addressing the flaws. But for a variety of psychological and political reasons—the 2004 presidential election was looming and, as always, American strategy was inextricably linked to the electoral cycle—administration officials were not inclined to do this, at least in the summer of 2003. It was easier to attribute the violence to "Saddamists" and extremists than to American mistakes.

As a result, the United States pursued tactical rather than strategic solutions, emphasizing military action and ceding the psychological initiative to the insurgents. Secretary Rumsfeld said, "We need to do whatever we need to do," but "that's up to the battlefield commanders."[26] So CENTCOM sent more military police and shifted a few infantrymen to police duties. Some combat units tackled infrastructure and public service problems on their own volition.[27] Many units, though, felt that they had accomplished what they were sent to do—remove Hussein's regime—and assumed a passive stance waiting to be relieved.[28] Units that did attempt to restore local order and stoke reconstruction found it a double-edged sword: they then were blamed by the Iraqi public when things went awry or when street violence and infrastructure problems interfered with daily life.

Almost immediately, questions arose about the adequacy of the U.S. troop numbers. This was the beginning of a long debate that reflected one of the enduring psychological dilemmas of counterinsurgency, particularly when it is undertaken by an outside force. Having more American forces would have deterred some insurgent operations and might have made some Iraqis feel more secure but would have antagonized others. It was a "damned if we do, damned if we don't" dilemma. Once Pentagon policymakers recognized that they could not count on Iraqis themselves to secure the country, they postponed the departure of some military units. Military commanders expanded patrols in Baghdad, seeking a continuous presence in key neighborhoods. They sent additional forces to the Sunni triangle. Some military commanders instinctively understood counterinsurgency and, on their own initiative, began implementing it. This did lead to some local (and short-term) successes. In Mosul, the 101st Airborne Division under the command of Maj. Gen. David Petraeus moved quickly into the political vacuum and worked vigorously to restore economic activity and a functioning Iraqi administration.

Elsewhere, though, U.S. forces went on the attack, staging raids and sweeps across the Sunni triangle. But the paradoxical logic again reared its head: tactical success had unintended psychological consequences. David Galula, a French veteran of Cold War–era counterinsurgency campaigns in Indochina and Algeria, noted that counterinsurgency often involves a "vicious cycle": when military operations turn the public against the military and the military, in turn, begins to see the public as the enemy, it thus amplifyies the mutual hostility and makes it more difficult to win public acceptance or support.[29] The June and July offensives suggested that just such a vicious cycle had begun in Iraq. They probably angered more Iraqis than they captured, leading to an aggregate increase in support for the insurgency and convincing much of the population (and Muslims outside Iraq) that the United States was an occupier, not a liberator. The methods American forces used when arresting suspected insurgents were particularly antagonizing. In a culture where personal honor is paramount, this created scores of new enemies bent on revenge.

Faced with hostility and violence, some American units began treating all Iraqis as potential insurgents. This became a self-fulfilling prophecy. By the end of his unit's tour, a company commander in the 4th Infantry Division advised officers coming after him to remember "most of the people here want us dead, they hate us and everything we stand for, and will take any opportunity to cause us harm."[30] After 227 years of independence, Americans had forgotten the humiliation of foreign occupation. U.S. troops in Iraq had as much difficulty understanding why Iraqis resisted efforts to help and protect them as eighteenth-century British authorities did understanding why their American colonists were so ungrateful for the protection provided them.

As U.S. military commanders struggled to find the most effective balance between eradicating insurgents and winning public support, they stressed intelligence gathering, "friendly persuasion," limiting civilian casualties, and minimizing destruction. The Commander's Emergency Response Program (CERP), which the CPA created with captured Iraqi money, allowed military commanders to undertake small projects with limited red tape.[31] Senior military leaders considered this program "highly important" and felt that had even more funds been available and restrictions on their use limited, it could have made a difference during the vital first months of occupation.[32] But despite this, significant sections of the Iraqi public remained hostile. Every arrest and sweep by American forces added to the sense of community dishonor. Ultimately counterinsurgency is shaped less by which side the public prefers to rule it than which side it blames for whatever has gone wrong. By the summer of 2003, it was clear that in the Sunni Arab community, the United States was held responsible.

As hopes for a quick withdrawal faded, U.S. military leaders recognized that they would need substantial troops in Iraq for an extended period of time. This required long-term rotation plans, addressing the problem of "high demand, low density" units such as military police and intelligence specialists, and building adequate military infrastructure. The rotation issue was particularly thorny. Neither the Army nor the Marine Corps was configured for large-scale, protracted counterinsurgency. A decade of defense transformation had created a force optimized for intense, short-duration operations, not stabilization or counterinsurgency. By September, the ground forces were feeling the stress. The Congressional Budget Office published a widely discussed report that questioned the ability of the Army to sustain its rotation in Iraq after March 2004 without extending tours beyond one year.[33] Doing so could adversely affect recruitment and retention, potentially forcing service leaders to compromise on the quality of people who entered the military and to spend additional funds keeping those they had. The military was akin to a finely trained sprinter entered in a marathon.

The Pentagon pursued several solutions. In the most immediate sense, it sought to squeeze as much as possible from available assets. The Army activated additional National Guard and reserve forces for service in Iraq. Nearly every active duty unit in the Army was added to the rotation schedule, tours were extended for both active and reserve units, and training and education cycles were adjusted to maximize the troops available for deployment. Even so, commanders could provide only a limited presence in parts of Iraq. Administration policymakers attempted to cover this shortfall by convincing other nations to send troops. A number did, but most provided only small contingents dependent on American support. The administration wooed those with more substantial military capability like India and Turkey but had no success. Most were unwilling to bear the costs of resolving a problem they did not cause. Some had decided that instability in Iraq was less of a threat than unchecked American power.

In June 2003 the CPA announced plans to create a new Iraqi military from scratch. It hoped for an initial force of 12,000 within a year with an ultimate goal of 40,000—a size deemed large enough for national defense but not large enough to threaten Iraq's neighbors.[34] While this made sense from the standpoint of regional comity, it was woefully inadequate for large-scale counterinsurgency operations. But the CPA and the administration clung to the idea that the violence in Iraq was the last gasp of "dead enders" rather than a serious insurgency. In October, U.S. officials announced a four-phase plan designed to turn responsibility over to Iraqi security forces as soon as they were ready.[35] A few weeks later the CPA increased the pace of Iraqi force development. This reflected the Cold War doctrine that stressed strengthening and supporting local forces, but it did not reflect the magnitude of the task at hand. There was a mismatch between the Bush administration's strategic objectives and the resources devoted to them.

In the Pentagon, Iraq began shaping and driving broader decisions about the future of the U.S. military. To some defense leaders, the conflict was shifting from an anomaly to a paradigm. However, Rumsfeld, his senior civilian advisers, and the service chiefs still seemed convinced that adjustments to existing programs, doctrine, and force structure would do. While the military was not optimized for counterinsurgency, it seemed flexible enough to be tolerably effective at that mission. "Rebalancing" and "modularizing" the Army were key. Rebalancing was a program to ensure that soldiers were placed where their skills were needed. It also involved "civilianizing" a number of jobs to free soldiers for other duties. Modularization was a new way to package forces, tailoring units to missions using brigade-based structure rather than the old division-based one.

Critics contended that even a modularized Army at its existing size could not undertake protracted stabilization operations, continue transformation, perform its other worldwide missions, and sustain the quality of its troops, leaders, and equipment. The only solution, they felt, was increasing the overall size of the American military, particularly its ground forces.[36] Congress, seeing this as a way to demonstrate its seriousness in the "war on terror," jumped on board.[37] Secretary Rumsfeld resisted, arguing that additional troops would draw resources from transformation. "The real problem," he wrote, "is not necessarily the size of our active and reserve military components, *per se*, but rather how forces have been managed, and the mix of capabilities at our disposal."[38] He continued to view the Iraqi insurgency as a temporary aberration, not a strategic paradigm or something that should be allowed to derail his long-term vision for the American military (which, as with much of American defense transformation, still used the Gulf War and the campaign to remove Hussein as its paradigm). Indeed, Rumsfeld and Abizaid both contended that sending additional U.S. forces to Iraq would simply stir up even more opposition and sidetrack the development of the Iraqi security forces.[39] This reflected a lesson the Bush administration had drawn from U.S. involvement in the Balkans: other nations are less inclined to assume responsibility for their own security if they believe the United States will do it for them. If the United States limited its role in Iraq, the Iraqis themselves would redouble their efforts. It was strategic "tough love."

As with so much of the Bush strategy, this was based on assumptions that proved inaccurate. While many Iraqis wanted control of their own security, they were not prepared for it in the months after the collapse of the Hussein regime. And the United States was equally unprepared to give them as much assistance as they needed. Some American defense analysts, members of Congress, and CPA administrator Bremer argued that the only solution was to deploy more American troops until the rebuilding of the Iraqi security forces was more successful.[40] While Secretary Rumsfeld and the president often stated that they never declined a request for more troops from their military commanders, it was clear that the administration's preference was for no additional deployments and instead doing more with what was already available. The military commanders understood this. "Tough love" applied to the U.S. military as well as to the Iraqis.

■ ■ ■

When conventional war looms, states often convince themselves that they are the victim of unjustified or unprovoked aggression and engage in armed conflict with a clean conscience. Counterinsurgency is different. By definition, an insurgency cannot form, consolidate, and continue unless the state has fundamental shortcomings. When the United States provides counterinsurgency support to a friendly regime, Washington must convince its partner that it has serious political, economic, social, and security sector problems that must be addressed. This is hard enough. But in Iraq, the United States itself was the regime. It thus had to admit that its own policies and approaches were flawed. Without such an admission, major change is impossible. During the vital first year of the Iraq insurgency the 2004 American presidential election loomed. This made it almost impossible for the Bush administration to admit its flaws. Had it done so, the admission would have been used as political ammunition. All it could do was downplay the growing challenges in Iraq, deny policy failure, and place responsibility for its strategy on the uniformed military.

This required continuing to describe the insurgency as a movement of "former Saddamists" and outside jihadists. Fortunately for the administration, this was credible. Many Iraqi males (perhaps even most Sunni Arabs) had ties of some sort to the former regime, having served in the military or other security forces, or relied on the Hussein regime for jobs or favors. While Iraqis themselves understood that this did not make them all "Saddamists," the Bush administration could make that claim, at least to domestic audiences. The charge that outside jihadists shaped or even dominated the insurgency was even easier. Foreign fighters, including many with an affiliation to al-Qaeda, did stream in. They were always a small portion of the insurgency but undertook many of the most violent and highly publicized attacks. This allowed the Bush administration to portray the conflict in Iraq as a battle against al-Qaeda and an integral part of the "war on terror." Again, this did not resonate with Iraqis, who had a clearer picture of the insurgency, but did play well with American audiences. And it had operational implications. To validate the portrayal, Lt. Gen. Ricardo Sanchez, commander of the U.S. forces, had to shift troops to finding and eradicating foreign fighters. This meant less time and fewer resources for other activities, including reconstruction.

As Americans grappled with these problems, the insurgents continued to evolve. They understood that combining regular, low-level violence with occasional large, high-profile attacks maximized fear and publicity. Humans can tolerate danger in constant and expected doses. Anticipation of a different kind or level of danger, though, increases anxiety, which, in turn, saps morale and will. Fear of the unknown is the most debilitating kind. Applying this idea, the insurgents launched a rocket attack on the Rashid Hotel in Baghdad during a visit by Deputy Secretary of Defense Paul Wolfowitz in October. This killed an American lieutenant colonel—the highest-ranking officer to die in the conflict to that point. More important, it demonstrated to the Americans that no place in Iraq was safe. As always in insurgency, the military effect of an operation was much less important than the psychological one. During the same time, insurgents struck three Baghdad police stations and the headquarters of the International Committee of the Red Cross simultaneously. This also served multiple psychological purposes, illustrating that the insurgents could coordinate complex operations, deterring relief and reconstruction efforts, and thus adding to the frustration of the Iraqi public. The worse, the better.

During October 2003, attacks surged in what American officials called the "Ramadan offensive." In November, insurgents downed a U.S. Army CH-47 transport helicopter, killing fifteen. At the time, this was the single worst attack on U.S. forces since the end of major combat operations. The insurgents stepped up assaults on less committed coalition members, including Spain, Japan, and South Korea. The fighting spread to regions that had been stable, particularly Mosul. By December, a third of the first battalion of the new Iraqi Army, which had been sworn in during October, had deserted. While it eventually died out, the Ramadan offensive showed new levels of coordination and resolve by the insurgents. After a pitched battle in Samarra, a U.S. Army officer said, "They had the training to stand and fight."[41]

Like the 1968 Tet Offensive in Vietnam or the January 1981 national offensive of the Frente Farabundo Marti de Liberación Nacional (FMLN) in El Salvador, the Ramadan offensive tried to demonstrate the insurgents' courage and power, expose the weakness of the United States and its allies, and galvanize support among the Iraqi public and other Muslims.[42] As in those earlier offensives, the insurgents suffered a tactical defeat but made psychological gains. A CIA assessment soon after the offensive provided a bleak picture, noting that a growing number of Iraqis believed the insurgents could defeat the United States.[43] Eventually November 2003 ended as the deadliest month for the United States to that point, surpassing the conventional battles of March and April. In response, U.S. military units increased force protection measures. Again, the paradoxical logic was at play: limiting casualties was good for morale and public support but hindered pacification. In November, Clay McManaway, a retired ambassador serving as CPA deputy, advised Paul Bremer that the Army had gone into a "passive mode."[44] The Bush administration realized that it had limited time before public and congressional support eroded. The dilemma was whether to seek the quickest possible transfer of responsibility to Iraqi security forces or a modulated pace of change that did not demand more of the new Iraqi forces than they could provide, thus maximizing the chances that Iraq would end up stable and democratic. Strategic failure, in other words, could come from two sources: the collapse of the new Iraqi government and security forces or the collapse of American support. The Bush administration had to navigate a treacherous course between these shoals.

The capture of Saddam Hussein in December 2003 briefly shifted the psychological initiative to the American side. Hopes were that it would convince the Iraqi public that the future lay with the new government. U.S. military leaders, though, recognized that Hussein's role in the insurgency was strictly symbolic. Attacks declined for a while but picked up again early in 2004, with an increase in the use of sophisticated roadside bombs. Assaults on Iraqis associated with the Americans, particularly serving and candidate police officers, were relentless, with more than 400 killed by March 2004. With some former regime officials demoralized by Hussein's capture, the role of foreign jihadists correspondingly increased. Once again, Fallujah was at the fore. Outside fighters, many linked to al-Qaeda in some way, poured into the city, forming working partnerships or loose alliances with locals. "The Fallujah region is filling up with Wahabis," said a tribal leader.[45] By February 2004, it was difficult to know who actually was in charge of the city—the U.S.-sanctioned local government or the insurgents.

This came at a treacherous time for the U.S. military, with 110,000 new troops scheduled to replace 130,000 who had finished their tour. The largest troop rotation since World War II involved eight of the Army's ten active divisions, a Marine Expeditionary Force (MEF), and 40,000 international troops. This raised several concerns among American military commanders. One was the loss of the local knowledge and expertise gained by the outgoing troops. Second, there would be fewer U.S. forces in Iraq after the rotation. Third, there was a greater proportion of reservists in the incoming forces, further stressing the services and complicating recruitment and retention. The sprinter turned marathoner was beginning to feel the strain.

Eventually the rotation went fairly well. The incoming units were better trained, organized, and equipped for stabilization and counterinsurgency than those they replaced, thus allowing them to adjust more quickly. Units scheduled for direct replacement—for instance, the 1st Cavalry Division and the 1st Armored Division, and the 101st Airborne and Task Force Olympia—established contact several months in advance of the rotation to share lessons and information. The commanders and some staff of incoming units arrived early and spent time with the departing units. Outgoing units left key staff members behind to help with continuity. An important step was what became known as "left seat/right seat rides" during the overlap, with incoming commanders participating in operations with the units they were to replace.[46] In addition, an extensive web of informal communications among junior officers and noncommissioned officers had emerged, relying on email and Internet sites. While this caused some concern among senior leaders, it did facilitate the handoff.

Insurgencies are always learning contests between the combatants. Success normally goes to the side that learns the fastest and most effectively. The first year of the Iraq counterinsurgency campaign was a time of rapid learning for the U.S. military. It had made great strides in many areas. Still, there were shortcomings. Mounting casualties and hostility from the Iraqi public, combined with the inherent aggressiveness of the U.S. military, led some units to concentrate more on eliminating insurgents than dominating the psychological battlespace. Such actions did eliminate enemy fighters, but they also amplified public anger and resentment. In many cases, operations that were successful militarily were political and psychological losses, inspiring new recruits or supporters for the insurgency. While most U.S. commanders understood the psychological priorities of counterinsurgency and acted accordingly, they were overshadowed by the negative effects of those who did not. To concentrate on eliminating enemy fighters rather than discrediting them or undercutting their support was within the U.S. military's tradition—it was a strategy of attrition in which victory came from killing or capturing enemy combatants until the opponent's will collapsed. This often worked in conventional war. It had led the United States to stunning victories in World War II and the Gulf War. But, history suggests, it seldom brings success in counterinsurgency.

In the vital political and economic spheres, the record was equally mixed. Some progress had been made on building a democratic government and a new constitution, but sectarianism imbued the process. Iraq's Shiites saw democracy as a means to use their numbers to dominate their country after centuries of repression. Sunni Arabs largely rejected the political process, viewing it as a means to solidify Iranian control of Iraq. The Kurds grudgingly went along while giving every indication that their ultimate goal was secession from Iraq. Economically, there had been a burst of activity. Consumer goods once in short supply or prohibited were suddenly abundant. But Iraq's dilapidated infrastructure was unrepaired. Electricity, water, health care, and other services were worse than they had been under Saddam Hussein. Unemployment was rampant as the CPA attempted to drag corrupt and inefficient state-owned enterprises' business to an open market. On top of it all, the violence dissuaded foreign investment and crippled Iraq's ability to exploit its petroleum. If the military glass was at least half full, the political and economic one was emptying fast. As James Stephenson, former mission director in Iraq for the U.S. Agency for International Development (USAID), put it, the United States lost the "golden hour" when an effective infusion of reconstruction assistance might have had a profound effect on the political and security situation.[47]

■ ■ ■

By the spring of 2004, the growing influence of foreign militants within the insurgency pushed it toward more extreme positions and a greater reliance on terrorism. Insurgent leaders had begun to believe that the Americans would soon be gone, leaving them to the second and decisive part of their struggle—war against the Shiites. A letter written by Abu Musab al-Zarqawi, the brutal Jordanian-born leader of "al-Qaeda in Iraq" said: "Shiism is the looming danger and the true challenge. They are the enemy. Beware of them. Fight them."[48] Zarqawi's followers put this concept into practice, and suicide bombers attacked participants at the religious festival of Ashura, killing 140. While Iraq's Shiites recognized the threat to their community from the Sunni Arabs, this did not translate into full support for the occupation and American-engineered transition. Their community was split on how to deal with the Americans. Many of them grudgingly accepted the U.S. presence, but others appeared to believe that, with Iranian support, they could take care of themselves. This made the conflict even more difficult for Americans to understand. As Barry Posen notes, most of the violent conflicts since the end of the Cold War have been based on identity politics. Because Americans view politics from the perspective of individual rather than group interests, they are often surprised by the outbreak of violence based on identity politics, the extent of group ambitions, the ferocity of the violence, the intensity of group loyalties, and the cost and duration of any American military intervention.[49] As Iraq demonstrated, incomprehension always derails strategic effectiveness.

The deadly learning contest thus lumbered on. For the American forces, much of the adaptation involved tactics, techniques, and procedures.

Within days of some insurgent innovation, countermeasures were in place and integrated into the training of units preparing for deployment. Newly deploying units used what then-Maj. Gen. Peter W. Chiarelli, commander of the 1st Cavalry Division, called "full spectrum operations," which tightly integrated combat with advisory and reconstruction efforts.[50]

Despite this, the insurgents also improved. Rather than "shoot and scoot" attacks, they undertook set-piece small unit actions. They attempted to create and hold "liberated areas." And they expanded their area of operations. By April 2004, violence had spread to previously quiet parts of Baghdad and the northern city of Kirkuk. In the south, Shiite militias under the control of Moqtada al-Sadr launched an offensive against the coalition. Major battles raged in half a dozen cities. Fighting in Fallujah reached a new peak as the coalition decided to clear the city after a well-publicized and particularly brutal attack on American security contractors. During the battle, Sunni Arab insurgents and Shiite militias openly cooperated for the first time. Facing bitterly hostile coverage from the Arab media and intense pressure from the Iraqi Governing Council and influential clerics like Grand Ayatollah Sistani, American officials feared a united Sunni-Shiite resistance, a nation-wide popular uprising, and derailment of the political transition. Washington called off the assault on Fallujah with parts of the city still under insurgent control. Responsibility for security was given to a cobbled-together Iraqi unit called the "Fallujah Brigade" that quickly proved worthless. Most of the hard-core militants simply faded away to fight another day. By June 2004, the Shiite uprising in Iraq's south had abated, but insurgents ruled the streets of Fallujah and implemented a Taliban-like, austere form of Islamic law. Foreign fighters controlled whole neighborhoods. The city became a major guerrilla base.

The insurgents heralded the battle for Fallujah as a major victory. As Anthony Cordesman noted, the battle "created the image of large innocent casualties, a 'heroic' Iraqi opposition, collateral damage, and U.S. advanced weapons hitting mosques."[51] Other observers talked of a "powerful, deeply symbolic myth" emerging from Fallujah.[52] This was an important idea: myth creation is often the goal of major insurgent offensives. Insurgency, after all, is armed theater. In past insurgencies, events such as the Battle of Algiers, Dien Bien Phu, and the Tet Offensive had symbolic impact far beyond their military effect. What became known as "first Fallujah" played a similar role. Conditions in Iraq made such myths particularly important. Hussein's tight control of information had left the Iraqi public poorly prepared to distinguish truth from disinformation, thus amplifying the effects of insurgent propaganda. Iraqis had not yet developed the mental filters necessary in a free market of ideas and information. This was the paradoxical logic at play again: crushing battlefield defeats do not deal decisive psychological blows to insurgents, but battlefield defeats that can be cast as "heroic" are transformed into psychological victories.

Ultimately, Fallujah did not have the strategic impact of Tet or Dien Bien Phu but did increase sympathy for the insurgents in Iraq and elsewhere in the Islamic world. It also had a polarizing effect, eroding the number of neutrals among the Iraqi public and driving many people to one camp or the other. In the United States, the furor of the April 2004 battles increased criticism of the counterinsurgency strategy and signaled a long decline in public and congressional support for American involvement. As always, trends and expectations were central in the evolution of the insurgency. Politically and psychologically Fallujah was an insurgent victory, creating a sense among the insurgents and their supporters that victory was possible and raising the idea within the United States that America could be defeated.

Fallujah and the other April battles were a wake-up call for U.S. military leaders. General Abizaid moved troops from other CENTCOM areas into Iraq. The Army again extended the tours of some units in Iraq, returned others to the country more quickly than planned, and began exploring other unpleasant measures such as shorter leaves. Gen. Peter Schoomaker, the Army chief of staff, admitted that Iraq was "stressing" the Army but advised that he could support at least three more years of involvement in Iraq at existing levels without a force increase.[53] Trouble lay ahead. "What keeps me awake at night," Gen. Richard Cody, Army vice chief of staff, told Congress, "is what will this all-volunteer force look like in 2007."[54] The April battles also showed the mixed quality of the new Iraqi security forces. While those trained by the British in the south or the 101st Airborne in the north did well, many others simply melted away. The Pentagon quickly dispatched Major General Petraeus back to Baghdad to energize the training program. But American counterinsurgency doctrine provided no guidance on what to do if training and advising local security forces failed.

Al-Sadr's April uprising illustrated the growing problem of sectarian militias. The country was full of them. Most important were the Kurdish *peshmergas*, a force of 70,000 that had emerged in the 1990s to protect the autonomous regions in Iraq's north from Hussein's forces; the Badr Corps of the Supreme Council for Islamic Revolution in Iraq (SCIRI), a Shiite movement with strong ties to Iran; and al-Sadr's "Mahdi Army." Ambassador Bremer wanted the militias dissolved and assigned veteran diplomat David Gompert to lead the effort. The leaders of the militias opposed this idea, recognizing that their armed groups were central to their authority and served as a check on both rival factions and the new government. As the CPA prepared to return sovereignty to the Iraqi government in June 2004, little progress had been made on this thorny problem.

In a broad sense, the militia issue showed one of the shortcomings in the way that the United States, armed with a concept of insurgency forged while fighting communist forces during the Cold War, thought about the Iraq conflict. In Cold War counterinsurgency, the antagonists themselves— the regime and the insurgents—and, in most cases, state sponsors of one side or the other determined the outcome. But one of the important defining features of twenty-first-century insurgency was the growing role of what might be called "third" and "fourth" forces.[55]

Third forces are armed organizations that are sometimes affiliated with either the insurgents or the regime and sometimes autonomous. They included militias, criminal gangs, warlord armies, and various kinds of death squads, all influencing the conduct and outcome of the insurgency. The Iraq conflict was not a binary insurgency in the Cold War model but multiple interlinked conflicts involving insurgents, terrorists, militias, and criminal gangs. U.S. doctrine did not account for this. And Iraq saw a new and important third force: security contractors who performed many of the functions that state counterinsurgent forces could not or would not. This raised new questions of morality, legality, and efficacy. It also added complexity to the paradoxical logic of counterinsurgency. Many security contractors, for instance, guarded coalition officials. Their mission was to protect their client by any means necessary. In many cases, the way they did this ran counter to the larger strategic objective of winning Iraqi support.

Fourth forces in insurgency were unarmed non-state organizations that affected the conduct and outcome of the conflict. They include international organizations, nongovernmental organizations involved in relief and reconstruction, private voluntary organizations, the international media, and international finance and business (which influence the conflict by deciding to support or not support the regime). Both third and fourth forces played a central role in Iraq: al Jazeera and other Arab and Iranian broadcasting organizations shaped public opinion. By criticizing the United States, they gained instant credibility. But neither the U.S. military nor the CPA had effective programs to deal with them. American counterinsurgency doctrine said almost nothing about fourth forces other than to advise commanders to be aware of them.

With the return of sovereignty to the Iraqi government approaching in June 2004, the U.S. military continued to shift from a leading to a supporting role, at least so far as the often-questionable competence of the Iraqi security forces would allow. U.S. units became involved more heavily in protecting Iraqi officials and infrastructure, gradually giving Iraqi security forces the lead on counterinsurgency strikes and sweeps. Unfortunately, though, the Iraqi security forces simply were not ready to replace U.S. units on a one-for-one basis. It was not so much a matter of raw numbers as of combat effectiveness. Few Iraqi units could undertake autonomous actions or even play a leading role in operations with American troops. Nor did they have the vital support they needed in terms of logistics, intelligence, and other functions. Scaling back U.S.-led combat operations left the insurgents unhindered in parts of Iraq, particularly the far western Anbar Province.

At this point, American strategy was more kicking the can down the road than resolving problems. In both Washington and Baghdad, American officials seemed to hope that the June 2004 handover of political authority to an Iraqi government would deflate the insurgency. But they also feared that the insurgents would launch another offensive during the transition. There was, in fact, an upsurge in violence. The week before the planned transfer on June 30, intense fighting raged in Fallujah, Ramadi, Baqubah, Mosul, and Baghdad. The offensive proved weaker than expected, though. In part, this reflected a schism within the insurgency. Some Sunni Arab nationalists had become convinced that foreign jihadists like Zarqawi had hijacked their movement and driven it toward objectives of little concern to them. Feelings about the political transition itself were mixed within the Sunni Arab community. Some favored allowing it because it would speed the withdrawal of the Americans. Others seemed to believe that interfering with the political transition (and sustaining the American presence) would work to their benefit by stoking public anger. As time wore on, most of the insurgents fell into the latter camp.

The attacks on civilians during preparations for the political transition illustrated one of the perennial challenges insurgents face: they also must modulate the form and extent of their violence, enflaming dissatisfaction with the regime, provoking overreaction, and deterring support for the government without alienating the public. Insurgents, too, must walk a fine line. The execution of hostages and suicide attacks on Shiite religious gatherings generated much publicity for the insurgents but also increased hostility. By the summer of 2004—with the insurgency a year old—most insurgents rejected the more grotesque acts such as broadcasting beheadings via the Internet, probably because the negative reaction outweighed the benefits. But for the time being, the Sunni nationalists within the insurgency were unwilling or unable to rein in Zarqawi or other foreign extremists as they hurled themselves against the Shiites.

■ ■ ■

Unfortunately the transfer of political power had little effect on the insurgency. Attacks continued on U.S. troops, on Iraqis associated with the Americans or the government, and on infrastructure. A massacre of fifty unarmed Iraqi National Guard recruits showed the brutal extent this could reach. As the autumn of 2004 began, American officials admitted that the insurgents had near control over important parts of central Iraq, especially the cities of Fallujah, Ramadi, Samarra, and Baqubah. Experts warned that the movement could be undertaking the classic development pattern of insurgencies, first creating "liberated zones" and then building a conventional capability. Fallujah was particularly worrisome and seen by both the insurgents and the counterinsurgents as the epicenter of the resistance. In November U.S. forces launched a second, larger, and better-planned offensive to clear it, driving the insurgents out after bitter fighting. Squeezed out of Fallujah, insurgents launched fierce counterattacks elsewhere, particularly in Mosul. Continuing the strategy of mayhem, they executed a number of Kurdish policemen and militia members. In January 2005, a group affiliated with al-Qaeda took credit for a bombing that killed Shiite cleric Sheikh Mahmoud al-Madaini, a senior aide to Grand Ayatollah Sistani. A few weeks later suicide bombers struck Shiite worshipers in and around Baghdad, killing at least thirty. Eventually the Shiite community lost patience. Its militias began engaging insurgents in gun battles and undertaking reprisals for insurgent attacks. Mysterious deaths of Sunnis were rumored to be the work of Shiite death squads linked to the police or other elements of the security services.

Despite this, the political process slowly continued. To help ensure security for the important January 2005 national elections, CENTCOM increased the American troop presence in Iraq from seventeen to twenty brigades, the highest level to that point. While the insurgents and radical clerics kept voter turnout light in Sunni areas, the election went smoothly in the rest of the country. The world press exploded with pictures of Iraqis jubilant over their first freely cast vote. Iraqis knew that it was mostly their own security forces that had kept order during the election. Public sentiment appeared to shift away from the insurgents. American leaders began talking of the "beginning of the end" of the insurgency, with Vice President Cheney claiming that it was in "the last throes."[56]

Once again this optimism was premature. Insurgents launched a new wave of attacks, including a car bomb in Al-Hillah that killed 125. They began trickling back into Fallujah. Foreign extremists assumed a greater role. An American military commander described Iraq as "an insurgency that's been hijacked by a terrorist campaign."[57] Suicide bombs—the weapon of choice for the foreign jihadists—began causing more deaths than any other insurgent activity. While the January 2005 election may have shifted some of the "undecideds" toward the government, there was little sign that support for the insurgency was dropping below the level needed to sustain it. After all, insurgents do not need all or most of the public to support them, only a foundation of active support and passivity from the rest.

The conflict began to have cascading effects on the U.S. military. The annual risk assessment by the chairman of the Joint Chiefs of Staff noted that commanders around the world were pressed to meet their obligations. Recruiting shortfalls slowed a temporary increase in the size of the Army that Congress had mandated. Concerns were growing that antiwar sentiment in the United States might damage troop morale. Reports surfaced of dissension within the senior ranks of the military. The dissidents were particularly worried that large security sweeps were not followed up with a long-term troop presence and thus allowed the insurgents to return soon after the operation ended. By the end of the summer, U.S. commanders no longer talked of clearing places like Anbar. Instead, they had to settle for holding a handful of cities and towns and disrupting insurgent activity elsewhere with periodic strikes. To many officers, this was frighteningly reminiscent of Vietnam.

Pummeled by criticism, the Bush administration released a document entitled *National Strategy for Victory in Iraq* in November 2005. This defined long-term victory as "an Iraq that has defeated the *terrorists* and neutralized the insurgency."[58] The distinction between "terrorists" and "insurgents" was important. With public support for involvement in Iraq fading, the administration placed greater emphasis on the relationship of that conflict to the wider struggle with Islamic extremism. "Prevailing in Iraq," *National Strategy for Victory in Iraq* stated, "will help us win the war on terror." As General Myers explained it, "As soon as we pull out, that would embolden this al-Qai'da organization, their violent extremist techniques, and surely the next 9/11 would be right around the corner."[59] It was a new domino theory. It meant that the most important enemies in Iraq—and the ones the United States would focus on—were those affiliated with al-Qaeda. Iraq's Sunni Arab insurgents were only important to the extent they affected America's war with al-Qaeda.

The Bush administration recognized that it faced a mounting problem in sustaining public and congressional support for what had become a monumentally expensive endeavor (both in monetary and blood terms). Having been promised quick and cheap success, the public was not psychologically prepared for what had become something different. Americans gradually understood that the conflict was not the dying spasm of the Hussein regime or the action of a few foreign terrorists but a sectarian struggle in which many Iraqis supported the insurgents. Traditionally Americans will support involvement in an armed conflict where there is demonstrable progress, moral clarity, and the hope of clear victory. These were in short supply in Iraq.

With the original rationale for intervention in Iraq—weapons of mass destruction—discredited, President Bush and his senior advisers had to recast the conflict. Fortunately for the administration, al-Qaeda provided a way to do this. It continued pathologically brutal attacks; bin Laden himself lauded the conflict as central to his struggle with the West. This allowed the administration to portray it as part of the "global war on terror." Again the Bush administration associated Iraq with September 11. In his May 2004 speech at the U.S. Army War College, for instance, President Bush ended a discussion of his strategy in Iraq with an emotional reminder of "the flames of September 11": "The troops here and across the world are fighting a global war on terror. The war reached our shores on September the 11th, 2001 . . . Iraq is the latest battlefield in this war . . . Our mission in Iraq is clear. We're hunting down the terrorists."[60] "Iraq is part of the global war on terror," he added in a speech in Wheeling, West Virginia. "In other words, it's a global war."[61] Later in 2005 he amplified: "The terrorists in Iraq share the same ideology as the terrorists who struck the United States on September

11th."[62] Then he linked the Iraqi insurgents to not only September 11, but also to terrorist attacks in Spain, Indonesia, Saudi Arabia, and Jordan.[63] Merging the full panoply of Islamic extremists into a unitary evil, President Bush stated, "When terrorists murder at the World Trade Center, or car bombers strike in Baghdad, or hijackers plot to blow up planes over the Atlantic, or terrorist militias shoot rockets at Israeli towns, they are all pursuing the same objective—to turn back the advance of freedom, and impose a dark vision of tyranny and terror across the world."[64]

While this resonated with President Bush's core supporters on the political Right, its effect was no longer as broad as it had been in 2002 and 2003. The public anger that had allowed the administration to mobilize support for the overthrow of Saddam Hussein had eased or, at least, could no longer be used to justify any action against any threat. Congress and the public were less deferential to the president on security policy. They questioned and criticized assumptions that they would have accepted easily in the months after September 11. The window of opportunity for boldness had closed. But the administration did not change the narrative used to justify its strategy, sticking doggedly to it through repeated reminders. President Bush's approach to strategic leadership leaned more heavily on persistence than adaptability. He remained the consummate "anti-Clinton."

While this depiction was necessary to sustain at least a working level of public support, it painted the administration into a corner. By casting the American effort in Iraq as a struggle with evil and unappeasable terrorists, linking it to the conflict with al-Qaeda, and refusing to countenance the idea that the insurgency was, to some extent, a result of flawed American policies, the administration made negotiation and reconciliation inconceivable despite the fact that they are among the most effective elements of successful counterinsurgency. For a brief time in late 2005, there was a change in the president's description of the conflict: he began talking of *three* components of the insurgents: "Saddamists," "terrorists affiliated with or inspired by al-Qaeda," and "rejectionists" (Sunni Arabs "who miss the privileged status they had under the regime of Saddam Hussein").[65] This suggested that the administration might be moving toward recognizing and addressing the grievances that motivated the majority of the insurgents. But then the portrayal changed again. After that, President Bush did not mention "rejectionists" but only "Saddamists" and "terrorists."

Counterinsurgency can be successful under two conditions. One is when the regime simply crushes the insurgents *and* its supporters. The other is when the conditions and policies that motivated the insurgents and their supporters are changed. This often leaves some small number of diehard insurgents in the field but causes enough of the insurgent cadre and its supporters to give up the fight that the insurgency becomes ineffective. The United States is unwilling to take the first approach. The Bush administration's portrayal of the conflict in Iraq obviated the second. The result was a slogging stalemate and a grinding battle of will, not only in Iraq itself but also within the American polity. The question was which could be sustained longer—the will of the insurgents or the will of the American public.

■ ■ ■

In February 2006, a powerful bomb shattered the Askariya Shrine in Samarra, one of the most important Shiite holy places. This set off a cycle of tit-for-tat sectarian violence. Shiites attacked Sunni mosques and clerics. A few weeks later, car bombs in Sadr City, the Shiite slum on the east side of Baghdad, killed at least forty-six people. Death squad killings became a nightly occurrence. As in El Salvador in the 1980s, gathering the corpses from the street became part of Baghdad's morning routine. Mixed neighborhoods underwent sectarian cleansing as one group or the other moved out or was forced to leave. In April, suicide bombers killed seventy-nine at the main Shiite mosque in Baghdad. Much of this was instigated by al-Qaeda in Iraq, which seemed to believe that by provoking Shiites into violence it could compel Sunni Arabs to support it. This practice of forcing the population to choose sides was a time-tested insurgent technique. When the population was neutral, insurgents did not know whom to attack and whom to trust. Once the population had cast its lot, the distinction between enemies and friends became clear.

The inability of the United States and its coalition partners to control sectarian violence eroded support even among Shiites. Cheering mobs surrounded a British helicopter downed by insurgents near the Shiite city of Basra in May 2006. Shiite militias increased their attacks on American forces. Hopes that Zarqawi's death in June would lessen sectarian violence proved unfounded. Within the Shiite community, armed conflict sputtered and raged between the Iranian-backed Supreme Council for Islamic Revolution in Iraq, the followers of Mogtada Sadr, and two smaller parties—the Islamic Dawa Party and Al Fadila al Islamiya. In the north, Kurdish and Arab militias clashed. A Department of Defense report to Congress noted that "the core conflict in Iraq [has] changed into a struggle between Sunni and Shi'ia extremists seeking to control key areas in Baghdad, create or protect sectarian enclaves, divert economic resources, and impose their own respective political and religious agendas."[66] As Solomon Moore and Louise Roug phrased it, Iraq had become "a nation of many wars, with the U.S. in the middle."[67]

As the violence mutated, the U.S. military altered its operational methods (even while the Bush administration's basic strategy and its justifying narrative remained constant). American commanders recognized that Baghdad was the fulcrum of the violence and that if U.S. and Iraqi security forces could not control militia violence there, they could not hope to in the rest of the country. In August, Iraq security forces and the American military began a long operation (called Together Forward) to clear the capital of insurgents, even shifting forces from other parts of the country. This failed and violence escalated. Gen. George Casey warned that he might need even more troops in the capital, possibly by increasing the overall U.S. force level in Iraq.[68] The concentration of security forces in Baghdad meant that gains made in other parts of Iraq, particularly Anbar, were lost with fewer American and Iraqi security forces available to protect them. Sadr's Mahdi Army renewed its offensive stance of 2004, briefly taking over the city of Amarah before being forced to withdraw by Iraqi police.

The other elements of the American strategy also faced challenges. The resources devoted to training the Iraqi security forces remained inadequate. The Iraqis had made strides but not enough to allow an American drawdown. Their military units occasionally refused to move outside their home areas. Many were simply inept, others under equipped and poorly supported. The police were even worse, with reports that up to 70 percent of its members were infiltrated by sectarian militias.[69] Most major construction projects begun by the United States were left unfinished. The Iraqi political leadership was unwilling or unable to rein in the militias. As James Lyons, former commander of the U.S. Pacific Command, phrased it, "It is an unhappy truth that, from the prime minister on down, no one in Iraq's government has so far demonstrated the backbone or grit necessary to bring

Still, the Bush administration remained convinced that its basic strategy was sound, but the tactics, military force levels, and operational methods to implement it needed fine-tuning. Ideas on how to do this began to emerge from experts inside and outside the military. In the autumn of 2005 Andrew Krepinevich, a former Army officer who headed an influential Washington think tank, argued that the American military "should concentrate on providing security and opportunity to the Iraqi people, thereby denying insurgents the popular support they need."[71] This was an old idea among counterinsurgency theorists. It required a different mind-set than the "warfighter" ethos that dominated the U.S. military. In its seminal twentieth-century campaigns—the world wars, Korea, Desert Storm—the U.S. military had focused on finding and destroying enemy armed formations and treated civilians as bystanders. But as Krepinevich noted, in counterinsurgency the population is not simply part of the background, but a resource that can determine success or failure for both sides. Even if the population was inclined to support the government and oppose the insurgents, it would not do so unless it felt secure from insurgent retribution.

As Krepinevich explained this idea to the Washington policy community, Col. H. R. McMaster, commander of the 3rd Armored Cavalry Regiment, was putting it into practice.[72] From the CENTCOM staff, where he had worked before assuming his command, Colonel McMaster had become convinced that the military's obsession with killing and capturing insurgents did little to undercut the insurgency. As Vietnam had shown, new insurgents appear faster than old ones can be eliminated. In the spring of 2005 Colonel McMaster's regiment was assigned an area of Anbar Province in western Iraq centered on the city of Tal Afar, a hotbed of insurgent activity and a transit point for foreign fighters entering from Syria. "The life was literally choked out of the city," Colonel McMaster said. "The terrorists had everyone living in abject fear."[73] He crafted a different approach based on understanding the intricacies of local culture and political power, sustaining the U.S. presence in areas cleared of insurgents, and treating detainees with all possible dignity to avoid dishonoring them and inspiring them (or their families) to seek revenge. This was so successful that President Bush described it in length during a March 2006 speech in Cleveland. The feeling grew in the administration and the U.S. military that after three years, it had finally discovered a workable approach to counterinsurgency. The problem was that providing security for the population was manpower intensive. McMaster had been able to do it with a regiment in a relatively sparsely populated area. What the administration needed was a way to apply and sustain the "lessons of Tal Afar" to the truly critical areas of Iraq, particularly Baghdad.

■　■　■

For more than a decade America's conflict with Iraq had shaped defense transformation. Now the counterinsurgency campaign and the broader "war on terror" inspired an adjustment in the trajectory of transformation and the evolution of American security strategy. One major step was the publication of the 2005 *National Defense Strategy*. This provided an innovative way of conceptualizing threats to American security, dividing them into *traditional* challenges (state militaries), *irregular* ones that rely primarily on insurgency and terrorism, *catastrophic* challenges based on WMDs, and *disruptive* challenges derived from breakthrough technologies. While it is possible to quibble with the words—irregular challenges actually are more "traditional" for the United States than war against state militaries—the idea was vitally important. For the first time in modern American history, irregular challenges were portrayed as something other than a secondary or peripheral concern. This codified an idea that defense thinkers had proposed since the end of the Cold War: American prowess in large-scale, conventional war was driving opponents to other forms of conflict. This conceptual adjustment was useful but flawed. While the document was a defense *strategy*, it defined enemies by their *operational methods* rather than the strategies they used. This reflects a long tradition within the U. S. military (and the government as a whole) to focus on operational concerns rather than on trategy.

Still, with the conflict in Iraq raging, the American defense establishment had become not only interested in irregular conflict, but nearly obsessed. Secretary Rumsfeld reinforced this through a directive that made stability operations a "core U.S. military mission" for the first time in history.[74] Stability operations, he instructed, "shall be given priority comparable to combat operations and be explicitly addressed and integrated across all DoD activities including doctrine, organizations, training, education, exercises, materiel, leadership, personnel, facilities, and planning." This was a sea change from the time when low-intensity conflict was a "lesser included contingency"—more accurately an afterthought—as the armed forces prepared for conventional war.

The 2006 *Quadrennial Defense Review* adopted and refined these themes. It noted that the United States was "in the fourth year of a long war, a war that is irregular in nature. The enemies in this war are not traditional conventional military forces but rather dispersed, global terrorist networks that exploit Islam to advance radical political aims."[75] This required the U.S. military to adopt unconventional and indirect approaches of its own and to operate in many locations simultaneously over long periods of time. While not using the words "insurgency" or "counterinsurgency," the 2006 QDR did address "irregular warfare." A few weeks later, the new *National Security Strategy of the United States* of America continued along the same lines,—describing an enemy that used a strategy of insurgency, but not using the word "insurgency" and instead relying on the more emotive "terror."[76] There were probably two reasons for this. One was the perception that labeling enemies "insurgents" gives them legitimacy. This was the paradoxical logic at play in the political realm: phrasing designed with the best intent—in this case, sustaining public and congressional support for U.S. involvement in Iraq— complicated the process of developing an effective counterinsurgency strategy. Insurgency is a holistic phenomenon with multiple dimensions. Focusing the American response on a single component, an operational method such as terrorism or irregular warfare, makes it difficult to formulate an equally holistic and multidimensional response—a *strategic* one.

A second reason was the idea that "irregular warfare" was a broader, more encompassing concept than "insurgency," more akin to the 1980s' concept of low-intensity conflict. A major Pentagon study preparing for the 2006 QDR listed insurgency as an "element" of irregular warfare. Unfortunately, this got it backward—insurgency is a strategy that includes irregular warfare but also includes political, psychological, and even economic dimensions. It is the non-state version of "unrestricted warfare," a concept described by members of the Chinese military.[77] As such, it is multidimensional and holistic; armed conflict is only a part and often not the decisive one. By making insurgency part of irregular warfare rather than the other way around, the Department of Defense kept its focus on armed violence, thus lessening the attention given to insurgency's more important political and psychological components. While a case could be made that some government agency other than the Department of Defense should bear primary responsibility for the political and psychological dimensions of insurgency (and that the Pentagon *should* concentrate on armed violence), none could, or did.

Given clear strategic guidance from the secretary of defense to improve capabilities for irregular warfare and stabilization, the U.S. military once again developed new programs and adjusted existing ones. The Pentagon again expanded its Special Operations Forces. The services were instructed to enhance language and cultural training, increase the number of commissioned and noncommissioned officers seconded to foreign militaries, and expand Foreign Area Officer programs.[78] Counterinsurgency reappeared in the curriculum at the U.S. Military Academy, the Command and

General Staff College, the School of Advanced Military Studies, and the Army War College. Unified Quest—the Army's major annual strategic war game—shifted from a focus on conventional warfighting with an insurgency sidebar to counterinsurgency. The Army created an Asymmetric Warfare Group to assess tactics and develop countermeasures. An Army program at Fort Riley began training mid-level officers as advisers to foreign militaries. The Army's Foreign Military Studies Office developed a program called the "Human Terrain System" to help brigade commanders understand social, ethnographic, cultural, economic, and political factors during irregular conflict.[79] The National Training Center—the Army's most important unit-level training facility—shifted from conventional combat on a "sterile" battlefield to a complex insurgency scenario complete with civilians and all of the other things a unit could expect to find in Iraq. Information technology allowed "virtual immersion," giving commanders a true "feel" for the situation in Iraq before they deployed.[80] And the Pentagon increased its exploration of technologies applicable to counterinsurgency such as nonlethal weapons and robotics.

In October 2004, the Army released its first new counterinsurgency doctrine in twenty years.[81] This was heavily influenced by the ongoing fighting in Iraq. By 2005, the new doctrine was already in use to prepare units for deployment to Iraq. When Major General Petraeus returned from Iraq to take command of the Army's Combined Arms Center, he pushed this even further. He consulted a wide range of experts from nontraditional sources such as the media, nongovernmental organizations, human rights specialists, and cultural anthropologists. When the final version appeared in December 2006, it received more attention than any U.S. military doctrine in history and was widely seen as innovative, even path-breaking.[82] Soon afterward, the Pentagon developed a Joint Operating Concept for Irregular Warfare and began work on joint doctrine to unify the service approaches. Even the U.S. Air Force became interested. Concerned that the shift to irregular challenges would lead to a cut in its force structure and budget, the Air Force proposed a greater reliance on airpower in activities like counterinsurgency.[83] As so often in the past, service interests were transmuted into strategic debates.

While other government agencies tried, they could not muster the same level of effort. In 2004 the State Department created the Office of the Coordinator for Reconstruction and Stabilization and named Ambassador

Carlos Pascual to head it. This was intended to tie together civilian and military efforts and prepare in advance of conflicts rather than simply re-acting to them.[84] Unfortunately the organization's funding was inadequate given its ambitious mission. Just as the military has difficulty breaking away from its "big war" mentality, the State Department's organizational culture tends to focus on diplomacy rather than the reconstruction or transforma-tion of other states. The small size of the Foreign Service added to the problem. There were not enough Foreign Service Officers to man major stabilization or counterinsurgency efforts. The U.S. Agency for International Development began its own institutional transformation. Because develop-ment and reconstruction are integral to addressing the root causes of in-surgency, USAID had played an important role in U.S. counterinsurgency strategy during the 1960s. But stung by the Vietnam experience, it had abandoned this. After the post–September 11 shifts in American strategy, the agency reversed its thinking. It began to include regional stability and counterterrorism among its programmatic priorities, sought greater involve-ment in security-related reconstruction, and pursued better coordination with the Department of Defense.[85]

With pressure growing for a "whole of government approach" to counterinsurgency, the State Department, Department of Defense, and the Agency for International Development began to work on a manual that would be the interagency equivalent of military doctrine. The problem was the lack of capacity in activities like policing, governance, civil society building, intelligence, and economic development more than it was disagreement on definitions. Counterinsurgency experts admitted that the single biggest short-fall for the United States was the lack of deployable police advisers and train-ers. But there were no major initiatives to address this. That most of the shortfalls faced by the United States were in the nonmilitary realm, yet the nonmilitary agencies of the government seemed unable to address them, posed a dilemma for the Department of Defense. Should it actively work to fill the vacuum even though doing so would involve it in realms better left to civilian agencies and, potentially, draw people and money away from the warfighting functions that only the military could do? Or should it simply "stay within its lane" and leave it to political leaders to address the capability shortfalls? The uniformed military and civilian defense policymakers re-mained torn on this issue.

■ ■ ■

While Washington reorganized, Iraq bordered on chaos. Two efforts early in 2006 failed to secure Baghdad. In areas without an American troop presence, insurgents had established training bases in areas. They had become financially self-sustaining, raising tens of millions of dollars a year from oil smuggling, kidnapping, counterfeiting, and tapping into Islamic charities. The government of Prime Minister Nuri Kamal al-Malaki gave no sign that it was willing or able to address the declining situation. History suggests that the effectiveness, energy, and vision of the political leadership in the nation facing insurgency determine its success or failure. As a November 2006 memo by National Security Adviser Stephen Hadley suggested, Malaki came up short on all counts.[86]

The mounting violence and political paralysis in Iraq fueled antiwar efforts in the United States. Through the 2004 election, opposition had been fairly muted. The Iraq plan of Senator John Kerry—the Democratic presidential nominee—differed little from Bush's strategy. Kerry simply vowed to implement it more effectively. But by 2006 opposition to continued American involvement had exploded. Democrats (and a handful of Republicans) argued that the administration had exploited September 11 to sell a weak or flawed case for removing Saddam Hussein. Iraq became the stalking horse for any opposition to President Bush and his policies. Its symbolic importance was greater than its actual significance. The outcome in Iraq would determine both George Bush's legacy and the future political power balance in the United States.

A number of factors helped sour the American public. The profusion of information technology made the human costs of the counterinsurgency campaign real and tangible. Images of the dead, the wounded, and their families were pervasive, making them more than simple casualty numbers. Americans felt a personal bond with their military. What the public saw as ingratitude from Iraqis made it worse. It was bad enough for an American service member to die, but televised gloating by the people he or she died to protect was infuriating. (Iraqis, of course, were convinced that the United States sought only to steal their oil and protect Israel so little gratitude was due.) Americans were also disillusioned by continued mismanagement of the reconstruction effort. President Bush's unwillingness to admit that he had made major errors and to compromise with Democrats on Iraqi policy further galvanized opposition. The mode of leadership that had served him well immediately after September 11 became a detriment when public and congressional deference faded. And, as in the past, the American people lost patience for a conflict without clear and demonstrable progress (or where every sign of progress was counterbalanced by violence, political paralysis, and corruption). Since the end of the Cold War the American public had been taught that U.S. military operations were quick and decisive. They expected steady progress toward victory. When the conflict in Iraq did not fit that mold, they were first confused, then angered.

By this point the president recognized that his strategy was spiraling toward "slow failure." He instructed the administration to conduct a wide-ranging review to explore other options that might lead toward victory as he defined it. While the National Security Council assessed the overall approach, Marine Gen. Peter Pace, who had replaced Richard Myers as chairman of the Joint Chiefs of Staff in September 2005, evaluated the military strategy. There were two broad positions among military leaders. One was that the American presence itself fed the insurgent narrative and allowed the insurgents to portray their actions as resistance against an outsider occupier. This suggested that the best approach was to focus on training the Iraqi military, shift U.S. forces to a secondary or supporting role, and diminish the number of Americans in the country. The second approach was based on the idea that violence was escalating faster than Iraqi security forces could be prepared to meet it. The longer it took to secure the Iraqi population, the less the chances of a desirable outcome. This suggested that the United States needed to *increase* its troop strength to secure Baghdad so the Iraqi security forces and government could address their shortcomings. Republicans like Senator John McCain of Arizona and conservative idealists in the policy community advocated this position.

As the strategic review moved forward, many Republican candidates for Congress were defeated in the November midterm elections. This was seen as a referendum on the administration's handling of Iraq and sent a clear signal that the American public had lost faith in the existing approach. The day after the election, Bush announced that Donald Rumsfeld was resigning as defense secretary and would be replaced by Robert Gates, a former director of the Central Intelligence Agency who was then serving as president of Texas A&M University. For many in Washington, Rumsfeld was reminiscent of Robert McNamara, Kennedy's and Lyndon Johnson's secretary of defense and one of the major architects of America's involvement in Vietnam. He was brilliant, innovative, and powerful yet "undone by policies that resulted in a quagmire in a distant land."[87]

Within Washington's policy community, the lines were much as they had been throughout the insurgency. Democrats advocated disengagement (although they disagreed on how soon to do it). But they were not alone. Colin Powell, in his first criticism of the Bush administration since leaving office, told Bob Schieffer of CBS News, "Nothing seems to be improving . . . . I am not persuaded that another surge of troops into Baghdad for the purpose of suppressing this communitarian violence, this civil war, will work."[88] But the conservative idealists remained committed to the idea that "victory" was within their grasp. The problem, they felt, was an inadequate effort and too few troops.[89]

As the president considered his options, two important external groups weighed in. The Iraq Study Group, a blue ribbon panel authorized by Congress and administered by the U.S. Institute for Peace, garnered the most attention, in part because of the stature of its co-chairmen—former secretary of state James A. Baker and former Congressman Lee Hamilton—and its high-profile, bipartisan composition.[90] It called for "new and enhanced diplomatic and political efforts in Iraq and the region," an acceleration of the transfer of responsibility for security to Iraq forces, and a shift of the U.S. military to a purely supportive role. American combat forces, the group thought, should be withdrawn from Iraq. At about the same time the Iraq Planning Group of the conservative American Enterprise Institute, led by Frederick W. Kagan and retired Army Gen. Jack Keane, released a report entitled "Choosing Victory: A Plan for Success in Iraq."[91] The AEI group was convinced that "the strategy of relying on a political process to eliminate the insurgency has failed." Rather than devoting more effort to training and advising Iraqi security forces as the Baker-Hamilton report advocated, the Kagan-Keane report urged a balance between the training and advising role and using the American military to secure the Iraqi population, particularly in Baghdad. This would require a temporary "surge" in the number of American forces in Iraq.

Neither report proposed ideas that the administration had not considered, but both helped crystallize the debate by providing articulate and powerful exposition of the alternatives. It was then up to President Bush to decide which way to go. As with most strategic decisions, this was shaped by his assessment of the likely outcome of the options and the risks associated with them. While the Baker-Hamilton plan promised to decrease casualties by removing the American military from normal operations, the president believed it might lead to the collapse of the Malaki government and hence

COUNTERINSURGENCY ————————————————————

defeat for the United States. For all of Malaki's flaws, he was the only part-ner the United States had. The "surge" advocated by Kagan and Keane also entailed risks. It would diminish the ability of the U.S. military to respond to crises elsewhere in the world, further stress the Army and Marine Corps, and possibly shatter the remaining public support for continued involve-ment in Iraq. But President Bush believed that it had a better chance of leading to a positive outcome. It was a final gambit for victory.

In the middle of December, military planners and White House bud-get analysts were asked to provide President Bush with options for sending more U.S. troops to Iraq. Securing the national capital may not ensure suc-cess in counterinsurgency, but not doing so ensures failure, so the addi-tional forces were to go to Baghdad. The president's decision to expand rather than decrease American involvement also reflected another lesson from past counterinsurgency campaigns: while the ultimate resolution of the conflict comes through political means, the underlying political causes of the conflict cannot be addressed without security. But a surge would in-crease the burden on an already-stressed military. After a series of consulta-tions with military leaders and defense experts, President Bush announced that he was increasing the size of the ground forces, reversing Rumsfeld's long resistance to the idea. A few weeks later, Gates proposed adding 92,000 troops to the Army and the Marine Corps over five years. Gen. James T. Conway, commandant of the Marine Corps, told Congress this would "go a long way towards reducing the strain on individual Marines and the institu-tion."[92]

In a January address to the nation, President Bush ordered five addi-tional combat brigades—about 20,000 troops—to Baghdad, extended the tours of some military units already there, and increased economic assis-tance and diplomatic efforts (a major recommendation of the Baker-Hamilton study group).[93] The new plan also called for a tighter integration of Iraqi and American units with an Iraqi in command of operations in Baghdad. Bush then appointed Lieutenant Petraeus to replace General Casey as the American commander in Iraq. There was no officer more qualified for this challenging task. As the commander of the 82d Airborne Division in 2003, Petraeus had stabilized the region under his control in an innovative, non-doctrinal way. He later returned to energize the training of the Iraqi security forces, so he was familiar with that effort. Then he led the develop-ment of the new Army–Marine Corps counterinsurgency doctrine. Accord-ing to Jim Hoagland of the *Washington Post*, "The appointment of Petraeus is another indication of Bush's willingness to go on the offensive and his dissatisfaction with the cautious, bureaucratic approach to the Iraqi campaign by General John Abizaid, who is departing as head of the Central Command."[94]

But the surge met with a rocky start both politically and on the ground. A February 2007 report by Steven Simon for the Council on Foreign Relations made a powerful case for disengagement.[95] The Center for a New American Security published a blueprint for disengagement, which resonated among Democrats.[96] Daniel Byman and Kenneth Pollack—two of the most astute analysts of Iraq—assessed the repercussions of regional spillover as "Iraq sinks deeper into the abyss of civil war."[97] At about the same time, the National Intelligence Council released a new, pessimistic assessment of the situation in Iraq.[98] Anthony Cordesman of the Center for Strategic and International Studies said that Bush "promised more than history is likely to deliver" in his January speech.[99]

In Congress, Democrats (and some moderate Republicans) mobilized in opposition to the surge. Even Republican senator John Warner, one of the most influential members of the GOP on military matters, expressed doubt, saying, "The American GI was not trained, not sent over there, certainly not by resolution of this institution [Congress], to be placed in the middle of a fight between the Sunni and the Shia and the wanton and just incomprehensible killing that's going on at this time."[100] Just as Congress had forced an end to American involvement in Vietnam in the 1970s, congressional Democrats sought to use the power of the purse to get their way. Since public sentiment was still behind "supporting the troops," the Democrats did not immediately move to cut off funds for Iraq but did seek to restrict spending for it.[101] This began a long struggle between Congress and the White House, with the legislature attempting to tie spending to a timetable for withdrawal and President Bush steadfastly resisting. But while this battle raged in Washington, in Iraq itself an unexpected turn of events began to change the contours of the conflict.

■   ■   ■

Traditional tribal rulers had long been important in Anbar Province. During the first few years of the insurgency, many of them cooperated with al-Qaeda and other foreign fighters (or at least tolerated them). By 2006, the Anbar sheiks were increasingly disillusioned with al-Qaeda's heavy-handed, Taliban-like behavior. They resented attempts to ban smoking and to force marriages between al-Qaeda fighters and local women. Others were unhappy that al-Qaeda had become a de facto occupier, shaking down truck drivers, extorting shop owners, and taking over the smuggling business. Anbar, after all, had resisted outsiders of all kinds for thousands of years. When U.S. forces drove the foreign fighters away in 2006, Abdul Sattar Buzaigh al-Rishawi, an important sheik, convinced his fellow tribal leaders to forge an alliance with the Americans and declare war on al-Qaeda. What became known as the "Anbar awakening" began in Ramadi, where improved population security measures by the 1st Brigade of the 1st Armored Division led the local population to reevaluate its ties to al-Qaeda and other foreign fighters. But the terrorists quickly struck back. In February, a car bomb killed thirty-seven Sunnis as they left a mosque in Habbaniya, forty miles west of Baghdad.[102] "I swear to God," said Sheik Sattar, "if we have good weapons, if we have good vehicles, if we have good support, I can fight al-Qaeda all the way to Afghanistan."[103] In April Sunni tribal leaders in Anbar created a party to oppose al-Qaeda and enter the national political process. American officials recognized the potential this offered and, despite concern from Prime Minister Malaki, developed deeper ties with the tribal leaders and began providing substantial assistance.[104]

While the schism between al-Qaeda and the local leaders was a positive development, the beginning of the troop surge saw escalated violence. In March, 220 Iraqis were killed by a wave of suicide bombs and gunfire as they converged on Karbala to mark the death of the first Shiite imam. In April, a suicide truck bomb loaded with chlorine gas exploded in Ramadi, killing thirty. As American troops patrolled deep into Baghdad's most dangerous neighborhoods and were stationed at small combat outposts, U.S. casualties increased. May 2007 was the deadliest month for U.S. troops since early 2005. Although President Bush's new approach called for an increase in development assistance, the State Department was unable to fully staff addition Provincial Reconstruction Teams. But Sunnis continued to join the counterinsurgency effort, not only in Anbar but also in Baghdad. By the summer of 2007, more than 30,000 were working with U.S. and Iraqi security forces.

Strictly speaking, the surge was never a "new strategy" (despite President Bush's insistence on calling it that). It was a change in operational methods designed to give Iraqi political leaders "breathing space" to address the root causes of the conflict. They showed little inclination to do so. The onus fell most heavily on Prime Minister Malaki. He failed to address the wide range of issues dividing Iraq's Shiite, Sunni Arab, Kurdish, and minority groups despite repeated implorations and warnings from American officials, including Adm.William Fallon, who had taken command of CENTCOM. The government careened close to collapse. Carlos Pascual and Kenneth Pollack described it as a "failed state."[105] Talk of removing Malaki circulated in Washington. But the Iraqi parliament was no better. It failed to enact key legislation and irritated the Bush administration and Congress by taking a long summer recess. Even President Bush acknowledged "a certain level of frustration" with the Iraqi government's failures.[106] Yet somehow it hung on.

By the beginning of the summer, the additional American troop deployments were complete. U.S. and Iraqi forces had pushed insurgents out of about a third of Baghdad's neighborhoods. Sectarian killings in Baghdad were down significantly, and the capital was moving toward normalcy. By the end of the summer, deaths of U.S. soldiers and Iraqi civilians had fallen to the lowest level in more than a year. An August 2007 National Intelligence Estimate noted "to the extent that Coalition forces continue to conduct robust counterinsurgent operations and mentor and support the Iraqi Security Forces (ISF) . . . Iraq's security will continue to improve modestly during the next six to twelve months."[107] While that was qualified praise after months of bad news, the administration's supporters bubbled with enthusiasm. Kimberly Kagan—a participant in the American Enterprise Institute's Iraq Planning Group—wrote that the "the tide in Iraq is clearly turning."[108] Max Boot claimed, "The surge is working."[109] "We're pushing them back," William Kristol added.[110] Even Michael O'Hanlon and Kenneth Pollack, two politically moderate security policy experts associated with the Brookings Institution, called it "a war we just might win."[111]

Congress remained unconvinced. Senator Harry Reid (D-NV) led the charge, stating in April, "This war is lost."[112] This heightened partisan tension in the Senate as Republicans responded angrily, stressing the potential effect of such defeatism on American troops. Despite the threat of a presidential veto, congressional Democrats added a requirement for withdrawal to a $124 billion war-spending bill. Without the votes to override a veto, they dropped this demand but tied further reconstruction assistance for Iraq to a series of benchmarks. In June, Republican senators Richard Lugar of Indiana, George Voinovich of Ohio, John Warner of Virginia, and Peter Domenici of New Mexico asked the administration to decrease the combat role of the U.S. military and place greater stress on diplomacy—recommendations made six months earlier by the Iraqi Study Group. Three other Republican senators—Olympia Snowe of Maine, Gordon Smith of Oregon, and Chuck Hagel of Nebraska—indicated that they were willing to support a Democratic proposal to withdraw all U.S. troops from Iraq by the spring of 2008. Other Republicans blocked this again, but the administration was deeply concerned. President Bush sent White House chief of staff Joshua B. Bolten, Secretary of State Rice, and National Security Adviser Hadley to the consult with GOP lawmakers. David Petraeus, now General Petraeus, added to the case, stating that a quick withdrawal of U.S. troops would cause "greatly increased sectarian violence."[113] Lt. Gen. Raymond Odierno, then serving as the number two commander in Iraq, made the same point in press conferences.

Congressional opposition to the war reflected the disillusionment of the public. Despite the signs of progress during the first half of 2007, 61 percent felt the conflict in Iraq was not worth fighting, nearly two-thirds believed the United States was not making progress, and 55 percent advocated either an immediate or phased withdrawal of American forces.[114] The administration was truly hanging on by its fingernails. Its great hope was that the September report to Congress by General Petraeus and Ryan Crocker, the U.S. ambassador in Baghdad, would sustain enough support to "stay the course." When the reports were presented, their conclusions were mixed. Petraeus stated that the "the military objectives of the surge are, in large measure, being met." Al-Qaeda in Iraq had been "dealt significant blows" and sectarian violence was down. The general predicted that U.S. forces could be reduced to pre-surge levels by the summer of 2008 without sacrificing the gains that had been made. Ambassador Crocker also showed guarded optimism, saying, "In my judgment, the cumulative trajectory of political, economic, and diplomatic developments in Iraq is upwards, although the slope of that line is not steep."

While congressional opponents attacked the reports as simply a justification for an open-ended commitment to Iraq, President Bush, in a nationally televised address, accepted Petraeus's recommendations. That he focused on General Petraeus to the exclusion of Ambassador Crocker was instructive. While counterinsurgency is won in the political and psychological realm, the Bush strategy continued to treat it as warfighting with a political veneer. Debate devolved on troop levels and withdrawal timetables rather than political progress and economic reconstruction. General Petraeus rather than Ambassador Crocker was the "face" of the U.S. effort. The address was instructive in another way as well. As is normally true in American strategy, President Bush was communicating with multiple (and diverse) audiences simultaneously. To the American public he promised eventual withdrawal but in a way less likely to lead to the collapse of the Iraqi government and full-scale civil war. To Iraq's leaders, he promised continued support but reminded them that time was running out. To the insurgents, he indicated that waiting the Americans out would not work.

Following the speech, public discontent eased a bit. Congressional Democrats dropped aggressive attempts to legislate a troop withdrawal and instead chipped away at the administration's Republican supporters on Capitol Hill. Commentary was less kind. The editors of the *New York Times* wrote, "Mr. Bush had no strategy to end his disastrous war and no strategy for containing the chaos he unleashed."[115] *New York Times* columnist Thomas Friedman said President Bush was simply "handing the baton, and probably the next election, to the Democrats."[116] From the other end of the political spectrum, William Kristol and Frederick Kagan blasted congressional critics of Petraeus and Bush, calling them "children at play."[117] Ultimately the editors of the *Washington Post* probably captured it best when they called the Bush strategy "the least bad plan."[118]

■ ■ ■

The lull in violence continued through the autumn of 2007. October saw the lowest civilian body count and American casualty figures since the Samarra mosque bombing in 2006. U.S. Army Maj. Gen. Joseph F. Fil Jr., commander of American forces in Baghdad, said that al-Qaeda had been routed in the city.[119] At the end of November the first drawdown of American forces began. U.S. commanders began shifting from combat operations to training and advising functions. In December the Senate finally approved an omnibus government-spending bill without the timeline for full withdrawal that the Democrats wanted. In a game of political "chicken," President Bush threatened to veto the bill if it included the stipulation. The Department of Defense said it would furlough hundreds of thousands of civilian workers as a result of the impasse. This was the third time the Democrats failed to pass a troop withdrawal measure.

Still, the Iraqi government remained unwilling or unable to make progress on the legislative, security, and economic issues that the United States had deemed crucial.[120] The Department of Defense's December 2007 quarterly report to Congress noted progress on bottom-up security measures with tribal leaders but only "marginal progress" on key national legislation, constitutional revisions, and other major issues.[121] After a trip to Iraq, retired U.S. Army Gen. Barry R. McCaffrey praised the security situation and even the maligned Iraqi security forces but stated bluntly, "There is no functioning central Iraqi Government."[122] U.S. military commanders and diplomats continued warning the Iraqi government that the progress brought by the troop surge would be reversed if it did not act, but it gave little sign of doing so. Many Iraqis remained convinced that the conflict in their nation was solely the work of outsiders, whether Americans or foreign militants.[123] Thus resolving it was someone else's responsibility. Four years after the end of the Hussein regime, the psychological hangover of his brutality—the lack of political of initiative and the tendency to defer to others for decisions and solutions—lingered in the Iraqi psyche.

In the United States there was growing concern that the bottom-up approach to security in Iraq was a recipe for long-term disaster. The creation of local militias or self-defense forces is a common and often essential part of counterinsurgency. Yet it has risks. While subcontracting security to sectarian militias in Iraq might create enough security to allow the United States to begin disengagement, it may create alternative (and armed) sources of power that can challenge the central government. The U.S. has always considered the militias a temporary expedient. "They were never intended to be permanent," according to Army Maj. Gen. Michael Jones, commander of the Civilian Police Assistance Training Team.[124] The government in Baghdad was to take over sponsorship of the groups and eventually disband them and integrate their members into the official security forces. But disbanding them will be extraordinarily difficult. They are a true Pandora's box, hard to close once opened. Local leaders may keep their militias, leading to a country where the central government has little authority outside Baghdad. This might allow American disengagement, but it would be different from the "victory" described in the Bush strategy. Basra, which saw the empowerment of local security forces even before Baghdad and the rest of the country, may offer an ominous preview of Iraq's future: multiple and interlinked forms of violence based on vigilantism, tribal and personal vendettas, and pervasive organized crime.[125] Given that many analysts already question the long-term viability of Iraq as a unitary nation, the devolution of security may contribute to political fragmentation or rule by warlords.

The stability in Iraq at the end of 2007 may have had less to do with the troop surge than with the need of the various factions to regroup, train, and equip.[126] The declining sectarian violence in Baghdad may have been more the result of sectarian cleansing than of increased security patrols. Neighborhoods that once mixed Sunnis and Shiites had become homogenous and walled. Ultimately the troop surge may prove analogous to the changes Gen. Creighton Abrams implemented when he replaced William Westmoreland as the U.S. commander in Vietnam: modestly useful steps undertaken several years too late. Even the reports of al-Qaeda's death may have been premature. Terrorism expert Abdul Hameed Bakier contended that it has simply broken into "unpredictable, incoherent and scattered groups adhering to the Salafi-jihadi ideology." He said, "These decentralized formations will attempt to attack soft targets and wait patiently for any slackening of security on the hard targets."[127]

In Washington, civilian and uniformed officials remained concerned about the effect that the Iraq counterinsurgency campaign had on the health of the U.S. military. It limited the Bush administration's options for dealing with other rising security threats such as the nuclear weapons program in North Korea and Iran. Hints or threats of regime change there were not credible so long as so much of the U.S. military was mired in Iraq. As Secretary Gates admitted, Iraq also hurt the multinational mission in Afghanistan, where al-Qaeda's Taliban allies were again on the rise.[128] He was also concerned that the military had assumed many tasks in Iraq and elsewhere that were better performed by civilian agencies, thus lowering the motivation of these agencies to develop their own capabilities or of Congress to fund them.[129] Adm. Michael Mullen, who became chairman of the Joint Chiefs of Staff in October 2007, was worried that Iraq left the military under prepared for other important missions.[130] The Army in particular had paid a high price for the conflict in Iraq. Even before the surge in September 2007, General Casey (who succeeded General Schoomaker as Army chief of staff) told Congress, "Our Army today is out of balance . . . The current demand for our forces exceeds the sustainable supply. We are consumed with meeting the demands of the current fight and are unable to provide ready forces as rapidly as necessary for other potential contingencies."[131]

Relief was far away; the planned expansion of the Army would take years to complete. And it did not address the growing exodus of talented mid-grade officers and noncommissioned officers. Crucial questions remained open. Would the enlargement make a difference in Iraq? Was the Iraq counter-insurgency campaign truly the paradigm for future U.S. military operations or was it a unique case growing from a combination of political and strategic conditions unlikely to be repeated in the future? Was the United States sacrificing long-term capabilities for short-term success in Iraq? If so, was that price worth paying? No one knew the answers to these pressing strategic questions.

CONCLUSION

The young lions roar after their prey, and seek their meat from God.
The Sun ariseth, they gather themselves together, and lay them down in their dens.
Man goeth forth unto his work, and to his labor until the evening.
—Psalms 104-21-23

raq has, to different degrees, affected the strategy of every U.S. president since Ronald Reagan. For Reagan, it was a peripheral issue. For the senior Bush, it was much more important, ranking second only to the dissolution of the Soviet Union. His expulsion of Iraqi forces from Kuwait is widely praised. The subsequent decision to leave Hussein in power as a counterweight to Iran is criticized. While it was understandable—too little time had passed after Vietnam for the United States to act confidently against the wishes of allies and partners—it set the stage for years of additional turmoil and violence. Bush's realism also helped fuel the emergence of Islamic extremism by associating the United States with corrupt, despotic regimes in the Gulf and elsewhere in the Arab world. Clinton's decision to focus on issues other than Iraq allowed the problem to fester. It was no closer to resolution at the end of his administration than it was at the beginning. His reliance on sanctions, partnerships with Gulf monarchies, and a growing U.S. military presence in the region provided additional political ammunition to Islamic extremists, allowing them to portray the United States as an imperial power with no regard for Muslims—only for their oil. The record of both the senior Bush and Clinton is mixed. Yet, both considered their approach to Iraq successful and used it to affirm or validate the broader contours of their strategy. Only with hindsight did flaws or problems become clear.

Iraq became the defining issue of George W. Bush's strategy. To a large extent, history will judge him by the outcome. It will always be impossible to know whether the intervention was necessary. Was Saddam Hussein really determined to acquire nuclear weapons and use them to renew aggression against his neighbors or to support terrorists? Could he have done so? Or was he simply struggling to keep his parasitic and pathological system from collapse? Political leanings will determine how a particular commentator or analyst answers these questions. Those on the political Right will be inclined to see the Bush strategy toward Iraq as averting a mounting threat; those on the Left will see it as a useless blunder.

One thing is beyond dispute: the Bush administration failed to gauge and prepare for the difficulties of stabilizing Iraq after Hussein. There are three explanations for this. The first is that mismanagement, incompetence, or bad decisions derailed what could have been a relatively successful transition from dictatorship to some form of democracy. The administration sent too few military forces, failed to plan, made major errors (such as the dissolution of the Iraqi Army), relied too much on the advice of exiles, refused to make concessions that might have attracted more partners to the stabilization effort, created unrealistic expectations in the American public, and tried to undertake a massive effort on the cheap. Those who subscribe to this position will search for culprits, from the president himself on down. Rumsfeld is likely to receive much of the blame, with Cheney, Bremer, Rice, Wolfowitz, Feith, and Franks getting a share as well. Generals Sanchez, Abizaid, and Casey may also be incriminated. Powell, Myers, and congressional Republicans may be seen as contributors to the failure since they could have influenced, perhaps even derailed, the march to war but did not.

The second explanation is that transforming Iraq from a parasitic dictatorship to a democracy was unachievable from the start. Even the best strategy could not have brought the easy success promised before the intervention. In one variant of this, President Bush is still to blame because he made the decision to undertake an impossible mission. Alternatively, the president's advisers are the culprits for not explaining the impossibility of the undertaking. The third explanation is the "stab in the back" theory—success was attainable had not some organization deliberately prevented it. Those who promote this insidious position—and they are likely to be diehard supporters of the Bush legacy from either within the administration or the conservative idealist community—will blame the U.S. military or the intelligence community or the media and Democrats for turning the public against the counterinsurgency campaign.

These explanations have more than scholarly importance. Whichever one is adopted will form a strategic "lesson." If policymakers, strategists, political leaders, and the wider strategic community accept the notion that the post-Hussein problems in Iraq were the result of mistakes or bad decisions by the Bush administration, then the implication is that future policymakers and strategists need only to be wiser. Experts within the military, the intelligence agencies, Congress, other components of the government, and the scholarly and strategic communities must be more assertive to ensure that policymakers understand the likely results of their decisions. There is nothing systemically flawed in the system by which Americans generate strategy. It was simply a matter of the wrong people in power at the wrong time, or a post–September 11 collective myopia. On the other hand, if the strategic and policymaking communities accept the idea that transforming Iraq into a democracy was an impossible mission, then the strategic "lesson" is that the United States should not undertake such actions. Rather than doing it better the next time, there should be no next time. This suggests that a strategy based on ameliorating the sources of conflict in the restive parts of the world is flawed and was not just badly executed. Some degree of disengagement, containment, and cauterization makes much more sense. The third explanation—the "stab in the back"—is unlikely to gain widespread support. If it did, however, the "lesson" would be that the guilty organization must be controlled or marginalized in the future.

That is the likely contour of the future debate over the George W. Bush strategy toward Iraq. Further implications can be drawn from the full span of this paradigmatic conflict. While the distinction is not perfect— there are overlaps and connections—these can be divided into things that the conflict tells us about the way Americans understand and interact with the world and things that it tells us about the way that Americans make strategy (or, as the case may be, fail to make it).

■   ■   ■

The long conflict with Iraq demonstrated that the more an opponent is unlike Americans in culture and psychology, the less effective is the U.S. strategy against it. This is true for any nation. The easier an enemy is to understand, the better the chances of countering it. When European colonial powers dealt with alien cultures and psychologies, they had a long learning period. As the newest great power to operate in alien cultures and psychologies, the United States is still learning. It does not have the luxury of a long and safe learning period. America is being educated under fire.

The Iraq conflict shows how difficulty understanding alien cultures and leaders complicates strategy. September 11 amplified both the importance of cross-cultural security interaction and its complexities. In their deadly strategic dance, neither George W. Bush nor Saddam Hussein fully understood each other or the political culture in which the other operated. Bush interpreted Hussein's deception and bluster as evidence that he sought weapons of mass destruction for purposes of regional domination. As it turned out, the United States was—to borrow a phrase from Islamic militants—Iraq's "far enemy." Hussein's "near enemies" were internal opponents, including the Kurds and Shiites, potential challengers within the Iraqi military, and Iran. He felt compelled to make these enemies believe that he had weapons of mass destruction as his conventional military power eroded. He may have assumed that the United States, with its massive intelligence capabilities, knew that he had few or no weapons of mass destruction and was simply trumpeting them for propaganda purposes. In psychological terms, both Bush and Hussein "mirror imaged" each other, with one assuming that his enemy's mind worked much as his own did.

All American presidents, George W. Bush in particular, misunderstood the Iraqi psyche and political culture. He underestimated the extent to which three decades of Saddam Hussein's pathological rule had damaged and distorted that society. A whole generation of Iraqis knew nothing except the skills needed to survive in a brutal, totalitarian system. A willingness to compromise, toleration, trust, civic responsibility, and personal initiative—all of which could get an Iraqi killed or exiled under the dictatorship—were in scarce supply. To preserve his grip on power after two disastrous wars, Hussein exacerbated sectarian hostility between Sunnis and Shiites, portraying Shiites as the puppets of Iran. Bush administration policymakers grossly underestimated the extent of this, sanguinely believing that the Sunnis, long accustomed to dominating Iraq, would accept minority status in a democratic country. Or, in an even more optimistic mode, Bush officials assumed that with Hussein gone, Iraqis would not approach politics through a sectarian lens. Phrased differently, the administration thought that Iraq was like

Czechoslovakia or Poland, where an essentially liberal society had a thin totalitarian veneer that could be stripped away.

Similarly, Bush administration policymakers did not understand the central role of honor and justice in Arab culture and the extent to which this was manifested as intolerance for outside intervention, particularly by non-Muslims. President Bush expected Americans to be seen as liberators and the leaders of the new Iraq to be publicly grateful for the removal of Hussein and his cronies. The administration was shocked when whatever gratitude existed quickly gave way to hostility. It failed to understand the power that honorable resistance to perceived injustice has in the Arab world. This misunderstanding of Iraqi culture and values was exacerbated by the virtual exclusion of regional experts from policymaking in the Bush administration, which was motivated, to some extent, out of concern that Arabists might have sympathies for the people of the region that would influence their thinking.[1] Instead administration policymakers relied on the advice of Iraqi exiles who had an even greater personal stake in the outcome.

Much of strategy is communicating intent. America's conflict with Iraq demonstrated the difficulty of such communication, particularly across cultural divides. The senior Bush's emphasis on multilateralism and the United Nations told Saddam Hussein that Washington would not act without a wide range of partners and the backing of the Security Council. He continued to believe this until 2003. Clinton's desire to downplay Iraq and to focus on other issues sent the unintended message that he was weak and could be intimidated. His withdrawal from Somalia—while it made perfect sense given the limited U.S. interests in that country—sent the message to Saddam Hussein (and al-Qaeda) that the United States did not have the stomach for bloodletting and could be compelled by guerrilla war or terrorism. Clinton's acceptance of the Joint Vision approach to military transformation sent the message that the United States was not interested in confronting protracted, asymmetric challenges. The George W. Bush strategy, on the other hand, sent the unintended message that the United States was imperialistic, dangerous, and hypocritical (since it held that America's power exempted it from the norms of international behavior).

Ultimately, strategic communication is most effective when backed by consistency. For centuries Roman strategy succeeded because the various tribes, clans, confederations, and states on the periphery of the republic and empire knew that if they became aggressive or caused instability, they would be punished. Because American strategy is shaped by so many variables, many of them arising from domestic politics, it does not have this degree of certainty. Enemies or potential enemies do not know whether involvement in terrorism or pursuit of nuclear weapons will bring an attack or concessions, whether they will deter Washington or provoke it. This inconsistency is inevitable given the American system for strategy formulation, but it means that enemies and potential enemies will continue to miscalculate just as Saddam Hussein did.

The Iraq conflict demonstrated shifts in what might be called the "tenor" of American strategy. Optimism is the norm. Americans assume that threats held in check will resolve themselves. The exception seems to be during transitional periods such as the opening years of the Cold War and the period immediately after September 11. New dangers breed fear and anxiety, thus tempering optimism. In terms of the conflict with Iraq, the senior Bush and Clinton believed that, if held in check, the Saddam Hussein problem would eventually go away. The darker worldview of George W. Bush (and Dick Cheney) assumed that the threat from Hussein would only get worse if not addressed. His perspective was more like the German Historian Oswald Spenglan who believed that all civilians began to decline than George Kennan who felt that freesocieties would win if they held dictators in check. It is not clear whether this is a permanent shift in the tenor of American strategy or simply one more pessimistic interlude.

The Iraq conflict demonstrated that the combination of weltanschauung and analogy play a major role in shaping strategy. The American weltanschauung is teleological. It encapsulates the liberal Enlightenment idea that history is the gradual spread of political and economic freedom. The end state—whether Hegel's "end of history" or Francis Fukuyama's "end of ideology"—is liberal democracy ascendant around the world. Reagan, the senior Bush, and Clinton all believed that if Saddam Hussein was held in check, this logic of history would play out. But just as Lenin sought to control and accelerate the laws of history rather than passively observe them, George W. Bush attempted to control and accelerate the progression toward liberal democracy. Since only evil despots prevent the natural flowering of liberal democracy, removing them would allow this flowering.

Strategy relies on precedents and analogies when new challenges and threats emerge. The key is selecting the right ones. When Saddam Hussein invaded Kuwait in 1990, the senior Bush had to decide whether Vietnam or the hypothetical analogy of a Warsaw Pact invasion of Western Europe applied. Although Vietnam was the most recent, the administration used the European analogy, deciding that cross-border invasion "will not stand." When the G. W. Bush administration contemplated intervention in Iraq, it decided that the removal of Manuel Noriega in Panama was a more apt analogy than Vietnam. As the insurgency developed, his administration had to fend off the idea that Iraq was "another Vietnam." Counterinsurgency experts within the military and the wider strategic community looked instead to the British experience in Malaya and the French experience in Algeria, both occurring from the late 1940s to early 1960s. These were, though, problematic analogies. In both cases the counterinsurgents were colonial powers with long experience in and extensive knowledge of the places where they fought. This did not apply to the American experience in Iraq. While the Algerian War (which seemed the most applicable precedent given that it occurred in an Arab Islamic country) was culled for such operational lessons as the focus on civilian security, policymakers overlooked the fact that the French ultimately failed. There was little or no analysis of whether French operational methods could lead to strategic success when applied by another outside power in another Arab Islamic nation. Formulating strategy *without* analogies or precedents is extremely difficult so the inclination is to find one even if it is problematic or inappropriate.

A strategy is no stronger than its assumptions. Assumptions include vital information that cannot be confirmed or disproven with existing information. Often they pertain to the future or to the way that a leader, a nation, or a people will react to a particular event or action. When dealing with Iraq, the senior Bush and Clinton adopted an assumption drawn from the Cold War strategy of containment: a dictator prevented from expanding would eventually fall. The younger Bush combined grimly pessimistic assumptions about the state of Iraq's weapons programs and Hussein's intentions with rosily optimistic assumptions about the ease with which Iraq could be rebuilt following intervention, the ease with which Iraq could form a stable democracy, the reaction to Iraq's political transformation in the rest of the Arab world, and the reaction of the world to American intervention. When most of these proved incorrect, the administration suffered a tremendous loss of deference and trust from both the American public and the world community. The price of unrealistic assumptions was a broader wounding of the president, which eroded his effectiveness and contributed to a major shift in the American political balance.

When the George W. Bush administration devoted so much of its attention to Iraq and gambled so much of the trust and deference that it had accumulated after September 11 it showed that focus is both a blessing and a curse for American strategy. Concentrating on a single enemy, threat, or issue makes it easier to mobilize and sustain support from the always-fickle public and Congress. It makes the strategy more coherent and convincing. An unfocused strategy complicates the task of mobilizing and sustaining support. Clinton's unwillingness to focus on Iraq or the Islamic world in general contributed to later trouble. The price of a focused strategy, though, is that other problems and issues may receive less effort than they should. The G. W. Bush administration's concentration on Iraq provided a textbook illustration of this. Little was done to stop the North Korean and Iranian nuclear programs until they were well under way. Afghanistan and Pakistan received less attention and resources than they would have. Emerging tensions in key petroleum producers like Nigeria and Venezuela were largely ignored. Little progress was made on the Israeli-Palestinian conflict. The American public, Congress, and foreign partners came to believe that not only was the Bush administration overly focused on a single problem, but that it was focused on the *wrong* problem. Bush had convinced the public that terrorism and proliferation were the most pressing security threats to the United States, but then it concentrated on a nation that was a marginal supporter of transnational terrorism and far from developing nuclear weapons. Again, the trust and deference so vital to leadership proved to be the casualties of administration's concentration on Iraq.

Because Americans see peace as the normal state of affairs in the world, at least in the absence of aggressive dictators, and because what the public thinks matters even in the realm of national security, policymakers must structure the U.S. military and military strategy in a way that can gain and sustain support. In broad terms, any use of military force must be in proportion to the perceived extent of the threat that it is intended to deter or defeat. If the threat is great, the public and its elected representatives are willing to tolerate even protracted and costly applications of armed force. If the threat is more modest, the public and Congress are only willing to tolerate quick, relatively low cost applications of force. Policymakers have addressed this in two ways. One is to minimize the length and cost of armed action. That was what the Joint Vision approach to transformation, programs to augment the capability of security partners, and improvements in the ability of the U.S. military to operate as part of coalitions were all about. They were intended to sustain the usability of the American military in a time when the threat was perceived as low. Speed, precision, and having someone else do things that the American public doesn't want its military to do were the keys. The second method is to persuade the public and

Congress that the threat is significant. This was what the G. W. Bush administration did when it opted to remove Saddam Hussein from power by military action. Both approaches have risks. Speed, precision, and relying on others risk a situation where the U.S. military (and government) is unprepared for the task at hand and no one else will do it. That is exactly what happened in Iraq when the insurgency emerged. Inflating the threat risks the deflation of public and congressional support if the portrayal proves false. That also happened in Iraq.

Since 2003 the Iraq conflict has shown that stressing usability in American military strategy came at the expense of effectiveness. Rather than having prepared for large-scale, protracted counterinsurgency, the strategy assumed that the United States would not become involved in such an action. Or, if it did, other nations and organizations would make up for the capability shortfalls in the U.S. military and in the nonmilitary components of the government. The U.S. military and American political leaders assumed that armed force would be used to defeat an enemy armed force or remove a hostile regime in a relatively quick, low-cost operation, and to support multinational stabilization or peacekeeping efforts. These assumptions, of course, did not hold. Current programs to augment the military's counterinsurgency capabilities are inadequate, in part because they are not matched by an equal effort to address nonmilitary capability shortfalls and also because they are based on an obsolete conceptualization of insurgency.[2] There is little indication that if the United States undertook regime removal and the wholesale political transformation of a major state in the near future, it would be markedly more successful than it has been in Iraq. Put simply, the conflict in Iraq illustrated an enduring means and ends mismatch in American strategy. But rather than undertake a fundamental examination of the assumptions and tenets of their strategy, Americans have concluded that a bit of reorganization and a few new programs will address the problems that Iraq laid bare. Iraq is seen as an aberration, not a symptom of deep flaws in national strategy.

As much as anything, the difficulties that the United States has faced in Iraq since 2003 demonstrate the shortcomings of a strategy that sees war and "not war" as discrete phenomena, one the primary purview of the military and the other of nonmilitary elements of the government. When faced with an opponent that did not fit neatly into this construct, the United States regressed to what it was comfortable with, stressing the one element of the global security system amenable to the type of military force it had: state support for terrorists. This has not worked and is less likely to in the future. Most experts believe that the dominant trends in the security environment are the blurring of traditional distinctions and the emergence of hybrid threats intermixing state and non-state components, economics and politics, crime and war, all shaped by new extremist ideologies. If so, the things done in response to the conflict in Iraq—enlargement of the ground forces, increased cultural training for the military, the development of a few interagency concepts, and so forth—will not be enough.

Finally, the conflict with and in Iraq suggests that the mode of leadership that the United States has exercised since the 1940s may have run its course. During the Cold War the United States was accepted as the leader of the "Free World" because the Soviet threat was pressing. Leadership was less an endorsement of Washington's style and effectiveness than a reflection of the fact that the Free World needed a leader and there was no other candidate. George W. Bush, conservative idealists, and even astute thinkers such as Colin Gray assumed that was sustainable.[3] In reality, Iraq may have shown that the world no longer wants a leader. The United States was effective when the challenge was aggressor states, whether the Soviet Union or the tinhorn dictatorships Moscow left in its wake. It is not clear that the United States can be an effective leader against hybrid threats in an environment of moral ambiguity. Events in Iraq since 2003 suggest that the world is drawing this conclusion and may come to see the United States as less than "indispensable." America's conflict with Iraq may be the last of its kind, at least for several decades.

■　■　■

The Iraq conflict is also rife with evidence of tensions and shortfalls in the way that Americans develop their strategy. The public and Congress play a larger role in the formulation of American strategy than in that of any other great power. The extent to which this constrains a president depends on the importance he attaches to strategy and the political price he is willing to pay for ignoring public and congressional opinion. The senior Bush and Clinton were unwilling to act on Iraq without congressional backing. This limited their options and, to an extent, was responsible for their inability to remove Saddam Hussein from power. The younger Bush placed great importance on confronting security threats to the United States. By conflating Saddam Hussein and the threat from transnational terrorism, Bush became willing to do whatever was necessary to remove the Iraqi dictator from power. He found it difficult, though, to send the desired message to the American public, Saddam Hussein, and other nations simultaneously. Any time he indicated moderation or a preference for diplomacy to the American public and other nations, Saddam Hussein took it as a sign of weakness. Any time he expressed the degree of belligerence necessary to compel Hussein, other nations and, to a lesser degree, the American public and Congress recoiled. This forced Bush to oversell the threat. The result was a deflation of support once the case for intervention fell apart. The public and Congress went from deference to obstructionism, hindering the administration's ability to execute its counterinsurgency strategy.

The conflict with Iraq demonstrated the effect that timing has on American strategy. The electoral cycle played a major role in strategic decisions. Rather than acting when it would maximize the effect, American presidents are forced to act when politics allow. No president wants to be mired in conflict during an election if it can be avoided. All American presidents know that the use of armed force faces a ticking clock. If they cannot show results within a few years, casualties are high, and the national interests at stake are questionable, public and congressional support will dry up. America's enemies seem to understand this and to believe that it is possible to wait the United States out. While George W. Bush elected to push ahead with his strategy despite faltering support, the price was undercutting the Republican Party and, in all likelihood, paving the way for Democratic domination of both the White House and Congress.

The Iraq conflict was shaped by a shifting relationship between policymakers and experts, whether regional or military ones. When policymakers defer to experts, it minimizes risk but also limits boldness and innovation. When policymakers ignore or exclude experts, boldness and innovation are possible. But so are the chances of major errors. Clinton clearly leaned toward deference to experts while the younger Bush tended to ignore them. The explosive growth in the community of strategic analysts and commentators provided alternative sources of ideas, further augmenting the potential for innovation and boldness (and the potential for mistakes). Just as the growth of congressional staffs several decades ago made the legislature less dependent on information and analysis from the executive branch and thus a stronger player in strategy formulation, the emergence of an independent (and often partisan) strategic community bolstered policymakers determined to buck government experts. Vice President

Cheney's role in developing American strategy toward Iraq is a perfect illustration. In all likelihood, without his marshalling of conservative idealist commentators working in parallel to sell the public and Congress on the idea of removing Saddam Hussein, Bush and his senior officials could not have mobilized enough support to do so. Whether one feels this is a good or a bad thing depends on one's olitical perspective. Conservative idealists might point out that without their contribution, Saddam Hussein would still be in power. Those on the other end of the political spectrum might reply that without the conservative idealists paving the way for intervention, thousands of young Americans might still be alive and billions of dollars of American money might be used for something other than the conflict in Iraq.

The Iraq conflict showed the degree to which idiosyncratic factors influence strategy. It comes as no surprise that personalities matter greatly. Had not George W. Bush been president and Donald Rumsfeld secretary of defense, the 2003 intervention would have been much less likely, probably impossible. But organizational idiosyncrasies matter as well. In the 1990s, each of the U.S. armed services promoted its own vision of the future security environment to shape defense transformation to their institutional advantage. For a variety of reasons, the Air Force and the Navy dominated. This lead to the Joint Vision model of transformation. The Army was dragged along, stressing that it too could perform with speed and precision rather than arguing that speed and precision were not panaceas for all security problems. As a result, when the U.S. military found itself in a type of conflict not amenable to speed and precision firepower—counterinsurgency—it was unprepared.

The Iraq conflict demonstrated that Americans remain more comfortable with technological, operational, and tactical innovation than with strategic adaptation. In a very real sense, American *strategy* toward Iraq changed little from 1990 to the present. When faced with challenges, the United States tends to reorganize and create new programs rather than alter or reconceptualize its strategy. In a broader sense, the Iraq conflict showed that outside the military, there is a dearth of strategic thinking and planning in the U.S. government. The National Security Council is not configured for developing true strategy with both a horizontal and vertical dimension. It formulates policies. While the State Department once had an impressive strategy-making capability in its Policy Planning Staff, there is little sign that the current manifestation of this plays anywhere near the role that its Cold War predecessor did when it included people like George Kennan and Paul Nitze.

In an even more general sense, the Iraq conflict demonstrated that the division of power ingrained in the American system for strategy development needs reevaluation. It was designed in a time when strategy could coalesce in a leisurely fashion. The public and Congress could be slowly educated on an issue and only then play an active role. Today, threats and challenges emerge quickly. It may be that America's essentially eighteenth-century method for deciding how to deal with the world is obsolete. The twenty-first century may be a time when boldness is necessary even given the risks it brings.

■ ■ ■

In all likelihood, America's conflict with Iraq will remain a strategic paradigm, shaping the way that future policymakers and strategists respond to new problems. Today, the general consensus seems to be that the military and the rest of the government need reform to deal more effectively with a large-scale stabilization challenge or counterinsurgency. Within a few years, the public and Congress may question the strategy that led the United States to remove Saddam Hussein and undertake counterinsurgency rather than simply believing that next time it can be done better. Only time will tell.

Many questions remain. Is America's conflict with and in Iraq nearly over? Was it always about Saddam Hussein or is it something deeper than that? Certainly there will be long-term regional and global effects from the conflict, but what will they be? Will they be lingering manifestations of Saddam Hussein's pathologies or the result of America's attempts to address Saddam Hussein's pathologies? The full effect of this long struggle will not become clear until the United States confronts its next, as yet unidentified, security challenge and the power or weakness of the Iraq paradigm is put to the test.

NOTES

INTRODUCTION

1. Barry R. Posen, "The Case for Restraint," *The American Interest* 3 (November–December 2007): 7.
2. Carl Von Clausewitz, *On War*, trans. Michael Howard and Peter Paret (Princeton, NJ: Princeton University Press, 1976), 177.
3. Colin S. Gray, *Modern Strategy* (Oxford: Oxford University Press, 1999), 16.
4. Edward N. Luttwak, *Strategy: The Logic of War and Peace* (Cambridge, MA: Belknap, 1987), 7–17. This is similar to Andrew Beaufre's emphasis on the dialectical nature of strategy given that it entails two opposing wills that use force to resolve disputes (*Introduction to Strategy* [New York: Praeger, 1965]). Gray captures the same idea as "nonlinearity" in strategy (Colin S. Gray, *Strategy for Chaos: Revolutions in Military Affairs and the Evidence of History* [London: Frank Cass, 2002], 5).
5. Russell F. Weigley, *The American Way of War: A History of United States Military Strategy and Policy* (Bloomington: Indiana University Press, 1973).
6. Max Boot, "The New American Way of War," *Foreign Affairs* 82 (July–August 2003): 41.
7. Antulio J. Echevarria II, *Toward an American Way of War* (Carlisle Barracks, PA: U.S. Army War College Strategic Studies Institute, 2004).

CHAPTER 1: ASCENT OF AN ENEMY

1. See Robert S. Litwak, *Détente and the Nixon Doctrine* (New York: Cambridge University Press, 1984).
2. Henry Kissinger, *White House Years* (Boston: Little, Brown, 1979), 255.
3. Michael A. Palmer, *Guardians of the Gulf: A History of America's Expanding Role in the Persian Gulf, 1833–1992* (New York: Free Press, 1992), 87–93.
4. Henry Kissinger, *Years of Upheaval* (Boston: Little, Brown, 1982), 675.
5. Zbigniew Brzezinski, *Power and Principle: Memoirs of the National Security Adviser, 1977–1981* (New York: Farrar, Straus, Giroux, 1983), 354.

6. Jimmy Carter, "State of the Union address to Congress," January 23, 1980.

7. Henry Kissinger, *Years of Renewal* (New York: Touchstone, 1999), 581.

8. Paul A. Gigot, "A Great American Screw-Up: The U.S. and Iraq, 1980–1990," *National Interest* 22 (Winter 1990–91): 4.

9. Milton Viorst, "Iraq at War," *Foreign Affairs* 65 (Winter 1986–87): 353; Bruce W. Jentleson, *With Friends Like These: Reagan, Bush, and Saddam, 1982–1990* (New York: W. W. Norton, 1994), 41; and Stephen C. Pelletiere, *The Iran–Iraq War: Chaos in a Vacuum* (Westport, CT: Praeger, 1992), 34.

10. Michael Sterner, "The Iran-Iraq War," *Foreign Affairs* 63 (Fall 1984): 130.

11. Brzezinski, *Power and Principle*, 452–54.

12. Palmer, *Guardians of the Gulf*, 113.

13. Barry Rubin, "The Reagan Administration and the Middle East," in *Eagle Defiant: United States Foreign Policy in the 1980s*, ed., Kenneth A. Oye, Robert J. Lieber, and Donald Rothchild (Boston: Little, Brown, 1983), 367, 370.

14. U.S. Interest Section in Baghdad, "Talking Points for Ambassador Rumsfeld's Meeting with Tariq Aziz and Saddam Hussein," telegram to American embassy in Amman, December 14, 1983, declassified document available from the National Security Archive, George Washington University, Washington, DC.

15. George P. Shultz, *Turmoil and Triumph: My Years as Secretary of State* (New York: Charles Scribner's Sons, 1993), 235.

16. *Implications of Iran's Victory Over Iraq*, Special National Intelligence Estimate 34/36, 2–82 (Washington, DC: Director of Central Intelligence, June 8, 1982), 1, declassified document available from the National Security Archive, George Washington University, Washington, DC.

17. Sterner, "The Iran-Iraq War," 129.

18. Jentleson, *With Friends Like These*, 42–47.

19. Ibid., 47–48.

20. Shultz, *Turmoil and Triumph*, 240.

21. Peter W. Galbraith, *The End of Iraq: How American Incompetence Created a War Without End* (New York: Simon and Schuster, 2006), 34.

22. *National Security Strategy of the United States* (Washington: The White House, January 1988), 5, 29.

23. Quoted in Michael R. Gordon and Bernard E. Trainor, *The Generals' War: The Inside Story of the Conflict in the Gulf* (Boston: Little, Brown, 1995), 14. For background on the formation of CENTCOM, see Amitav Acharya, *U.S. Military Strategy in the Gulf* (London: Routledge, 1989), 63–88; and Jay E. Hines, "From Desert One to Southern Watch: History of the U.S. Central Command," *Joint Force Quarterly* 24 (Spring 2000): 42–48.

24. Anthony H. Cordesman, *The Gulf and the West: Strategic Relations and Military Realities* (Boulder, CO: Westview, 1988), 93.

25. Adeed I. Dawisha, "Iraq: The West's Opportunity," *Foreign Policy* 41 (Winter 1980–81): 148. Dawisha is an Iraqi who at the time the article was published was at the Royal Institute of International Affairs in London.

26. Daniel Pipes and Laurie Mylroie, "Back Iraq," *The New Republic*, April 27, 1987, 15.

27. Frederick W. Axelgard, "War and Oil: Implications for Iraq's Postwar Role in Gulf Security," in *Iraq in Transition: A Political, Economic, and Strategic Perspective*, ed. Frederick W. Axelgard (Boulder, CO: Westview, 1986), 1.

28. Frederick W. Axelgard, *A New Iraq? The Gulf War and Implications for U.S. Policy* (New York: Praeger, 1988), 100–103.

29. Edmund Ghareeb, "Iraq in the Gulf," in *Iraq in Transition*, ed., Axelgard, 77, 79.

30. Robert H. Johnson, "The Persian Gulf in U.S. Strategy," *International Security* 14 (Summer 1989): 146.

31. Jentleson, *With Friends Like These*, 50–51.

32. Cited in Jentleson, *With Friends Like These*, 90; Gordon and Trainor, *The Generals' War*, 9; and Gigot, "A Great American Screw-Up," 6.

33. George H. W. Bush, "Remarks at the Aspen Institute Symposium," Aspen, CO, August 2, 1990.

34. George H. W. Bush, "State of the Union Address Before a Joint Session of Congress," January 29, 1991.

35. Bush, "Remarks at the Aspen Institute."

36. *National Security Strategy of the United States* (Washington, DC: The White House, 1991), p. 25.

37. Colin Powell, "U.S. Forces: Challenges Ahead," *Foreign Affairs* 71 (Winter 1992–1993): 35.

38. *Certain Victory: United States Army in the Gulf War* (Washington, DC: United States Army, Office of the Chief of Staff, 1993), 6.

39. The speech is reprinted in Caspar W. Weinberger, *Fighting for Peace: Seven Critical Years in the Pentagon* (New York: Warner, 1990), 433–45.

40. Terry L. Deibel, "Bush's Foreign Policy: Mastery and Inaction," *Foreign Policy* 84 (Fall 1991): 20.

41. "U.S. Policy Toward the Persian Gulf," *National Security Directive 26*, October 2, 1989, declassified document available from the Federation of American Scientists, Washington, DC, 1.

42. Jentleson, *With Friends Like These*, 94–95.

43. "U.S. Policy Toward the Persian Gulf," *National Security Directive 26*, 2.

44. *National Security Strategy of the United States* (Washington, DC: The White House, 1990), 13.

45. Barry Rubin, "The Gulf Crisis: Origins and Course of Events," in *Middle East Contemporary Survey*, Vol. 14, ed. Ami Ayalon (Boulder, CO: Westview, 1990), 79.

46. George Bush and Brent Scowcroft, *A World Transformed* (New York: Alfred A. Knopf, 1998), 307.

47. Gordon and Trainor, *The Generals' War*, 4–6, 14–20; and Bob Woodward, *The Commanders* (New York: Touchstone, 1991), 205–22.

48. *Conduct of the Persian Gulf War: Final Report to Congress* (Washington, DC: Department of Defense, 1992), 8.

49. Palmer, *Guardians of the Gulf*, 159.

50. Woodward, *The Commanders*, 211.

51. Thomas A. Keaney and Eliot A. Cohen, *Revolution in Warfare: Air Power in the*

Persian Gulf (Annapolis, MD: Naval Institute Press, 1995), 4. This document was originally published as the official *Gulf War Air Power Summary Report*.

CHAPTER 2: THE TEST OF BATTLE

1. *1989 Joint Military Assessment,* 2–5.
2. President George H. W. Bush, "Address Before a Joint Session of Congress," September 11, 1990.
3. Bush and Scowcroft, *A World Transformed,* 305.
4. See Woodward, *The Commanders,* 306–07, 347, and 355; and Bush and Scowcroft, *A World Transformed,* 354.
5. *Conduct of the Persian Gulf War,* 32.
6. John Keegan, "The Lessons of the Gulf War," *Los Angeles Times Magazine,* April 9, 1991, 21.
7. President George H. W. Bush, "Remarks and an Exchange with Reporters on the Iraqi Invasion of Kuwait," August 5, 1990.
8. H. Norman Schwarzkopf with Peter Petre, *It Doesn't Take a Hero* (New York: Bantam, 1993), 345–46.
9. Lally Weymouth, "How Bush Went to War," *Washington Post,* March 31, 1991.
10. Woodward, *The Commanders,* 237.
11. *Conduct of the Persian Gulf War,* 31.
12. Bush and Scowcroft, *A World Transformed,* 335.
13. Bush and Scowcroft, *A World Transformed,* 303.
14. Bush, Address Before a Joint Session of Congress, September 11, 1990.
15. James Mann, *Rise of the Vulcans: The History of Bush's War Cabinet* (New York: Penguin, 2004), 184; Woodward, *The Commanders,* 229; and Colin Powell with Joseph E. Persico, *My American Journey* (New York: Ballantine, 1995), 479–80. After the meeting where Powell made this point, Cheney chastised him for making a policy point rather than a purely military one. The implication was the General Powell had forgotten that as chairman of the Joint Chiefs of Staff, his job was not to proffer policy advice as it had been when he was Reagan's national security adviser.
16. Quoted in Gordon and Trainor, *The Generals' War,* 33.
17. Woodward, *The Commanders,* 249; and Schwarzkopf, *It Doesn't Take a Hero,* 349–50.
18. Bush and Scowcroft, *A World Restored,* 328.
19. Powell, *My American Journey,* 476.
20. Ibid., 469.
21. Palmer, *Guardians of the Gulf,* 169.
22. Woodward, *The Commanders,* 262.
23. *Conduct of the Persian Gulf War,* 252.
24. Gordon and Trainor, *The Generals' War,* 163.
25. See John K. Cooley, "Pre-War Gulf Diplomacy," *Survival* 33 (March–April 1991): 125–39.
26. Powell, *My American Journey,* 487–89.
27. John A. Warden III, *The Air Campaign: Planning for Combat* (Washington, DC: Pergamon–Brassey's, 1989). The air planning is described in *Conduct of the Persian Gulf War,* 91–101; and Alexander S. Cochran, et. al., *Gulf Air*

Power Survey, vol. 1 (Washington, DC: Government Printing Office, 1993), 1–233.

28. P.L. 102-1 (H.J.Res. 77), *Authorization for Use of Military Force Against Iraq Resolution*, gave congressional authorization to expel Iraq from Kuwait in accordance with United Nations Security Council Resolution 678, which called for the implementation of eleven previous Security Council resolutions. This became public law on January 12, 1991.

29. *Conduct of the Persian Gulf War*, 131.

30. The official histories of the ground campaign are *Certain Victory* and *Conduct of the Persian Gulf War*, 226–97. A good summary is William J. Taylor Jr. and James Blackwell, "The Ground War in the Gulf," *Survival* 33 (May–June 1991), 230–45.

31. Bush and Scowcroft, *A World Transformed*, 490–1.

32. Harry G. Summers Jr., *On Strategy II: A Critical Analysis of the Gulf War* (New York: Dell, 1992), 7–8.

33. Bush and Scowcroft, *A World Transformed*, 492.

34. The phrase was from Charles Krauthammer, "The Unipolar Moment," *Foreign Affairs* 70 (Summer 1991), 23–33.

35. *National Security Strategy of the United States* (1991), 1.

36. Ibid., v.

37. Ibid., 13.

38. Christopher M. Gacek, *The Logic of Force: The Dilemma of Limited War in American Foreign Policy* (New York: Columbia University Press, 1994), 294–95.

39. Carl E. Vuono, "Desert Storm and the Future of Conventional Forces," *Foreign Affairs* 70 (Spring 1991): 49.

40. William J. Perry, "Desert Storm and Deterrence in the Future," in *After the Storm: Lessons From the Gulf War*, ed. Joseph S. Nye Jr. and Roger K. Smith (Lanham, MD: Madison, 1992), 244; and Bobby R. Inman, Joseph S. Nye Jr., William J. Perry, and Roger K. Smith, "Lessons From the Gulf War," *Washington Quarterly* 15 (Winter 1992): 68.

41. Michael J. Mazarr, Don M. Snider, and James A. Blackwell Jr., *Desert Storm: The Gulf War and What We Learned* (Boulder, CO: Westview, 1993), 151–52.

42. Stephen Biddle develops the idea that "skill differential" explains military success in *Military Power: Explaining Victory and Defeat in Modern Battle* (Princeton, NJ: Princeton University Press, 2004).

43. The classic study of service cultures in the U.S. military and their effect on strategy is Carl Builder, *The Masks of War: Military Styles in Strategy and Analysis* (Baltimore: Johns Hopkins University Press, 1989).

44. Public Law 99–433. For background, see *Defense Organization: The Need For Change*, Staff Report to the Committee on Armed Service, United States Senate, October 15, 1985. Analysis of the development of the bill is found in James R. Locher III, *Victory on the Potomac: The Goldwater–Nichols Act Unifies the Pentagon* (College Station: Texas A&M University Press, 2002). Locher was one of the primary Senate staffers who helped develop the legislation.

45. Lawrence J. Korb, "The Impact of the Persian Gulf War on Military Budgets and Force Structure," in *After the Storm*, ed. Nye and Smith, 221–23.

46. Stephen Biddle, "Victory Misunderstood: What the Gulf Tells Us About the Future of Conflict," *International Security* 21 (Fall 1996): 139–179.

47. *1992 Joint Military Net Assessment* (Washington, DC: Joint Chiefs of Staff, 1992), 1–6.

48. Dennis M. Drew, "Desert Storm as a Symbol: Implications of the Air War in the Desert," *Airpower Journal* 10 (Fall 1992): 13.

49. . . . *From the Sea: Preparing the Naval Service for the 21st Century* (Washington, DC: Department of the Navy, 1992).

50. See *Operational Maneuver From the Sea* and *United States Marine Corps Warfighting Concepts for the 21st Century* (Quantico, VA: Marine Corps Combat Development Command, 1996), I-3 through I-22.

51. Jeffrey Record, *Hollow Victory: A Contrary View of the Gulf War* (Washington: Brassey's, Inc., 1993), 136.

52. William J. Taylor Jr. and James Blackwell, "The Ground War in the Gulf," *Survival* 33 (May–June 1991): 245.

53. George H. W. Bush, "Remarks of President Bush to the American Association for the Advancement of Science on Iraq's Withdrawal Statement," February 15, 1991.

54. Bush and Scowcroft, *A World Restored,* 471.

55. Ibid., *A World Restored,* 472.

56. Galbraith, *The End of Iraq,* 36–69.

57. Gordon and Trainor, *The Generals' War,* 454–55.

58. *1992 Joint Military Net Assessment,* 1–2.

59. *Triumph Without Victory: The Unreported History of the Persian Gulf War* (New York: Times Books, 1992); and Record, *Hollow Victory.*

60. *Certain Victory,* 314.

61. Strobe Talbott, "Post-Victory Blues," *Foreign Affairs* 71 (1991–1992): 59.

62. Gordon and Trainor, *The Generals' War,* 444–46. On the helicopter issue, Schwarzkopf contends that he was duped since the Iraqi negotiator asked only for helicopter flights to carry government officials in regions where roads and bridges were out (*It Doesn't Take a Hero,* 566). Be that as it may, the fact remains that someone more versed in negotiations, particularly with Iraqis, should have been present.

63. Shultz, *Turmoil and Triumph,* 345.

64. Record, *Hollow Victory,* 126. Emphasis in original.

65. Niall Ferguson, *Colossus: The Rise and Fall of the American Empire* (New York: Penguin, 2004), 6.

66. Ivo H. Daalder and James M. Lindsay, "American Empire, Not 'If' but 'What Kind,'" *New York Times,* May 10, 2003.

67. Record, *Hollow Victory,* p. 135; and Michael Mandelbaum, "The Bush Foreign Policy," *Foreign Affairs* 70 (Summer 1991), 10.

68. Powell, "U.S. Forces," 34.

CHAPTER 3: TRANSFORMATION AND CONTAINMENT

1. Elaine Sciolnio, "New Iraqi Site Raided as White House Vows Firmness," *New York Times,* January 23, 1993.

2. William Clinton, "Address to the Nation," Washington, DC, June 26, 1993.

3. Secretary of State Warren Christopher, "The Strategic Priorities of American Foreign Policy," statement before the Senate Foreign Relations Committee, Washington, DC, November 4, 1993.

4. William J. Perry, "Defense in an Age of Hope," *Foreign Affairs* 75 (November–December 1996): 64–79.

5. Anthony Lake, "The Need For Engagement," address to the Woodrow Wilson School, Princeton University, November 30, 1994; and Anthony Lake, "The Price of Leadership," address before the National Press Club, Washington, DC, April 27, 1995.

6. Richard K. Kohn, "Out of Control: The Crisis in Civil-Military Relations," *The National Interest* 35 (Spring 1994): 3–17. See also Don M. Snider and Miranda A. Carlton-Carew, eds., *U.S. Civil-Military Relations: In Crisis or Transition?* (Washington, DC: Center for Strategic and International Studies, 1995); and Michael C. Desch, *Civilian Control of the Military: The Changing Security Environment* (Baltimore: Johns Hopkins University Press, 2001).

7. *Military Transformation: A Strategic Approach* (Washington, DC: Department of Defense Office of Force Transformation, 2003), 12.

8. Marshall was the consummate behind-the-scenes player and normally did not give interviews, publish his thoughts, or make public presentations. One seminal early work that has been circulated is "Some Thoughts on Military Revolutions—Second Version," Memorandum for the Record, Office of the Secretary of Defense, Office of Net Assessment, August 23, 1993. See Debra O. Maddrell, *Quiet Transformation: The Role of the Office of Net Assessment* (Washington, DC: National Defense University, 2003); and James Kitfield, *War and Destiny: How the Bush Revolution in Foreign and Military Affairs Redefined American Power* (Washington, DC: Potomac Books, 2005), 28. The most influential of the early conceptualizers was Dr. Andrew Krepinevich, a retired lieutenant colonel who had worked for Marshall and later headed the Center for Strategic and Budgetary Assessments, a Washington consulting firm. See Andrew Krepinevich, *Transforming the American Military* (Washington, DC: Center for Strategic and Budgetary Assessments, 1997); "Cavalry to Computer: The Pattern of Military Revolutions," *National Interest* 37 (Fall 1994): 30–42; and *The Military-Technical Revolution: A Preliminary Assessment* (Washington, DC: Center for Strategic and Budgetary Assessments, 2002, reprint of a 1991 report prepared for the Office of Net Assessment). For other early analyses, see Jeffrey R. Cooper, *Another View of the Revolution in Military Affairs*; Michael Mazarr, et. al., *The Military Technical Revolution: A Structural Framework*, final report of the CSIS Study Group on the MTR (Washington, DC: Center for Strategic and International Studies, Washington, 1993); Daniel Gouré, "Is There a Military-Technical Revolution in America's Future?" *Washington Quarterly* 16 (Autumn 1993): 175–92; and John W. Bodnar, "The Military Technical Revolution: From Hardware to Information," *Naval War College Review* 46 (Summer 1993): 7–21. Early attempts by the military services to grapple with the concept can be found in *The U.S. Air Force Roundtable on the Revolution in Military Affairs* (McLean, VA: Science Applications International Corporation, January 1994); *The U.S. Navy*

Roundtable on the Revolution in Military Affairs (McLean, VA: Science Applications International Corporation, July 1994); and *The Summary Roundtable on the Revolution in Military Affairs* (McLean, VA: Science Applications International Corporation, October 1994). The most comprehensive (and critical) treatment of the RMA idea as cultivated by the American military is Colin Gray, *Strategy for Chaos: Revolutions in Military Affairs and the Evidence of History* (London: Frank Cass, 2002). His more recent ideas are in *Recognizing and Understanding Revolutionary Change in Warfare: The Sovereignty of Context* (Carlisle Barracks, PA: U.S. Army War College Strategic Studies Institute, 2006).

9. After leaving military service, Owens explained his experience and ideas in *Lifting the Fog of War* (Baltimore, MD: Johns Hopkins University Press, 2000).

10. *Joint Vision 2010* appeared in 1997; *Joint Vision 2020* in 2000.

11. The most comprehensive history and assessment of this is Frederick W. Kagan, *Finding the Target: The Transformation of American Military Policy* (New York: Encounter, 2006).

12. The National Defense Panel was chaired by Philip A. Odeen and included Richard L. Armitage. Gen. Richard D. Hearney, USMC (ret); Adm. David E. Jeremiah, USN (ret); Robert M. Kimmitt; Andrew F. Krepinevich; Gen. James P. McCarthy, USAF (ret); Janne E. Nolan; and Gen. Robert W. RisCassi, USA (ret).

13. *Transforming Defense: National Security in the 21st Century*, Report of the National Defense Panel, December 1997, 1.

14. *Shape, Respond, Prepare Now—a Military Strategy for a New Era* (Washington, DC: Joint Chiefs of Staff, 1997).

15. *A National Security Strategy for a New Century* (Washington, DC: The White House, 1998), 24.

16. *A National Security Strategy for a New Century* (Washington, DC: The White House, 1999), 21.

17. *A National Security Strategy for a Global Age* (Washington, DC: The White House, 2000), 29. These are developed in greater detail in Secretary of Defense William S. Cohen, *Annual Report to the President and Congress* (Washington, DC: Department of Defense, 2000), 123–34.

18. See David A. Ochmanek, "The Air Force: The Next Round," in *Transforming America's Military*, ed. Hans Binnendijk (Washington, DC: National Defense University Center for Technology and National Security Policy, 2002).

19. See Phillip S. Meilinger, "The Origins of Effects-Based Operations," *Joint Force Quarterly* 35 (October 2004): 116–22; Price T. Bingham, "Transforming Warfare With Effects-Based Operations," *Aerospace Power Journal* 15 (Spring 2001): 58–66; and Paul Davis, *Effects Based Operations* (Santa Monica, CA: RAND Corporation, 2001).

20. See Arthur K. Cebrowski and John J. Garstka, "Network-Centric Warfare: Its Origin and Future," *Proceedings of the U.S. Naval Institute* 124 (January 1998): 28–35; and David S. Alberts, John J. Garstka, and Frederic P. Stein, *Network Centric Warfare: Developing and Leveraging Information Superiority* (Washington, DC: Department of Defense C4ISR Cooperative Research Program, 1998).

21. See William D. O'Neil, "The Naval Services: Network-Centric Warfare," in *Transforming America's Military*, ed. Binnendijk.

22. See *Operational Maneuver From the Sea* and *Warfighting Concepts for the 21st Century* (Quantico, VA: U.S. Marine Corps Combat Development Command, 1996).

23. Thomas X. Hammes, *The Sling and the Stone: On War in the 21st Century* (St. Paul, MN: Zenith, 2004), 2. While the notion of fourth-generation warfare has evolved, it has conceptual shortcomings. See Antulio J. Echevarria II, *Fourth-Generation War and Other Myths* (Carlisle Barracks, PA: U.S. Army War College Strategic Studies Institute, 2005).

24. Charles C. Krulak, "The Strategic Corporal: Leadership in the Three Block War," *Marines* 28 (May 1999): 28–34.

25. The Pentagon's notion of asymmetry is traced in Steven Metz and Douglas V. Johnson II, *Asymmetry and U.S. Military Strategy: Definition, Background, and Strategic Concepts* (Carlisle Barracks, PA: U.S. Army War College Strategic Studies Institute, 2001), 2–4. See also Bruce R. Nardulli and Thomas L. McNaugher, "The Army: Toward the Objective Force," in *Transforming America's Military*, ed. Binnendijk.

26. *Army Vision 2010* (Washington, DC: Headquarters, Department of the Army, 1996), 2.

27. *Speed and Knowledge*, the annual report on the Army After Next Project to the Chief of Staff of the Army (Fort Monroe, VA: U.S. Army Training and Doctrine Command, 1997), 9–10.

28. This downward trend, which began during the George H. W. Bush administration, was reversed toward the end of the Clinton administration.

29. William A. Owens, "JROC: Harnessing the Revolution in Military Affairs," *Joint Force Quarterly* 5 (Summer 1994): 56.

30. While the complete PDD was classified, the U.S. Department of State Bureau of International Organization Affairs released an unclassified summary on February 22, 1996.

31. See Dan Henk and Steven Metz, *The United States and the Transformation of African Security: The African Crisis Response Initiative and Beyond* (Carlisle Barracks, PA: U.S. Army War College Strategic Studies Institute, 1997).

32. Leslie H. Gelb, "Quelling the Teacup Wars: The New World's Constant Challenge," *Foreign Affairs* 73 (November–December 1994): 2–6.

33. Michael Mandelbaum, "Foreign Policy as Social Work," *Foreign Affairs* 75 (January–February 1996): 16–32; and Richard K. Betts, "The Delusion of Impartial Intervention," *Foreign Affairs* 73 (November–December 1994): 20–33.

34. For instance, Don M. Snider, Daniel Gouré, and Stephen A. Cambone, *Defense in the Late 1990s: Avoiding the Train Wreck* (Washington, DC: Center for Strategic and International Studies), 1995; John Hillen, "Defense's Death Spiral," *Foreign Affairs* 78 (July–August 1999): 2–7. One of the most detailed and powerful analyses of this was Daniel Gouré, Jeffrey M. Ranney, and James R. Schlesinger, *Averting the Defense Train Wreck in the New Millennium* (Washington, DC: Center for Strategic and International Studies, 1999).

35. Daniel L. Byman and Matthew C. Waxman, *Confronting Iraq: U.S. Policy and the Use of Force Since the Gulf War* (Santa Monica, CA: RAND Corporation, 2000), 26.

36. Kenneth M. Pollack, *The Threatening Storm: The Case for Invading Iraq* (New York: Random House, 2002), 87.

37. William Clinton, "Address to the Nation on Iraq," October 10, 1994.

38. See statement signed by Sheikh Usamah Bin-Muhammad Bin-Ladin; Ayman al-Zawahiri, leader of the Jihad Group in Egypt; Abu-Yasir Rifa'i Ahmad Taha, a leader of the Islamic Group; Sheikh Mir Hamzah, secretary of the Jamiat-ul-Ulema-e-Pakistan; and Fazlul Rahman, leader of the Jihad Movement in Bangladesh, published in *Al-Quds al-'Arabi* on February 23, 1998.

39. Noam Chomsky, *Iraq Under Siege: The Deadly Impact of Sanctions and War* (Boston: South End Press, 2000); David Cortright, "A Hard Look at Iraq Sanctions," *The Nation*, November 15, 2001; and Peace Action Education Fund, "End Sanctions on Iraq," n.d.

40. John Mueller and Karl Mueller, "Sanctions of Mass Destruction," *Foreign Affairs* 78 (May–June 1999): 43–53; F. Gregory Gause III, "Getting It Backwards on Iraq," *Foreign Affairs* 78 (May–June 1999): 54–65; and Congressman Cynthia McKinney (D-GA), "Must Children Die for Hussein's Defeat?" *Detroit Free Press*, September 20, 1999. Other examples include George Capaccio, "Sanctions Harm Ordinary Iraqis," *Baltimore Sun*, November 23, 1997; Stephen Kinzer, "Smart Bombs, Dumb Sanctions," *New York Times*, January 3, 1999; Sam Husseini, "Twisted Policy on Iraq," *Washington Post*, January 26, 1999; Denis Halliday, "End the Catastrophe of Sanctions Against Iraq," *Seattle Post-Intelligencer*, February 12, 1999; Charley Reese, "Embargo Makes Deathbeds of Hospital Beds for Children," *Orlando Sentinel*, March 2, 1999; Mary K. Meyer, "In Iraq, Children Carry the Burden of Sanctions," *Kansas City Star*, September 16, 1999; "A Morally Unsustainable Iraq Policy," *Chicago Tribune*, September 17, 1999; Steve Chapman, "Persisting in Futility on the Iraq Sanctions," *Chicago Tribune*, March 2, 2000; and Lewis W. Diuguid, "Punish Hussein, Not Iraqis," *Kansas City Star*, June 8, 2000.

41. William Clinton, "Address to the Nation Announcing Military Strikes on Iraq," December 16, 1998.

42. Byman and Waxman, *Confronting Iraq*, 68.

43. Stephen J. Glain, "Iraq Refuses to Readmit U.N. Inspectors," *New York Times*, December 22, 1998.

44. Pollack, *The Threatening Storm*, 72–73.

45. Daniel Byman, Kenneth Pollack, and Gideon Rose, "The Rollback Fantasy," *Foreign Affairs* 78 (January–February 1999): 24.

46. Public Law 105-338, codified in a note to 22 USCS § 2151.

47. William Clinton, "Statement on Signing the Iraq Liberation Act of 1998," *Weekly Compilation of Presidential Documents*, November 9, 1998.

48. Samuel R. Berger, remarks on Iraq at Stanford University, Palo Alto, CA, December 8, 1998.

49. Daniel Byman, "After the Storm: U.S. Policy Toward Iraq Since 1991," *Political Science Quarterly* 115 (Winter 2000–2001): 514.

50. Joshua Muravchik, *Apply the Reagan Doctrine to Iraq* (Washington, DC: American Enterprise Institute, 1999).

51. See Byman, Pollack, and Rose, "The Rollback Fantasy," 24–41; Pollack, *The Threatening Storm*, 117–118; and Daniel Byman, "Proceed With Caution: U.S. Support for the Iraqi Opposition," *Washington Quarterly* 22 (Summer 1999): 23–38.

52. Anthony Zinni (USMC), testimony before the Senate Armed Services Committee, January 28, 1999.

53. In the final months of the Clinton administration, Vice President Gore did press for and gain some funding for the Iraqi opposition. (Jim Hoagland, "Don't Fear Saddam," *Washington Post*, October 10, 2000; and Pollack, *The Threatening Storm*, 99–100.

54. Daniel Byman, "A Farewell to Arms Inspections," *Foreign Affairs* 79 (January–February 2000), 119–32.

55. Andrew J. Bacevich, "Saddam Is Reversing Gulf War Defeat," *Wall Street Journal*, January 20, 2000.

56. Daniel Byman, "All Talk, No Action May Be Best With Iraq," *Washington Post*, January 2, 2000.

CHAPTER 4: TERRORISM AND FORCE

1. Ivo H. Daalder and James M. Lindsay, *America Unbound: The Bush Revolution in Foreign Policy* (Washington, DC: Brookings Institution Press, 2003), 37. The "Vulcans" included Condoleezza Rice, Paul Wolfowitz, Dov Zakheim, Richard Armitage, Richard Perle, Stephen Hadley, Robert Blackwill, and Robert Zoellick. For their backgrounds, see Mann, *Rise of the Vulcans*.

2. George W. Bush, "A Period of Consequences," speech at the Citadel, Charleston, SC, September 23, 1999.

3. Condoleezza Rice, "Promoting the National Interest," *Foreign Affairs* 79 (January–February 2000): 45–62. Similar themes appeared in Robert B. Zoellick, "A Republican Foreign Policy," *Foreign Affairs* 79 (January–February 2000): 63–78.

4. Rice, "Promoting the National Interest," 53.

5. Daalder and Lindsay insist that the phrase "democratic imperialists" is more accurate. For a detailed but highly critical assessment of the origins and development of this group, see Stefan Halper and Jonathan Clarke, *America Alone: The Neo-Conservatives and the Global Order* (New York: Cambridge University Press, 2004). For a defense, see Robert G. Kaufman, *In Defense of the Bush Doctrine* (Lexington: University Press of Kentucky, 2007). For a balanced treatment by a scholar often considered a "neo-conservative," see Francis Fukuyama, *America at the Crossroads: Democracy, Power, and the Neoconservative Legacy* (New Haven, CT: Yale University Press, 2006).

6. William Kristol and Robert Kagan, "Toward a Neo-Reaganite Foreign Policy," *Foreign Affairs* 75 (July–August 1996): 23.

7. Charles Krauthammer, "The Unipolar Moment Revisited," *The National Interest* 70 (Winter 2002–2003): 5.

8. Kristol and Kagan, "Toward a Neo-Reaganite Foreign Policy," 18–32.

9. Robert Kagan and William Kristol, eds., *Present Dangers: Crisis and Opportunity in American Foreign and Defense Policy* (San Francisco: Encounter, 2000).

10. Douglas J. Feith, "U.S. Strategy for the War on Terrorism," speech at the University of Chicago Political Union, April 14, 2004.

11. George W. H. Bush, "Address to a Joint Session of Congress and the American People," September 21, 2001.

12. Ibid.

13. Wang Gungwu, "City, and Citadel, on the Hill," *National Interest* 69 (Fall 2002): 23.

14. See, for instance, *Seeking a National Strategy: A Concert for Preserving Security and Promoting Freedom*, the Phase II report of the United States Commission on National Security, 21st Century, 2000.

15. Richard A. Clarke, *Against All Enemies: Inside America's War on Terror* (New York: Free Press, 2004), 155.

16. Presidential Decision Directive 39, "U.S. Policy on Counterterrorism," June 21, 1995.

17. Carla Anne Robbins and Jeanne Cummings, "New Doctrine: How Bush Decided That Iraq's Hussein Must Be Ousted," *Wall Street Journal*, June 14, 2002.

18. Journalist Ron Suskind argues that Vice President Cheney was the driving force in this shift (*The One Percent Doctrine: Deep Inside America's Pursuit of Its Enemies Since 9/11* [New York: Simon and Schuster, 2006]).

19. George W. Bush, "President Bush Delivers Graduation Speech at West Point, U.S. Military Academy, West point, NY, June1, 2002 " Emphasis added.

20. Donald H. Rumsfeld, prepared testimony for the Senate Armed Services Committee hearings on Iraq, September 19, 2002. Emphasis added.

21. Richard Cheney, "Vice President Speaks at the Veterans of Foreign Wars 103rd National Convention, Nashville, TN, August 26, 2002." Emphasis added.

22. "Remarks by the Vice President to the Heritage Foundation," Washington, DC, October 11, 2003.

23. *Quadrennial Defense Review Report* (Washington, DC: Department of Defense, 2001), 5. (Henceforth *QDR 2001*).

24. Ibid., 13.

25. Ibid., 14.

26. Stephen Biddle assesses the strengths and shortcomings of the "Afghan model" in *Afghanistan and the Future of Warfare: Implications for Army and Defense Policy* (Carlisle Barracks, PA: U.S. Army War College Strategic Studies Institute, 2002).

27. *National Security Strategy of the United States of America* (Washington, DC: The White house, September 2002), ix.

28. See Norman Podhoretz, *World War IV: The Long Struggle Against Islamofascism* (New York: Doubleday, 2007); David Frum and Richard Perle, *An End to Evil: How to Win the War on Terror* (New York: Ballantine, 2004); and Newt Gingrich on NBC's *Meet the Press*, July 16, 2006.

29. Michael Howard, "What Friends Are For," *National Interest* 69 (Fall 2002): 8.

30. Quoted in Bob Woodward, *Bush at War* (New York: Simon and Schuster, 2002), 42.
31. Robert W. Tucker, "The End of a Contradiction?" *National Interest* 69 (Fall 2002): 7.
32. *National Strategy for Combating Terrorism* (Washington DC: The White House, 2003) 22.
33. *National Strategy for Combating Terrorism* (Washington, DC: The White House, 2006) 9.
34. Fareed Zakaria, *The Future of Freedom: Illiberal Democracy at Home and Abroad* (New York: W. W. Norton, 2004).
35. *National Strategy for Combating Terrorism*, September 2006, 9.
36. Ibid., 10.
37. This was noted and assessed in David Kilcullen, "Countering Global Insurgency," *Journal of Strategic Studies* 28 (August 2005): 597–617.

CHAPTER 5: DECISION AND TRIUMPH
1. Quoted in "Iraq: 'Evil Policy' Caused Attack," *Washington Post*, September 13, 2001.
2. Michael R. Gordon and Bernard E. Trainor, *Cobra II: The Inside Story of the Invasion and Occupation of Iraq* (New York: Pantheon, 2006), 10.
3. *Final Report of the National Commission on Terrorist Attacks Upon the United States*, July 24, 2004, 334.
4. Clarke, *Against All Enemies*, 32.
5. Robin Wright and Doyle McManus, "After the Attack, Military Options," *Los Angeles Times*, September 21, 2001; Patrick E. Tyler and Elaine Sciolino, "Bush's Advisers Split on Scope of Retaliation," *New York Times*, September 20, 2001; Woodward, *Bush at War*, 81; and Bob Woodward, *Plan of Attack* (New York: Simon and Schuster, 2004), 25.
6. *Final Report of the National Commission on Terrorist Attacks Upon the United States*, 335.
7. For instance, Laurie Mylroie, *Study of Revenge: Saddam Hussein's Unfinished War Against America* (Washington, DC: American Enterprise Institute Press, 2000).
8. R. James Woolsey, "The Iraq Connection," *Wall Street Journal*, October 18, 2001.
9. Richard Perle, "The U.S. Must Strike at Saddam Hussein," *New York Times*, December 28, 2001.
10. Charles Krauthammer, "The War: A Roadmap," *Washington Post*, September 28, 2001.
11. William F. Buckley Jr., "Evidence Against Iraq?" *National Review*, November 19, 2001, 62.
12. Richard Lowry, "End Iraq," *National Review*, October 15, 2001, 33.
13. Quoted in Karen DeYoung and Rick Weiss, "U.S. Seems to Ease Rhetoric on Iraq," *Washington Post*, October 24, 2001.
14. Quoted in Ronald Brownstein, "Hawks Urge Bush to Extend Military Campaign to Iraq," *Los Angeles Times*, November 20, 2001.
15. Woodward, *Plan of Attack*, 4.

16. George Tenet, *At the Center of the Storm: My Years at the CIA* (New York: HarperCollins, 2007), 341–56.
17. George W. Bush, "President Welcomes Aid Workers Rescued From Afghanistan," remarks at the White House, Washington, DC, November 26, 2001.
18. L. Paul Bremer, "Iraq Shouldn't Be the Next Stop in War on Terror," *Wall Street Journal*, December 6, 2001.
19. Brent Scowcroft, "Build a Coalition," *Washington Post*, October 16, 2001.
20. Tenet, *At the Center of the Storm*, 301.
21. Woodward, *Bush at War*, 329; and Woodward, *Plan of Attack*, 108–9.
22. Tenet, *At the Center of the Storm*, 304.
23. George W. Bush, "President Discusses the Future of Iraq," remarks to the American Enterprise Institute, Washington Hilton, Washington, DC, February 23, 2003.
24. Quoted in Bill Keller, "The Sunshine Warrior," *New York Times*, September 22, 2002.
25. Bush, "President Discusses the Future of Iraq," February 23, 2003.
26. George W. Bush, "President Delivers State of the Union Address," January 29, 2002.
27. George W. Bush, "President Holds Press Conference," the White House, Washington, DC, March 13, 2002.
28. In February 2002 congressional testimony, Secretary of State Powell had stated, "With respect to the nuclear program, there is no doubt that the Iraqis are pursuing it. The best intelligence we have suggests that it isn't something they have ready to pop out in the next year or so. It would take them quite a bit longer than that in the absence of external help" (*The President's International Affairs Budget Request for FY 2003*, hearing before the U.S. House of Representatives Committee on International Relations, 107th Congr., 2d sess., February 6, 2002).
29. Michael R. Gordon, "U.S. Seen as Likely to Stay on Collision Path With Iraq," *New York Times*, March 9, 2002; and Woodward, *Plan of Attack*, 111–112.
30. Jeanne Cummings, "Bush Shifts Focus to State Links With Terrorists," *Wall Street Journal*, May 24, 2002.
31. Thomas E. Ricks, "Some Top Military Brass Favor Status Quo in Iraq," *Washington Post*, July 28, 2001.
32. Quoted in Thomas E. Ricks, "Timing, Tactics on Iraq War Disputed," *Washington Post*, August 1, 2002.
33. Tommy Franks with Malcom McConnell, *American Soldier* (New York: Regan, 2004), 329.
34. The most rigorous assessment of attempts to apply the Afghan model to Iraq is in Pollack, *The Threatening Storm*, 293–334. Pollack demonstrates the infeasibility of this and hence advocates a full-scale invasion.
35. Michael Dobbs, "Old Strategy on Iraq Sparks New Debate," *Washington Post*, December 27, 2001.
36. Franks, *American Soldier*, 373.
37. For an explanation of the U.S. military's deliberate planning process, see *The Joint Staff Officer's Guide* (Norfolk, VA: Joint Forces Staff College, 2000), chapter 4.

38. U.S. Central Command briefing slides, August 15, 2002, available from the National Security Archive, Washington, DC.
39. Franks, *American Soldier*, 339–40.
40. Thomas E. Ricks, "War Plans Target Hussein Power Base," *Washington Post*, September 22, 2002.
41. Quoted in Ricks, "War Plans Target Hussein Power Base."
42. According to an interview by the author with a former Republican Guard noncommissioned officer in April 2003, the Republican Guard received no training in urban operations. This also holds for the regular Army. Until the moment of his demise, Hussein clearly feared his own military as much or more than the Americans.
43. Franks, *American Soldier*, 367.
44. Matthew Rycroft, Private Secretary to Prime Minister Tony Blair, memo to David Manning, U.K. ambassador to the United States, July 23, 2002 (the "Downing Street memo").
45. George W. Bush, "Remarks by the President in Address to the United Nations General Assembly," New York, NY, September 12, 2002.
46. George W. Bush, "President Bush, Colombia President Uribe Discuss Terrorism," the White House, Washington, DC, September 25, 2002.
47. Vice President Dick Cheney interviewed by Tim Russert on NBC News *Meet the Press*, September 8, 2002.
48. National Security Adviser Condoleezza Rice interviewed by Margaret Warner on *PBS NewsHour*, September 25, 2002.
49. George W. Bush, "President's Radio Address," February 8, 2003.
50. George W. Bush, "President's Radio Address," March 8, 2003.
51. George W. Bush, "President George Bush Discusses Iraq in National Press Conference," March 6, 2003.
52. Colin Powell, "Address to the U.N. Security Council," February 5, 2003.
53. Rumsfeld, prepared testimony for the Senate Armed Services Committee Hearings on Iraq.
54. There were a few bold exceptions such as Jeffrey Record, *Bounding the Global War on Terrorism* (Carlisle Barracks, PA: U.S. Army War College, 2003). Secretary Rumsfeld scoffed at this scholarly analysis in a press conference.
55. Inspector General, United States Department of Defense, Deputy Inspector General for Intelligence, *Review of the Pre–Iraqi War Activities of the Under Secretary of Defense for Policy*, Report No. 07-INTEL-04, February 9, 2007, 4. See also Jesse Nunes, "Pentagon Report Debunks Prewar Iraq–al Qaeda Connection," *Christian Science Monitor*, April 6, 2007; Tom Regan, "Pentagon: Prewar Intel on al Qaeda–Hussein Link Not Illegal But 'Dubious,'" *Christian Science Monitor*, February 9, 2007; R. Jeffrey Smith, "Hussein's Prewar Ties to Al-Qaeda Discounted," *Washington Post*, April 6, 2007; "Prewar Report Doubted Iraq–al Qaeda Tie," CNN, November 6, 2005; and "Prewar CIA Report Doubted Claim That al Qaeda Sought WMD in Iraq," CNN, November 11, 2005.
56. Stephen F. Hayes, "Target Iraq?" *The Weekly Standard*, October 1, 2001, 23–24. Hayes continued making the point in *The Weekly Standard* and, later, in

The Connection: How al Qaeda's Collaboration With Saddam Hussein Has Endangered America (New York: HarperCollins, 2004).

57. George Tenet, "Evolving Dangers in a Complex World" (as prepared for delivery), Testimony for the Senate Select Committee on Intelligence on the Worldwide Threat 2003, February 11, 2003.

58. Cheney, "Vice President Speaks at the Veterans of Foreign Wars 103rd National Convention," and Vice President Dick Cheney interviewed by Tim Russert on NBC News *Meet the Press*, March 16, 2003.

59. Powell, "Addresses U.N. Security Council."

60. George W. Bush, "President's Remarks at the United Nations General Assembly," September 12, 2003.

61. Deputy Secretary of Defense Paul Wolfowitz, response to questions in Department of Defense Budget Priorities for Fiscal Year 2004, hearing before the Committee on the Budget, House of Representatives, 108th Congr., 1st ses., February 27, 2003. There is a myth that Shinseki was fired after this, spread by people like Congressman Nancy Pelosi and Senator John Kerry (Pelosi on Comedy Central's *The Daily Show*, November 30, 2005; Kerry, Press Conference, Tipton, IA, October 5, 2004). In reality, General Shinseki had already set a retirement date well before his testimony, in large part because of tensions with Rumsfeld. Secretary of the Army Thomas White was fired after agreeing with Shinseki's assessment for Iraq but this too was simply the straw that broke the camel's back. The bigger issue was Rumsfeld's contention that the Army leadership was hidebound and resistant to change.

62. Secretary Rumsfeld Media Availability with Afghan President Karzai, the Pentagon, February 27, 2003.

63. Cheney interviewed by Tim Russert.

64. Wolfowitz, testimony, Committee on the Budget, House of Representatives.

65. Cheney interviewed by Tim Russert.

66. Rumsfeld, testimony for the Senate Armed Services Committee Hearings on Iraq.

67. Woodward, *Plan of Attack*, 149.

68. I am indebted to Don Snider for this observation.

69. Thomas E. Ricks, *Fiasco: The American Military Adventure in Iraq* (New York: Penguin, 2006), 42; Thomas E. Ricks, "Military Bids to Postpone Iraq Invasion," *Washington Post*, May 24, 2002; Christopher Marquis, "Bush Officials Differ on Way to Force Out Iraqi Leader," *New York Times*, June 19, 2002; Ricks, "Some Top Military Brass Favor Status Quo in Iraq"; and Ricks, "Timing, Tactics on Iraq War Disputed.

70. See H. R. McMaster, *Dereliction of Duty: Johnson, McNamara, the Joint Chiefs of Staff, and the Lies That Led to Vietnam* (New York: HarperCollins, 1997).

71. Joseph H. Biden Jr., "Opening statement," *Hearings to Examine Threats, Responses, and Regional Considerations Surrounding Iraq*, United States Senate Committee on Foreign Relations, 107th Congr., 2d ses., July 31 and August 1, 2002, 1.

72. Richard Butler, testimony in *Hearings to Examine Threats, Responses, and Regional Considerations Surrounding Iraq*, 10.

73. Khidhir Hamza, testimony in *Hearings to Examine Threats, Responses, and Regional Considerations Surrounding Iraq*, 18–19. Butler repeated the claim that "there are detailed accounts available now of the throughput through that center [Salman Pak] of a variety of nationalities, most of them from countries in the Middle East" (p. 57). Postwar assessments supported a 2002 report by the Defense Intelligence Agency that found that there was no evidence to support the claim that Iraq trained al-Qaeda or other transnational terrorists at Salman Pak (*Report of the Senate Select Committee on Postwar Findings About Iraq's WMD Programs and Links to Terrorism and How They Compare With Prewar Assessments*, 109th Congr., 2d sess., September 8, 2006). As with many of the Iraqi exiles that the Bush administration used to build its case for war, Hamza's credentials and information were disputed (Robert Collier, "Bush's Evidence of Threat Disputed," *San Francisco Chronicle*, October 12, 2002). For a good summary of the prewar intelligence on Hussein's WMD programs, see Kenneth M. Pollack, "Spies, Lies, and Weapons: What Went Wrong," *Atlantic Monthly*, January–February 2004, 78–92.

74. Morton Halperin, testimony in *Hearings to Examine Threats, Responses, and Regional Considerations Surrounding Iraq*, 82.

75. Lt. Gen. Thomas G. McInerney, USAF (ret), in *Hearings to Examine Threats, Responses, and Regional Considerations Surrounding Iraq*, 91.

76. Fouad Ajami, testimony in *Hearings to Examine Threats, Responses, and Regional Considerations Surrounding Iraq*, 126.

77. Samuel R. Berger, testimony in *Hearings to Examine Threats, Responses, and Regional Considerations Surrounding Iraq*, 239.

78. Richard C. Holbrooke, testimony in *Next Steps in Iraq*, hearings before the United States Senate Committee on Foreign Relations, 107th Congr., 2d sess., September 25 and 26, 2002, 6.

79. Madeleine Albright, testimony in *Next Steps in Iraq*, p. 53.

80. Ken Adelman, "Cakewalk in Iraq," *Washington Post*, February 13, 2002.

81. Lawrence F. Kaplan and William Kristol, *The War Over Iraq: Saddam's Tyranny and America's* Mission (San Francisco: Encounter, 2003); Kenneth M. Pollack, "Next Stop Baghdad?" *Foreign Affairs* 81 (March–April 2002): 32–47; and Pollack, *The Threatening Storm*.

82. Joshua Micah Marshall, "The Reluctant Hawk: The Skeptical Case for Regime Change in Iraq," *Washington Monthly*, November 2002, 43.

83. Elisabeth Bumiller, "Bush Aides Set Strategy to Sell Policy on Iraq," *New York Times*, September 7, 2002.

84. Galbraith, *The End of Iraq*, 76–77.

85. George W. Bush, "President Bush to Send Iraq Resolution to Congress Today," remarks by the president in photo opportunity with Secretary of State Colin Powell, September 19, 2002.

86. Colin Powell on Fox News *Sunday*, September 8, 2002.

87. Colin Powell, testimony before the Senate Foreign Relations Committee, September 26, 2002.

88. Bush, "President Bush to Send Iraq Resolution to Congress."

89. Colin Powell, testimony before the Senate Foreign Relations Committee, September 26, 2002.

222

90. Tenet, *At the Center of the Storm*, 321.
91. Only the State Department's Bureau of Intelligence and Research (INR) rejected the notion that Iraq had resumed its nuclear weapons program.
92. Ricks, *Fiasco*, 61; and Tenet, *At the Center of the Storm*, 334–35.
93. United Nations Security Council Resolution 1441, adopted November 8, 2002.
94. Donald Rumsfeld quoted in Woodward, *Plan of Attack*, 234.
95. Franks, *American Soldier*, 342–45.
96. John Hendren, "Punishing Airstrikes Are First Stage of War, Analysts Say," *Los Angeles Times*, September 27, 2002.
97. Thomas E. Ricks, "War Plan for Iraq Largely in Place," *Washington Post*, March 2, 2003.
98. Paul Wolfowitz interviewed by Melissa Block on National Public Radio, February 19, 2003.
99. For instance, the administration never released a March 2003 report by the State Department's Bureau of Intelligence and Research that was skeptical of both the prospects for democracy in Iraq and that attempting to build a democracy in Iraq would promote reform elsewhere in the Islamic world (Greg Miller, "A State Department Report Disputes Bush's Claim That Ousting Hussein Will Spur Reform in the Mideast, Intelligence Officials Say," *Los Angeles Times*, March 14, 2003).
100. Marc I. Grossman, under secretary of state for political affairs, statement before the Senate Foreign Relations Committee in the *Future of Iraq* hearing, 108th Congr., 1st sess., February 11, 2003.
101. David Rieff, "Blueprint for a Mess," *New York Times Magazine*, November 2, 2003, 31.
102. The working groups were Transitional Justice; Public Finance; Public Outreach Development; Democratic Principles; Water, Agriculture, and the Environment; Public Health and Humanitarian Needs; Defense Policy; Local Government; Economy and Infrastructure; Civil Society Capacity-Building; Transparency and Anti-Corruption; Education; Return of Refugees; Building a Free Media; Foreign Policy; Oil and Energy; and Preserving Cultural Heritage. This information is drawn from U.S. Department of State briefing entitled "Future of Iraq Project," May 12, 2003, available from the National Security Archive, Washington, DC.
103. "Pre-War Planning for Post-War Iraq," undated fact sheet from the Office of Near Eastern and South Asian Affairs, Office of the Assistant Secretary of Defense for International Security Affairs.
104. Douglas J. Feith, under secretary of defense for policy, interview with the *Washington Post*, February 21, 2003 (transcript from the U.S. Department of Defense, Office of the Assistant Secretary of Defense for Public Affairs).
105. Douglas J. Feith, statement before the Senate Foreign Relations Committee in the *Future of Iraq* hearing, February 11, 2003.
106. Jay Garner, conversations with the author, Baghdad, May 2003. Col. Kevin Benson (ret) told me that Garner had a signed letter from president Bush that gave him the full authority of the President (conversation with the

author, McLean, VA, November 2007). Clearly Franks, Rumsfeld, and others never gave Garner this degree of power.

107. Quoted in James Fallows, "Blind Into Baghdad," *Atlantic Monthly,* January–February 2004, 58.

108. Future of Iraq Project, Report of the Democratic Principles Working Group, November 2002, 16 (available from the National Security Archive, Washington, DC).

109. Neil King Jr., "Bush Has an Audacious Plan to Rebuild Iraq Within a Year," *Wall Street Journal,* March 17, 2003; and Joseph J. Collins, deputy assistant secretary of defense for stability operations, briefing on Humanitarian Relief Planning for Iraq, the Pentagon, February 25, 2003.

110. Kellogg Brown and Root officially separated from Halliburton in April 2007 to become a stand-alone company called KBR, Inc.

111. Elizabeth Becker, "U.S. Business Will Get Role in Rebuilding Occupied Iraq," *New York Times,* March 18, 2003. There seems to have been little consideration that the distinction between a reconstruction project run by the U.S. military and one run by a U.S. contractor might be lost on most Iraqis.

112. During the 1991 war Norman Schwarzkopf, the CENTCOM commander, exercised overall command of the operation himself. Because Franks was still responsible for operations in Afghanistan and other elements of the war on terror, he delegated command of the war to a subordinate organization—CFLCC.

113. Kevin C. M. Benson, "'Phase IV' CFLCC Stability Operations Planning," in *Turning Victory Into Success: Military Operations After the Campaign* Brian M. DeToy ed. (Fort Leavenworth, KS: Combat Studies Institute Press, 2004), 184. Colonel Benson was CFLCC's lead planner. See also Kevin C. M. Benson, "OIF Phase IV: A Planner's Reply to Brigadier Aylwin-Foster," *Military Review* 86 (March–April 2006): 61–67; and Kevin Benson interviewed by John McCool, Operational Leadership Experiences Project, Fort Leavenworth, KS, October 10, 2006.

114. Benson, conversation with the author.

115. Tyler Marshall and David Lamb, "Other Nations, and Especially the Arab World, Fear the Start of an American Empire," *Los Angeles Times,* March 16, 2003.

116. Ronald Brownstein, "U.S. Has Severe Image Problem in Much of Europe, Poll Finds," *Los Angeles Times,* March 19, 2003; Robin Wright, "Polls Find Arabs Are Extremely Antiwar," *Los Angeles Times,* March 15, 2003; Sonni Efron, "U.S. Losing Popularity in the World," *Los Angeles Times,* December 5, 2002; William Boston, "European Leaders, Public at Odds Over War With Iraq," *Christian Science Monitor,* January 17, 2003; Glenn Frankel, "Sneers From Across the Atlantic," *Washington Post,* February 11, 2003; and Glenn Kessler and Mike Allen, "Bush Faces Increasingly Poor Image Overseas," *Washington Post,* February 24, 2003.

117. Michael Dobbs, "On Iraq, Chorus of Criticism Is Loud but Not Clear," *Washington Post,* February 3, 2003.

118. Bill Bradley, "Bush Has Not Made the Case," *Washington Post,* February 2, 2003.

119. John J. Mearsheimer and Stephen M. Walt, "An Unnecessary War," *Foreign Policy* 134 (January–February 2003): 50–59.
120. *Iraq: The Day After*, report of an independent task force sponsored by the Council on Foreign Relations, January 2003; and *A Wiser Peace: An Action Strategy for a Post-Conflict Iraq* (Washington, DC: Center for Strategic and International Studies, January 2003).
121. Anthony H. Cordesman, *Planning for a Self-Inflicted Wound: US Policy to Reshape a Post–Saddam Iraq* (Washington, DC: Center for Strategic and International Studies, revision 3, December 31, 2002).
122. Janet Hook, "On Iraq, Congress Cedes All the Authority to Bush," *Los Angeles Times*, March 9, 2003.
123. John Keegan, *The Iraq War* (New York: Alfred A. Knopf, 2004), 119; and Woodward, *Plan of Attack*, 292.
124. Woodward, *Plan of Attack*, 346.
125. Steven R. Weisman, "A Long, Winding Road to a Diplomatic Dead End," *New York Times*, March 17, 2003.
126. Maura Reynolds, "Most Unconvinced on Iraq War," *Los Angeles Times*, December 17, 2002; and Richard Morin and Claudia Deane, "71% of Americans Support War, Poll Shows," *Washington Post*, March 19, 2003.
127. This was reminiscent of CENTCOM's ability to convince Hussein that it was launching an amphibious operation to recapture Kuwait in the 1991 war. Throughout its conflict with the United States, Iraq suffered from a pervasive lack of intelligence and from Hussein's own misperceptions and prejudices.
128. While in captivity before his execution, Hussein told his American interrogator that the stories of look-alikes were not true.
129. Franks, *American Solder*, 450–61. It later turned out that Hussein was not at that location. In fact, the information that he was to be there may have been a scam to smoke out those within the Iraqi security forces who were providing information to the CIA.
130. As it turned out, the Iraqis had done relatively little to sabotage the oil fields. As part of a research team in Iraq in late April and early May 2003, my colleagues and I asked a number of Iraqi military prisoners being held at the detention center at Camp Bucca, Iraq, why this was not done. We were not able to ascertain whether Hussein had no intention of destroying the fields in the first place or his orders were simply ignored.
131. I was told by captured Iraqi officers at Camp Bucca, Iraq, that their units were deployed with inadequate weapons, limited stocks of ammunition, no hope of artillery support or reinforcement, and no real mission other than fighting as long as they could. An Iraqi artillery officer told me that some of his troops had never fired a live round in training. Most of the officers either ordered their troops to go home, ignored it when the troops deserted, or abandoned the troops themselves.
132. Franks, *American Soldier*, 486.
133. See Tim Pritchard, *Ambush Alley: The Most Extraordinary Battle of the Iraq War* (New York: Random House, 2005).

134. Quoted in Rajiv Chandrasekaran and William Branigin, "Suicide Bombing Kills Four Soldiers," *Washington Post*, March 30, 2003.

135. Quoted in John F. Burns, "Iraqis Threatening New Suicide Strikes Against U.S. Forces," *New York Times*, March 30, 2003.

136. George W. Bush, "President Rallies the Troops at MacDill Air Force Base in Tampa," March 26, 2003.

137. DOD News Briefing—Secretary Rumsfeld and General Myers, the Pentagon, March 28, 2003.

138. Iraqi prisoners interviewed by the author and colleagues, Camp Bucca, Iraq, April 2003.

139. I interviewed a former Republican Guard noncommissioned officer in Camp Bucca, Iraq, in April 2003 who described a major movement of his division that CFLCC was unaware of.

140. Quoted in Rajiv Chandrasekaran and Peter Baker, "Baghdad-Bound Forces Pass Outer Defenses," *Washington Post*, April 3, 2003.

141. For an excellent account of the Marines' campaign, see Bing West, *The March Up: Taking Baghdad With the United States Marines* (New York: Bantam, 2004).

142. Venon Loeb and Bradley Graham, "Military to Impose Cordon on Baghdad," *Washington Post*, April 6, 2003. The U.S. Army had explored this method of urban combat, which it called the "indirect approach," beginning in the late 1990s and relied heavily on war-games. See, for instance, Robert H. Scales, Jr., *Future Warfare Anthology*, rev. ed. (Carlisle Barracks, PA: U.S. Army War College Strategic Studies Institute, 2001), 203–16.

143. Republican Guard noncommissioned officer, interview with the author, Camp Bucca, Iraq, April 2003.

144. Maj. Gen. James Thurman, C3 (Operations) director, CFLCC, interview with the author, Camp Doha, Kuwait, April 2003.

145. Col. David Perkins, interview with the author and colleagues, Baghdad, May 2003.

CHAPTER 6: COUNTERINSURGENCY

1. Accounts of who fired first are conflicting. See Ian Fisher, "U.S. Force Said to Kill 15 Iraqis During an Anti-American Rally," *New York Times*, April 30, 2003.

2. Amy Waldman, "Cleric Wants Iraqis to Write Constitution," *New York Times*, July 1, 2003; Neil MacFarquhar, "In Najaf, a Sudden Anti-U.S. Storm," *New York Times*, July 21, 2003; L. Paul Bremer, *My Year in Iraq: The Struggle to Build a Future of Hope* (New York: Simon and Schuster, 2006), 94; Larry Diamond, *Squandered Victory: The American Occupation and the Bungled Effort to Bring Democracy to Iraq* (New York: Henry Holt, 2005), 44; and W. Andrew Terrill, *The United States and Iraq's Shiite Clergy: Partners or Adversaries?* (Carlisle Barracks, PA: U.S. Army War College Strategic Studies Institute, 2004), 11.

3. Donald H. Rumsfeld, prepared testimony for the Senate Armed Services Committee, Washington, DC, July 9, 2003.

4. Maj. Gen. Raymond Odierno, video news briefing from Baghdad, June 18, 2003. A year later General Odierno reiterated that he did not think the

Iraqi resistance constituted an insurgency until about July 2003 (Ricks, *Fiasco*, 171).

5. "DOD News Briefing—Mr. Di Rita and General Abizaid," U.S. Department of Defense news transcript, July 16, 2003. See also Vernon Loeb, "'Guerrilla' War Acknowledged," *Washington Post*, July 17, 2003.

6. Ricks, *Fiasco*, 215.

7. An important exception was then-Maj. John Nagl, who wrote a Ph.D. dissertation at Oxford University that was later published as *Learning to Eat Soup With a Knife: Counterinsurgency Lessons From Malaya and Vietnam* (New York: Praeger, 2002). When the United States became involved in Iraq, this book became very popular within the military and defense communities, and was later released in paperback by the University of Chicago Press.

8. Since most Kurds are also Sunni, I have elected to follow the lead of many Iraq experts and use the phrase "Sunni Arab insurgents."

9. "In Their Own Words: Reading the Iraqi Insurgency," *Middle East Report* 50 (Brussels: International Crisis Group, 2006), 23–25. Michael Eisenstadt and Jeffrey White explain it in a slightly different way, dividing military operations into counter-coalition, counter-collaboration, counter-mobility, counter-reconstruction, and counter-stability activities. (*Assessing Iraq's Sunni Arab Insurgency* [Washington, DC: Washington Institute for Near East Studies, 2005], 19).

10. Bremer, *My Year in Iraq*, 26. Emphasis in original.

11. Email correspondence with the author, June 2004. The Operation Iraqi Freedom after-action report of the 3rd Infantry Division (Mechanized), for example, admits that the unit did not have a fully developed plan for the transition to stabilization and support operations (p. 17). This undoubtedly held for others as well.

12. Email correspondence with the author, June 2004.

13. Michael Kilian, "Areas Bypassed in War Are Problem, Rumsfeld Explains," *Chicago Tribune*, June 19, 2003.

14. Rajiv Chandrasekaran, *Imperial Life in the Emerald City: Inside Iraq's Green Zone* (New York: Alfred A. Knopf, 2006), 28–37; and George Packer, *The Assassins' Gate: America in Iraq* (New York: Farrar, Straus, and Giroux, 2005), 120–135.

15. This was reinforced in discussions the author held with ORHA personnel in Baghdad, May 2003, and multiple email interviews with brigade and battalion commanders and staff officers who served in Iraq from 2003 to 2004.

16. Quoted in Timothy Carney, "We're Getting in Our Own Way," *Washington Post*, June 22, 2003. Ambassador Carney was a senior member of the ORHA–CPA staff. The arrival of Ambassador Bremer in May 2003 and the reorganization of ORHA into the CPA did not resolve the civil-military problems. See Rajiv Chandrasekaran, "Who Killed Iraq?" *Foreign Policy* 156 (September–October 2006): 36–43; and Sharon Behn, "General Assails CPA Bureaucracy as Unresponsive," *Washington Times*, July 1, 2004.

17. Email correspondence with the author, June 2004.

18. S3 (battalion operations officer) from the 1st Infantry Division, email correspondence with the author, June 2004.

19. CPA did move forward on strategic and operational planning after the arrival of L. Paul Bremer in May 2003. See Andrew Rathmell, "Planning Post-Conflict Reconstruction in Iraq: What Can We Learn?" *International Affairs* 81 (October 2005): 1026–30. Rathmell served on the CPA staff.

20. CPA, order number 1, "De-Ba'athification of Iraqi Society," signed by Ambassador Bremer on May 16, 2003.

21. Ambassador Bremer and Walter Slocombe, the former Clinton administration Pentagon official who served as director for national security and defense in the Coalition Provisional Authority, have since defended this decision. Slocombe contended that the Iraqi Army had "self demobilized" and no longer existed, so CPA's decision simply accepted that reality (Walter B. Slocombe, "To Build an Army," *Washington Post*, November 5, 2003). Bremer echoes the same point and attempts to shift some of the responsibility to General Abizaid, who was CENTCOM deputy commander at the time the decision was made (L. Paul Bremer III, "I Didn't Dismantle Iraq's Army," *New York Times*, September 6, 2007). Two facts, though, are clear: General Franks was not informed in advance of the decision (but did not resist it strenuously once it was announced). And, more important, the Iraqi Army did not consider itself "self demobilized" but simply felt that it was following the instructions given to it by CENTCOM before the war and awaiting recall. CPA's later decision to continue paying the Army did not change the anger and resentment that its dissolution caused.

22. Secretary of Defense Donald H. Rumsfeld, interview with Todd McDermott, WCBS-TV, New York City, May 27, 2003.

23. DOD news briefing from the Pentagon, Washington, DC, May 20, 2003.

24. Ambassador Paul Bremer, video news briefing from Baghdad on post-war reconstruction and stabilization efforts, June 12, 2003; and Lt. Gen. David McKiernan, Coalition Joint Task Force (CJTF) 7 commander, video news briefing from Baghdad, June 13, 2003. CJTF 7 had replaced CFLCC as the primary military headquarters in Iraq. McKiernan, who had been the CFLCC commander, initially led CJTF 7 as well.

25. George W. Bush, "President Addresses Nation, Discusses Iraq, War on Terror," address at Fort Bragg, NC, June 28, 2005.

26. Secretary Rumsfeld interview with *Fox and Friends*, November 11, 2003.

27. Interview by the author with Lt. Col. John Charlton, battalion commander in the 3rd Infantry Division, Baghdad, May 3, 2003; interview by the author with Col. Martin Stanton, Coalition Forces Land Component Command C9 (Civil-Military Affairs Staff Section), Baghdad, May 14, 2003; and Dion Nissenbaum, "Marines Play Awkward Role as a Nation Building Force," *San Jose Mercury News*, May 1, 2003.

28. This is based on the author's observations in and around Baghdad during May 2003, and on correspondence and discussions with a wide range of officers and noncommissioned officers during 2003.

29. David Galula, *Pacification in Algeria, 1956–1958* (Santa Monica, CA: RAND Corporation, 2006; reprint of a 1963 publication), 218.

30. Quoted in Ricks, *Fiasco*, 303.

31. David H. Petraeus, "Learning Counterinsurgency: Observations From Soldiering in Iraq," *Military Review* 84 (January–February 2006): 5; Michael Toner, "Commander's Emergency Response Program (CERP)," *The Armed Forces Comptroller* 49 (Summer 2004): 30–31; and Mark Martins, "No Small Change of Soldiering: The Commander's Emergency Response Program (CERP) in Iraq and Afghanistan," *Army Lawyer*, February 2004, 1–20.

32. Discussions by the author with a senior Army commander who was in Iraq during 2003.

33. *An Analysis of the U.S. Military's Ability to Sustain an Occupation of Iraq* (Washington, DC: Congressional Budget Office, September 3, 2003).

34. Coalition Provisional Authority, order number 22, "Creation of a New Iraqi Army," August 7, 2003.

35. "Rebuilding Iraq: Preliminary Observations on Challenges in Transferring Security Responsibilities to Iraqi Military and Police," statement of Joseph A. Christoff, director of international affairs and trade at the Government Accountability Office, submitted to the U.S. House of Representatives Subcommittee on National Security, Emerging Threats, and International Relations on March 14, 2005. At about the same time, CPA also announced an escalated process for the transition to Iraqi self-governance, thus abandoning Ambassador Bremer's notion of a period of extended tutelage while Iraqi's mastered the intricacies of democracy.

36. Michael O'Hanlon of the Brookings Institution and Frederick Kagan of the American Enterprise Institute have been among the most persistent in calling for an increase in the size of the Army. See, for instance, O'Hanlon's "Breaking the Army," *Washington Post*, July 3, 2003; "The Need to Increase the Size of the Deployable Army," *Parameters* 34 (Autumn 2004): 4–17; and *Defense Policy for the Post-Saddam Era* (Washington, DC: Brookings Institution, 2005); and Kagan's "The Army We Have: It's Too Small," *The Weekly Standard*, December 27, 2004; "Army Needs More Strength in Numbers," *New York Daily News*, August 24, 2006; and "The U.S. Military's Manpower Crisis," *Foreign Affairs* 85 (July–August 2006): 97–110. Other organizations and individuals took a similar line. In January 2005, for instance, the Project for the New American Century sent a letter to leading members of Congress regarding the number of U.S. ground forces. The signatories included defense experts from both ends of the political spectrum, retired senior military leaders, and former officials of the Clinton and G. H. W. Bush administrations.

37. Mark Sappenfield, "Dueling Views on Army Size: Congress vs. Rumsfeld," *Christian Science Monitor*, May 17, 2005. In early 2004 a bipartisan group of 128 members of the House, led by Heather Wilson (R-NM), called on President Bush to increase the Army's overall size, called end strength, and to reduce the time reservists must spend on active duty. In October 2004 the FY2005 Defense Authorization Act increased Army "end strength" by 20,000 and Marine Corps end strength by 3,000 for FY2005, with additional increases authorized in future years. For background, see Edward F. Bruner, *Military Forces: What Is the Appropriate Size for the United States?* Congressional

Research Service Report for Congress, May 28, 2004. The National Defense Authorization Act for Fiscal Year 2006 (Public Law 109–163) authorized active duty end strength for the Army at 512,400 and 179,000 for the Marine Corps. Additional authority also was provided in section 403 of that act to increase active duty end strength for the Army by up to 20,000 and increase Marine Corps active duty end strength by up to 5,000 above these levels during fiscal years 2007 through 2009.

38. Donald H. Rumsfeld, "New Model Army," *Wall Street Journal*, February 3, 2004.

39. Eric Schmitt, "Rumsfeld Says More G.I.'s Would Not Help In Iraq," *New York Times*, September 11, 2003; and Eric Schmitt, "General in Iraq Says More G.I.'s Are Not Needed," *New York Times*, August 29, 2003.

40. Ronald Brownstein and Richard Simon, "U.S. Military Strength Called Lacking in Iraq," *Los Angeles Times*, August 25, 2003. Ambassador Bremer told National Security Adviser Rice that the coalition only had about half the number it needed. Bremer, *My Year in Iraq*, 106.

41. Quoted in Sabah Jerges, "Guerrillas Now 'Stand and Fight,'" *Washington Times*, December 2, 2003.

42. Journalists quickly drew the comparison to Tet. See, for instance, James Kitfield, "Ramadan Offensive," *National Journal*, November 1, 2003, 3326–32. Ultimately, though, the Iraqi insurgents proved unable to undertake a nationwide offensive on the scale that the Viet Cong or other more hierarchical insurgents' movements were. The loose, networked configuration of the Iraqi insurgency made it adaptable and difficult to eradicate, but it was an impediment to coordination.

43. Jonathan S. Landay, "CIA Has a Bleak Analysis of Iraq," *Philadelphia Inquirer*, November 12, 2003; Douglas Jehl, "C.I.A. Report Suggests Iraqis Are Losing Faith in U.S. Efforts," *New York Times*, November 13, 2003; and Warren P. Strobel and Jonathan S. Landay, "CIA: Iraq at Risk of Civil War," *Philadelphia Inquirer*, January 22, 2004.

44. Bremer, *My Year in Iraq*, 221.

45. Quoted in Stephen Schwartz, "Jihadists In Iraq," *The Weekly Standard*, February 2, 2004.

46. Lt. Gen. Peter W. Chiarelli, commander, Multinational Corps–Iraq, email correspondence to the author, October 6, 2006.

47. James Stephenson, *Losing the Golden Hour: An Insider's View of Iraq's Reconstruction* (Washington, DC: Potomac Books, 2007).

48. Coalition Provisional Authority, English translation of terrorist Musab al-Zarqawi letter obtained by United States Government in Iraq, February 2004. See also Dexter Filkins, "U.S. Says Files Seek Qaeda Aid in Iraq Conflict," *New York Times*, February 9, 2004; and Rowan Scarborough, "U.S. Adjusts to 'Changing' Tactics of Iraqi Rebels," *Washington Times*, March 8, 2004.

49. Posen, "The Case for Restraint," 10.

50. Peter W. Chiarelli and Patrick R. Michaelis, "Winning the Peace: The Requirement for Full-Spectrum Operations," *Military Review* 85 (July–August 2005): 4–17.

51. Anthony H. Cordesman, *The Implications of the Current Fighting in Iraq*, working paper, Washington, DC: Center for Strategic and International Studies, April 8, 2004, 5.
52. Karl Vick and Anthony Shadid, "Fallujah Gains Mythic Air," *Washington Post*, April 13, 2003.
53. Esther Schrader, "Army Says It Has Enough Troops for Three More Years," *Los Angeles Times*, June 16, 2004.
54. Quoted in Ann Scott Tyson, "Two Years Later, Iraq War Drains Military," *Washington Post*, March 19, 2005.
55. I explore this concept in some detail in *Rethinking Insurgency* (Carlisle Barracks, PA: U.S. Army War College Strategic Studies Institute, 2007).
56. Rowan Scarborough, "Pentagon Begins to See Iraq Momentum Shift," *Washington Times*, March 28, 2005; Bill Gertz, "Myers Says U.S. Winning in Iraq," *Washington Times*, April 27, 2005; Mark Mazzetti, "Insurgency Is Waning, a Top U.S. General Says," *Los Angeles Times*, March 2, 2005; "The Beginning of the End for Sunni Insurgents?" *Stratfor.com*, April 1, 2005; and Vice President Dick Cheney, interviewed on CNN's *Larry King Live*, June 20, 2005.
57. Maj. Gen. Richard Zahner, quoted in Bradley Graham, "Zarqawi 'Hijacked' Insurgency," *Washington Post*, September 28, 2005.
58. *National Strategy for Victory in Iraq* (Washington, DC: National Security Council, 2005), 3. Emphasis added.
59. Gen. Richard B. Myers, chairman of the Joint Chiefs of Staff, testimony before the Senate Armed Services Committee, Washington, DC, September 29, 2005.
60. Bush, "President Addresses Nation, Discusses Iraq, War on Terror."
61. George W. Bush, "President Discusses War on Terror, Progress in Iraq in West Virginia," Capitol Music Hall, Wheeling, WV, March 22, 2006.
62. George W. Bush, "President Outlines Strategy for Victory in Iraq," United States Naval Academy, Annapolis, MD, November 30, 2005.
63. George W. Bush, "President Discusses War on Terror and Rebuilding Iraq," Omni Shoreham Hotel, Washington, DC, December 7, 2005.
64. George W. Bush, "President Bush Addresses American Legion National Convention," Salt Palace Convention Center, Salt Lake City, UT, August 31, 2006.
65. Bush, "President Outlines Strategy for Victory in Iraq."
66. Department of Defense, *Measuring Stability and Security in Iraq*, Report to Congress, August 2006, 26.
67. Solomon Moore and Louise Roug, "Deaths Across Iraq Show It Is a Nation of Many Wars, With U.S. in the Middle," *Los Angles Times*, October 7, 2006, 1.
68. John F. Burns, "General Weighs 2d Troop Shift to Calm Baghdad," *New York Times*, October 25, 2006; and Ellen Knickmeyer, "More U.S. Troops May Be Iraq-Bound," *Washington Post*, October 25, 2006.
69. Amit R. Paley, "In Baghdad, a Force Under the Militias' Sway," *Washington Post*, October 31, 2006.
70. James Lyons, "Multifaceted Strategy for Iraq," *Washington Times*, October 16, 2006.

71. Andrew F. Krepinevich, Jr., "How to Win in Iraq," *Foreign Affairs* 84 (September–October 2005): 88–89.

72. See George Packer, "The Lesson of Tal Afar," *New Yorker*, April 10, 2006, 9–62.

73. Col. H. R. McMaster, interviewed by PBS *Frontline*, February 21, 2006.

74. *Department of Defense Directive 3000.05*, "Military Support for Stability, Security, Transition, and Reconstruction Operations," November 28, 2005.

75. *Quadrennial Defense Review Report* (Washington, DC: Department of Defense, 2006), 1.

76. *The National Security Strategy of the United States of America* (Washington, DC: The White House, 2006).

77. Qiao Liang and Wang Xiangsui, *Unrestricted Warfare* (Beijing: PLA Literature and Arts Publishing House, 1999). Nathan Freier drew my attention to this similarity between unrestricted warfare and insurgency.

78. *QDR*, 2006, 78.

79. Jacob Kipp, Lester Grau, Karl Prinslow, and Don Smith, "The Human Terrain System: A CORDS for the 21st Century," *Military Review* 86 (September–October 2006): 8–15.

80. Discussion with a senior Army commander, October 7, 2006.

81. FMI (Field Manual Interim) 3-07.22, *Counterinsurgency Operations*, October 2004.

82. Field Manual (FM) 3-24, Marine Corps Warfighting Pamphlet (MCWP) 3-33.5, *Counterinsurgency*, December 2006. In another unprecedented move, the University of Chicago Press published a reprint of the manual.

83. For instance, Charles J. Dunlap, Jr., "Air-Minded Considerations for Joint Counterinsurgency Doctrine," *Air and Space Power Journal* 20 (Winter 2007): 63–74. See also Adam J. Vick et al., *Air Power in the New Counterinsurgency Era: The Strategic Importance of the USAF Advisory and Assistance Missions* (Santa Monica, CA: RAND Corporation, 2006).

84. Ambassador Carlos Pascual, prepared statement for the Senate Foreign Relations Committee, June 16, 2005; and "An Interview with Carlos Pascual, Vice President and Director of Foreign Policy Studies of the Brookings Institution," *Joint Force Quarterly* 42 (2006): 80–85.

85. In 2004, for instance, USAID approached the author about preparing a study of the nature of counterinsurgency and the role of USAID in it for the agency's senior managers.

86. Michael R. Gordon, "Bush Adviser's Memo Cites Doubt About Iraqi Leader," *New York Times*, November 29, 2006. The text of Hadley's leaked memo was reprinted in *New York Times*, November 29, 2006.

87. Michael Gordon, "Rumsfeld, a Force for Change, Did Not Change With the Times Amid Iraq Tumult," *New York Times*, November 9, 2006.

88. Colin Powell interviewed by Bob Schieffer on CBS News *Face the Nation*, December 17, 2006.

89. For instance, Robert Kagan and William Kristol, "It's Up to Bush," *The Weekly Standard*, December 18, 2006, 9.

90. The group also included Lawrence Eagleburger, Vernon Jordan, Edwin

Meese, Sandra Day O'Connor, Leon Paneta, William Perry, Charles Robb, and Alan Simpson. It was supported by a wide range of subject matter experts.

91. The AEI Iraq Planning Group also included Army Lt. Gen. David Barno (ret), Danielle Pletka, Rend al-Rahim, Army Col. Joel Armstrong (ret), Army Maj. Daniel Dwyer (ret), Larry Crandall, Larry Sampler, Michael Eisenstadt, Kimberly Kagan, Michael Rubin, Reuel Marc Gerecht, Thomas Donnelly, Gary Schmitt, Mauro De Lorenzo, and Vance Serchuk. Unlike the bipartisan Baker-Hamilton commission, the AEI group was solidly conservative. Its members were all associated with such conservative institutions as AEI itself, the Project for the New American Century, and *The Weekly Standard.*

92. Gen. James T. Conway, prepared statement for testimony before the U.S. House of Representatives Armed Services Committee, January 23, 2007.

93. George W. Bush, "President's Address to the Nation," January 10, 2007.

94. Jim Hoagland, "In Baghdad, a Test of the Petraeus Principles," *Washington Post,* January 14, 2007. Adm. William Fallon replaced Abizaid as the CENTCOM commander—the first time a Navy officer held that position.

95. Steven N. Simon, *After the Surge: The Case for U.S. Military Disengagement From Iraq* (New York: Council on Foreign Relations, February 2007).

96. James N. Miller and Shawn W. Brimley, *Phased Transition: A Responsible Way Forward and Out of Iraq* (Washington, DC: Center for a New American Security, June 2007).

97. Daniel L. Byman and Kenneth M. Pollack, *Things Fall Apart: Containing the Spillover From an Iraqi Civil War* (Washington, DC: Brookings Institution Saban Center for Middle East Policy, January 2007).

98. National Intelligence Council, *Prospects for Iraq's Stability: A Challenging Road Ahead,* January 2007.

99. Anthony H. Cordesman, *The New Bush Strategy for Iraq: What Are the Chances of "Victory"?* (Washington, DC: Center for Strategic and International Studies, February 5, 2007).

100. David Rogers, "More Republicans Join Critics of Bush Troop-Surge Strategy," *Wall Street Journal,* January 23, 2007.

101. Thom Shanker and David S. Cloud, "Bush's Plan for Iraq Runs Into Opposition in Congress," *New York Times,* January 12, 2007.

102. Christian Berthelsen and Borzou Daragahi, "Insurgents Turn on Sunnis," *Los Angeles Times,* February 25, 2007.

103. Quoted in Edward Wong, "In Lawless Sunni Heartland of Iraq, a Tribal Chief Opposes the Jihadists and Prays," *New York Times,* March 3, 2007. Sattar was killed by a car bomb in September 2007.

104. Ned Parker, "Iraqi Schism Targeted by U.S.," *Los Angeles Times,* March 27, 2007.

105. Carlos Pascual and Kenneth M. Pollack, "The Critical Battles: Political Reconciliation and Reconstruction in Iraq," *Washington Quarterly* 30 (Summer 2007): 7.

106. George W. Bush, "President Bush Participates in Joint Press Availability with Prime Minister Harper of Canada, and President Calderón of Mexico,"

Fairmont Le Chateau Montebello, Montebello, Canada, August 21, 2007. See also Sheryl Gay Stolberg and Jim Rutenberg, "A Step Away From Malaki," *New York Times*, August 22, 2007.

107. National Intelligence Council, *Prospects for Iraq's Stability: Some Security Progress but Political Reconciliation Elusive*, August 2007, 1.

108. Kimberly Kagan, "The Tide Is Turning in Iraq," *Wall Street Journal*, September 4, 2007.

109. Max Boot, "The 'Surge' Is Working," *Los Angeles Times*, September 8, 2007.

110. William Kristol, "Keep on Surgin'," *The Weekly Standard*, July 25, 2007, 9.

111. Michael E. O'Hanlon and Kenneth M. Pollack, "A War We Just Might Win," *New York Times*, July 30, 2007.

112. Quoted in Jeff Zeleny, "Leading Democrat in Senate Tells Reporters, 'This War Is Lost,'" *New York Times*, April 20, 2007. Senator Reid had a penchant for bizarre claims on Iraq. In June, commenting from the safety of his Washington office, Reid said that General Petraeus "isn't in touch with what's going on in Baghdad" (quoted in Thomas E. Ricks, "Reid Faults Petraeus as 'Not in Touch,'" *Washington Post*, June 15, 2007).

113. Quoted in Leslie Sabbagh, "General Petraeus Warns of a Hasty US Pullout From Iraq," *Christian Science Monitor*, July 13, 2007.

114. Dan Balz and Jon Cohen, "Discontent Over Iraq Increasing, Polls Find," *Washington Post*, June 5, 2007.

115. "No Exit, No Strategy," *New York Times*, September 14, 2007.

116. Thomas L. Friedman, "Somebody Else's Mess," *New York Times*, September 16, 2007.

117. Frederick W. Kagan and William Kristol, "Men at Work, Children at Play," *The Weekly Standard*, September 24, 2007, 7.

118. "The Least Bad Plan: President Bush's Long-Shot Strategy for Iraq Is Less Risky Than the Alternatives," *Washington Post*, September 14, 2007, p. A12.

119. Damien Cave, "Militant Group Is Out of Baghdad, U.S. Says," *New York Times*, November 8, 2007, p. A19.

120. Government Accountability Office, *Securing, Stabilizing, and Rebuilding Iraq: Iraqi Government Has Not Met Most Legislative, Security, and Economic Benchmarks*, Report to Congressional Committees, September 2007.

121. Department of Defense, *Measuring Stability and Security in Iraq*, Report to Congress, December 2007, 1.

122. Barry R. McCaffrey, memorandum for Col. Michael Meese, Department of Social Sciences, U.S. Military Academy, December 18, 2007.

123. Multi-National Forces–Iraq, *Focus Groups on Reconciliation in Iraq*, executive summary of findings, December 2007.

124. Quoted in Jim Michaels, "U.S. Hails Iraq Bid to Unite Security," *USA Today*, December 18, 2007.

125. International Crisis Group, "Where Is Iraq Heading? Lessons From Basra," *Middle East Report* 67 (June 25, 2007).

126. See, for instance, Douglas Macgregor, "Will Iraq's Great Awakening Lead to a Nightmare?" *Mother Jones*, December 11, 2007.

127. Abdul Bakier, "Al-Qaeda Adapts Its Methods in Iraq as Part of a Global

Strategy," *The Jamestown Foundation Terrorism Monitor* 5 (December 20, 2007): 7.

128. Hans Nichols, "Gates Tells Lawmakers Iraq War Is Hurting Afghanistan Mission," Bloomberg.com, October 1, 2007.

129. Secretary of Defense Robert M. Gates, "Landon Lecture," Kansas State University, Manhattan, KS, November 26, 2007.

130. Thom Shanker, "Joint Chiefs Chairman Looks Beyond Current Wars," *New York Times*, October 22, 2007.

131. Gen. George W. Casey Jr., statement before the U.S. House of Representatives Armed Services Committee, September 26, 2007.

CONCLUSION

1. W. Patrick Lang, "Drinking the Kool-Aid," *Middle East Policy* 9 (Summer 2004): 41.

2. I develop this idea in *Rethinking Insurgency*.

3. Colin S. Gray, *The Sheriff: America's Defense of the New World Order* (Lexington: University Press of Kentucky, 2004).

SELECTED BIBLIOGRAPHY

Acharya, Amitav. *U.S. Military Strategy in the Gulf.* London: Routledge, 1989.

Adelman, Ken. "Cakewalk in Iraq." *Washington Post,* February 13, 2002.

Ajami, Fouad. Testimony in *Hearings to Examine Threats, Responses, and Regional Considerations Surrounding Iraq,* United States Senate Committee on Foreign Relations, 107th Congr., 2d sess., July 31 and August 1, 2002.

Alberts, David S., John J. Garstka, and Frederic P. Stein. *Network Centric Warfare: Developing and Leveraging Information Superiority.* Washington, DC: Department of Defense C4ISR Cooperative Research Program, 1998.

Albright, Madeleine K. Testimony in *Next Steps in Iraq,* hearings before the United States Senate Committee on Foreign Relations, 107th Congr., 2d sess., September 25 and 26, 2002.

Allawi, Ali A. *The Occupation of Iraq: Winning the War, Losing the Peace.* New Haven, CT: Yale University Press, 2007.

An Analysis of the U.S. Military's Ability to Sustain an Occupation of Iraq. Washington, DC: Congressional Budget Office, September 3, 2003.

Army Vision 2010. Washington, DC: Headquarters, Department of the Army, 1996.

Atkinson, Rick. *Crusade: The Untold Story of the Persian Gulf War.* Boston: Houghton Mifflin, 1993.

Axelgard, Frederick W., ed. *Iraq in Transition: A Political, Economic, and Strategic Perspective.* Boulder, CO: Westview, 1986.

————. *A New Iraq? The Gulf War and Implications for U.S. Policy.* New York: Praeger, 1988.

Bacevich, Andrew J. *The New American Militarism: How Americans Are Seduced by War.* Oxford: Oxford University Press, 2005.

Bengio, Ofra. "Iraq." In *Middle East Contemporary Survey,* Vol. 14, edited by Ami Ayalon. Boulder, CO: Westview, 1990.

Benson, Kevin C. M. "'Phase IV' CFLCC Stability Operations Planning." In *Turning Victory Into Success: Military Operations After the Campaign,* edited by Brian M. DeToy. Fort Leavenworth, KS: Combat Studies Institute Press, 2004.

————. "OIF Phase IV: A Planner's Reply to Brigadier Aylwin-Foster." *Military Review* 86 (March–April 2006): 61–67.

————. Interviewed by John McCool, Operational Leadership Experiences Project, Fort Leavenworth, KS, October 10, 2006.

Berger, Samuel R. "Remarks on Iraq at Stanford University," Palo Alto, CA, December 8, 1998.

————. Testimony in *Hearings to Examine Threats, Responses, and Regional Considerations Surrounding Iraq*, United States Senate Committee on Foreign Relations, 107th Congr., 2d sess., July 31 and August 1, 2002.

Betts, Richard K. "The Delusion of Impartial Intervention." *Foreign Affairs* 73 (November–December 1994): 20–33.

Biddle, Stephen. "Victory Misunderstood: What the Gulf Tells Us About the Future of Conflict." *International Security* 21 (Fall 1996): 139–79.

————. *Afghanistan and the Future of Warfare: Implications for Army and Defense Policy*. Carlisle Barracks, PA: U.S. Army War College Strategic Studies Institute, 2002.

————. *Military Power: Explaining Victory and Defeat in Modern Battle*. Princeton, NJ: Princeton University Press, 2004.

Biden, Joseph H. Jr. "Opening Statement." *Hearings to Examine Threats, Responses, and Regional Considerations Surrounding Iraq*, United States Senate Committee on Foreign Relations, 107th Congr., 2d sess., July 31 and August 1, 2002.

Bingham, Price T. "Transforming Warfare With Effects-Based Operations," *Aerospace Power Journal* 15 (Spring 2001): 58–66.

Binnendijk, Hans, ed. *Transforming America's Military*. Washington, DC: National Defense University Center for Technology and National Security Policy, 2002.

Bodnar, John W. "The Military Technical Revolution: From Hardware to Information." *Naval War College Review* 46 (Summer 1993): 7–21.

Boot, Max. "The 'Surge' Is Working." *Los Angeles Times*, September 8, 2007.

Borer, Douglas A. "Inverse Engagement: Lessons from US-Iraq Relations, 1982-1990." *Parameters* 33 (Summer 2003): 51–65.

Bowman, Steve. *Iraq: U.S. Military Operations*. Congressional Research Service Report for Congress, October 2, 2003.

————. *Iraq: U.S. Military Operations*. Congressional Research Service Report for Congress, July 5, 2005.

Brands, Hal. *From Berlin to Baghdad: America's Search for Purpose in the Post–Cold War World*. Lexington: University Press of Kentucky, 2008.

Bremer, L. Paul. "Iraq Shouldn't Be the Next Stop in War on Terror." *Wall Street Journal*, December 6, 2001.

————. *My Year In Iraq: The Struggle to Build a Future of Hope*. New York: Simon and Schuster, 2006.

————. "I Didn't Dismantle Iraq's Army," *New York Times*, September 6, 2007.

Bruner, Edward F. *Military Forces: What Is the Appropriate Size for the United States?* Congressional Research Service Report for Congress, May 28, 2004.

Brzezinski, Zbigniew. *Power and Principle: Memoirs of the National Security Adviser, 1977–1981*. New York: Farrar, Straus, Giroux, 1983.

Buckley, William F., Jr. "Evidence Against Iraq?" *National Review* (November 19, 2001): 62.

Builder, Carl. *The Masks of War: Military Styles in Strategy and Analysis*. Baltimore: Johns Hopkins University Press, 1989.

Bush, George H. W. "Remarks at the Aspen Institute Symposium," Aspen, CO, August 2, 1990.

———."Remarks and an Exchange With Reporters on the Iraqi Invasion of Kuwait," August 5, 1990.

———. "Address Before a Joint Session of Congress," September 11, 1990.

———. "State of the Union Address Before a Joint Session of Congress," January 29, 1991.

———. "Remarks to the American Association for the Advancement of Science on Iraq's Withdrawal Statement," February 15, 1991.

Bush, George H. W., and Brent Scowcroft. *A World Transformed.* New York: Alfred A. Knopf, 1998.

Bush, George W. "A Period of Consequences," speech at the Citadel, Charleston, SC, September 23, 1999.

———. "Address to a Joint Session of Congress and the American People," September 21, 2001.

———. "President Welcomes Aid Workers Rescued From Afghanistan," remarks at the White House, Washington, DC, November 26, 2001.

———. "President Delivers State of the Union Address," January 29, 2002.

———. "President Holds Press Conference," the White House, Washington, DC, March 13, 2002.

———. "Remarks by the President in Address to the United Nations General Assembly," New York, NY, September 12, 2002.

———. "President Bush to Send Iraq Resolution to Congress Today," remarks by the president in photo opportunity with Secretary of State Colin Powell, September 19, 2002.

———. "President Bush Delivers Graduation Speech at West Point," United States Military Academy, West Point, NY, June 1, 2002.

———. "President Bush, Colombia President Uribe Discuss Terrorism," the White House, Washington, DC, September 25, 2002.

———. "President's Radio Address," February 8, 2003.

———. "President Discusses the Future of Iraq," remarks to the American Enterprise Institute, Washington Hilton, Washington, DC, February 23, 2003.

———. "President George Bush Discusses Iraq in National Press Conference," March 6, 2003.

———. "President's Radio Address," March 8, 2003.

———. "President Addresses Nation, Discusses Iraq, War on Terror," address at Fort Bragg, NC, June 28, 2005.

———. "President Outlines Strategy for Victory in Iraq," United States Naval Academy, Annapolis, MD, November 30, 2005.

———. "President Discusses War on Terror and Rebuilding Iraq," Omni Shoreham Hotel, Washington, DC, December 7, 2005.

———. "President Discusses War on Terror, Progress in Iraq in West Virginia," Capitol Music Hall, Wheeling, WV, March 22, 2006.

———. "President Bush Addresses American Legion National Convention," Salt Palace Convention Center, Salt Lake City, UT, August 31, 2006.

———. "President's Address to the Nation," January 10, 2007.

———. "President Bush Participates in Joint Press Availability with Prime Minister Harper of Canada, and President Calderón of Mexico," Fairmont Le Chateau Montebello, Montebello, Canada, August 21, 2007.

Butler, Richard. Testimony in *Hearings to Examine Threats, Responses, and Regional Considerations Surrounding Iraq,* United States Senate Committee on Foreign Relations, 107th Congr., 2d sess., July 31 and August 1, 2002.

Byman, Daniel. "Proceed With Caution: U.S. Support for the Iraqi Opposition." *Washington Quarterly* 22 (Summer 1999): 23–38.

———. "A Farewell to Arms Inspections." *Foreign Affairs* 79 (January–February 2000): 119–32.

———. "After the Storm: U.S. Policy Toward Iraq Since 1991." *Political Science Quarterly* 115 (Winter 2000–2001): 493–516.

Byman, Daniel L. and Kenneth M. Pollack. *Things Fall Apart: Containing the Spillover From an Iraqi Civil War.* Washington, DC: Brookings Institution Saban Center for Middle East Policy, January 2007.

Byman, Daniel, Kenneth Pollack, and Gideon Rose. "The Rollback Fantasy." *Foreign Affairs* 78 (January–February 1999): 24–41.

Byman, Daniel L., and Matthew C. Waxman. *Confronting Iraq: U.S. Policy and the Use of Force Since the Gulf War.* Santa Monica, CA: RAND Corporation, 2000.

Carney, Timothy. "We're Getting in Our Own Way." *Washington Post,* June 22, 2003.

Carter, Jimmy. "State of the Union Address to Congress," January 23, 1980.

———. *Keeping Faith: Memoirs of a President.* New York: Bantam, 1982.

Carus, W. Seth. *The Genie Unleashed: Iraq's Chemical and Biological Weapons Production.* Washington, DC: Washington Institute for Near East Policy, 1989.

Casey, George W., Jr. Statement before the U.S. House of Representatives Armed Services Committee, September 26, 2007.

Cebrowski, Arthur K., and John J. Garstka. "Network-Centric Warfare: Its Origin and Future." *Proceedings of the U.S. Naval Institute* 124 (January 1998): 28–35.

Certain Victory: United States Army in the Gulf War. Washington, DC: United States Army, Office of the Chief of Staff, 1993.

Chandrasekaran, Rajiv. *Imperial Life in the Emerald City: Inside Iraq's Green Zone.* New York: Alfred A. Knopf, 2006.

———. "Who Killed Iraq?" *Foreign Policy* 156 (September–October, 2006): 36–43.

Cheney, Richard. "Vice President Speaks at the Veterans of Foreign Wars 103rd National Convention," Nashville, TN, August 26, 2002.

———. Interviewed by Tim Russert on NBC News *Meet the Press,* September 8, 2002.

———. "Remarks by the Vice President to the Heritage Foundation," Washington, DC, October 11, 2003.

Chiarelli, Peter W., and Patrick R. Michaelis. "Winning the Peace: The Requirement for Full-Spectrum Operations." *Military Review* 85 (July–August 2005): 4–17.

Choosing Victory: A Plan for Success in Iraq, Report of the American Enterprise Institute Iraq Study Group, January 2007.

Christopher, Warren. "The Strategic Priorities of American Foreign Policy." Statement before the Senate Foreign Relations Committee, November 4, 1993.

Chubin, Shahram. "Post-War Gulf Security." *Survival* 33 (March/April 1991): 140-157.

Clarke, Richard A. *Against All Enemies: Inside America's War on Terror.* New York: Free Press, 2004.

Clinton, William. "Address to the Nation on Iraq," October 10, 1994.

———. "Statement on Signing the Iraq Liberation Act of 1998." *Weekly Compilation of Presidential Documents,* November 9, 1998.

———. "Address to the Nation Announcing Military Strikes on Iraq," December 16, 1998.

Coalition Provisional Authority. Order number 1, "De-Ba'athification of Iraqi Society," May 16, 2003.

———. Order number 22, "Creation of a New Iraqi Army," August 7, 2003.

Cochran, Alexander S., et. al. *Gulf Air Power Survey.* Washington, DC: Government Printing Office, 1993.

Conduct of the Persian Gulf War: Final Report to Congress. Washington, DC: Department of Defense, 1992.

Conway, James T. Prepared statement for testimony before the U.S. House of Representatives Armed Services Committee, January 23, 2007.

Cooley, John K. "Pre-War Gulf Diplomacy." *Survival* 33 (March–April 1991): 125–39.

Cordesman, Anthony H. *The Gulf and the West: Strategic Relations and Military Realities.* Boulder, CO: Westview, 1988.

———. *Planning for a Self-Inflicted Wound: US Policy to Reshape a Post-Saddam Iraq.* Washington, DC: Center for Strategic and International Studies, revision 3, 2002.

———. *The Implications of the Current Fighting in Iraq.* Washington, DC: Center for Strategic and International Studies, 2004.

———. *Iraq and Foreign Volunteers.* Washington, DC: Center for Strategic and International Studies, 2005.

———. *Iraq's Evolving Insurgency and the Risk of Civil War.* Washington, DC: Center for Strategic and International Studies, 2006.

———. *Iraqi Force Development and the Challenge of Civil War: Can Iraqi Forces Do the Job?* Washington, DC: Center for Strategic and International Studies, 2006.

———. *Iraqi Force Development and the Challenge of Civil War: The Critical Problems and Failures the US Must Address if Iraqi Forces Are to Do the Job.* Washington, DC: Center for Strategic and International Studies, 2007.

———. *Iraq's Insurgency and Civil Violence.* Washington, DC: Center for Strategic and International Studies, 2007.

———. *Iraq's Sectarian and Ethnic Violence and Its Evolving Insurgency.* Washington, DC: Center for Strategic and International Studies, 2007.

———. *The New Bush Strategy for Iraq: What Are the Chances of "Victory"?* Washington, DC: Center for Strategic and International Studies, 2007.

Daalder, Ivo H., and James M. Lindsay. *America Unbound: The Bush Revolution in Foreign Policy.* Washington, DC: Brookings Institution Press, 2003.

Davis, Lynn E., et. al. *Stretched Thin: Army Forces for Sustained Operations.* Santa Monica, CA: RAND Corporation, 2005.

Davis, Paul. *Effects Based Operations.* Santa Monica, CA: RAND Corporation, 2001.

Dawisha, Adeed I. "Iraq: The West's Opportunity." *Foreign Policy* 41 (Winter 1980–81): 134–53.

Deibel, Terry L. "Bush's Foreign Policy: Mastery and Inaction." *Foreign Policy* 84 (Fall 1991): 3-23.

Department of Defense Directive 3000.05, "Military Support for Stability, Security, Transition, and Reconstruction Operations," November 28, 2005.

Desch, Michael C. *Civilian Control of the Military: The Changing Security Environment.* Baltimore: Johns Hopkins University Press, 2001.

Diamond, Larry. *Squandered Victory: The American Occupation and the Bungled Effort to Bring Democracy to Iraq.* New York: Henry Holt, 2005.

Dicker, Paul F. "Effectiveness of Stability Operations During the Initial Implementation of the Transition Phase for Operation Iraqi Freedom." U.S. Army War College Strategy Research Project, March 19, 2004.

Director of Central Intelligence. *Iraq's Role in the Middle East.* National Intelligence Estimate 36.2-1-79, June 21, 1979.

———. *Implications of Iran's Victory Over Iraq.* Special National Intelligence Estimate 34/36. 2-82, June 8, 1982.

———. *Prospects for Iraq.* Special National Intelligence Estimate 36.2-83, July 19, 1983.

Dobbins, James. "Who Lost Iraq? Lessons From the Debacle." *Foreign Affairs* 86 (September–October 2007): 61–74.

Donnelly, Thomas. *Operation Iraqi Freedom: A Strategic Assessment.* Washington, DC: American Enterprise Institute, 2004.

Drew, Dennis M. "Desert Storm as a Symbol: Implications of the Air War in the Desert." *Airpower Journal* 6 (Fall 1992): 4–13.

Dunlap, Charles J., Jr. "Air-Minded Considerations for Joint Counterinsurgency Doctrine." *Air and Space Power Journal* 20 (Winter 2007): 63–74.

Echevarria, Antulio J., II. *Toward an American Way of War.* Carlisle Barracks, PA: U.S. Army War College Strategic Studies Institute, 2004.

———. *Fourth-Generation War and Other Myths.* Carlisle Barracks, PA: U.S. Army War College Strategic Studies Institute, 2005.

Eisenstadt, Michael, and Jeffrey White. *Assessing Iraq's Sunni Arab Insurgency.* Washington, DC: Washington Institute for Near East Studies, 2005.

El-Shazly, Nadia El-Sayed. *The Gulf Tanker War: Iran and Iraq's Maritime Swordplay.* New York: St. Martin's, 1998.

Fallows, James. "Blind Into Baghdad." *Atlantic Monthly,* January–February 2004, 52–74.

———. "Why Iraq Has No Army." *Atlantic Monthly,* December 2005, 60–77.

Feith, Douglas J. Interview with the *Washington Post,* February 21, 2003 (transcript from the U.S. Department of Defense, Office of the Assistant Secretary of Defense for Public Affairs).

———. "U.S. Strategy for the War on Terrorism," speech at the University of Chicago Political Union, April 14, 2004.

Feldman, Noah. *What We Owe Iraq: War and the Ethics of Nation Building.* Princeton, NJ: Princeton University Press, 2004.

Ferguson, Niall. *Colossus: The Price of America's Empire.* New York: Penguin, 2004.

Field Manual (FM) 3-24, Marine Corps Warfighting Pamphlet (MCWP) 3-33.5, *Counterinsurgency,* December 2006.

Final Report of the National Commission on Terrorist Attacks Upon the United States, July 24, 2004.

Franks, Tommy. *American Soldier.* With Malcolm McConnell. New York: Regan, 2004.

Freedman, Lawrence. "The Gulf War and the New World Order." *Survival* 33 (May–June 1991): 195–209.

. . . *From the Sea: Preparing the Naval Service for the 21st Century.* Washington, DC: Department of the Navy, 1992.

Fukuyama, Francis. *America at the Crossroads: Democracy, Power, and the Neoconservative Legacy.* New Haven, CT: Yale University Press, 2006.

Future of Iraq Project. Report of the Democratic Principles Working Group, November 2002.

Gacek, Christopher M. *The Logic of Force: The Dilemma of Limited War in American Foreign Policy.* New York: Columbia University Press, 1994.

Gaddis, John Lewis. "Toward the Post-Cold War World." *Foreign Affairs* 70 (Spring 1991): 102–22.

Galbraith, Peter W. *The End of Iraq: How American Incompetence Created a War Without End.* New York: Simon and Schuster, 2006.

Gates, Robert M. "Landon Lecture," Kansas State University, Manhattan, KS, November 26, 2007.

Gause, F. Gregory, III. "Getting It Backwards on Iraq." *Foreign Affairs* 78 (May–June 1999): 54–65.

Gelb, Leslie H. "Quelling the Teacup Wars: The New World's Constant Challenge." *Foreign Affairs* 73 (November–December 1994): 2–6.

Gigot, Paul A. "A Great American Screw-Up: The U.S. and Iraq, 1980–1990." *The National Interest* 22 (Winter 1990–91): 3–10.

Gordon Michael R., and Bernard E. Trainor. *The Generals' War: The Inside Story of the Conflict in the Gulf.* Boston: Little, Brown, 1995.

———. *Cobra II: The Inside Story of the Invasion and Occupation of Iraq.* New York: Pantheon, 2006.

Gouré, Daniel. "Is There a Military-Technical Revolution in America's Future?" *Washington Quarterly* 16 (Autumn 1993): 175–92.

Gouré, Daniel, Jeffrey M. Ranney, and James R. Schlesinger. *Averting the Defense Train Wreck in the New Millennium.* Washington, DC: Center for Strategic and International Studies, 1999.

Government Accountability Office. *Securing, Stabilizing, and Rebuilding Iraq: Iraqi Government Has Not Met Most Legislative, Security, and Economic Benchmarks,* Report to Congressional Committees, September 2007.

Gray, Colin S. *Modern Strategy.* Oxford: Oxford University Press, 1999.

———. *Strategy for Chaos: Revolutions in Military Affairs and the Evidence of History.* London: Frank Cass, 2002.

———. *Another Bloody Century: Future Warfare.* London: Weidenfeld and Nicolson, 2005.

———. *Recognizing and Understanding Revolutionary Change in Warfare: The Sovereignty of Context.* Carlisle Barracks, PA: U.S. Army War College Strategic Studies Institute, 2006.

Haig, Alexander M., Jr. *Caveat: Realism, Reagan and Foreign Policy.* New York: Macmillan, 1984.

Halper, Stefan, and Jonathan Clarke. *America Alone: The Neo-Conservatives and the Global Order.* New York: Cambridge University Press, 2004.

Halperin, Morton. Testimony in *Hearings to Examine Threats, Responses, and Regional Considerations Surrounding Iraq,* United States Senate Committee on Foreign Relations, 107th Congr., 2d sess., July 31 and August 1, 2002.

Hammes, Thomas X. *The Sling and the Stone: On War in the 21st Century.* St. Paul, MN: Zenith, 2004.

Hammond, Grant T. "Myths of the Gulf War: Some 'Lessons' Not to Learn." *Airpower Journal* 12 (Fall 1998): 6–18.

Hamre, John. *Iraq's Post-Conflict Reconstruction: A Field Review and Recommendations.* Washington, DC: Center for Strategic and International Studies, July 2003.

Hamza, Khidhir. Testimony in *Hearings to Examine Threats, Responses, and Regional*

Considerations Surrounding Iraq, United States Senate Committee on Foreign Relations, 107th Congr., 2d sess., July 31 and August 1, 2002.

Hashim, Ahmed S. *Insurgency and Counter-Insurgency in Iraq.* Ithaca, NY: Cornell University Press, 2006.

Hayes, Stephen F. *The Connection: How al Qaeda's Collaboration With Saddam Hussein Has Endangered America.* New York: HarperCollins, 2004.

Hillen, John. "Defense's Death Spiral." *Foreign Affairs* 78 (July–August 1999): 2–7.

Hines, Jay E. "From Desert One to Southern Watch: History of the U.S. Central Command." *Joint Force Quarterly* 24 (Spring 2000): 42–48.

Holbrooke, Richard C. Testimony in *Next Steps in Iraq,* hearings before the United States Senate Committee on Foreign Relations, 107th Congr., 2d sess., September 25 and 26, 2002.

Hoffman, Bruce. *Insurgency and Counterinsurgency in Iraq.* Santa Monica, CA: RAND Corporation, 2004.

Howard, Michael. "What Friends Are For." *National Interest* 69 (Fall 2002): 8–10.

Hubbard, Andrew. "Plague and Paradox: Militias in Iraq." *Small Wars and Insurgencies* 18 (September 2007): 345–62.

Hurst, Steven. *The Foreign Policy of the Bush Administration: In Search of a New World Order.* London: Cassell, 1999.

Inman, Bobby R., Joseph S. Nye Jr., William J. Perry, and Roger K. Smith. "Lessons From the Gulf War." *Washington Quarterly* 15 (Winter 1992): 57–74.

Inspector General, United States Department of Defense, Deputy Inspector General for Intelligence. *Review of the Pre–Iraqi War Activities of the Under Secretary of Defense for Policy,* Report No. 07-INTEL-04, February 9, 2007.

International Crisis Group. "In Their Own Words: Reading the Iraqi Insurgency." *Middle East Report* 50 (Brussels: February 15, 2006).

———. "The Next Iraqi War? Sectarianism and Civil Conflict." *Middle East Report* 52 (Brussels: February 27, 2006).

———. "Where Is Iraq Heading? Lessons From Basra." *Middle East Report* 67 (Brussels: June 25, 2007).

Iraq: The Day After. Report of an Independent Task Force Sponsored by the Council on Foreign Relations, January 2003.

Iraq: One Year After. Report of an Independent Task Force sponsored by the Council on Foreign Relations, March 2004.

Iraq Study Group Report: The Way Forward—A New Approach, December 2006.

Jaffe, Lorna S. *The Development of the Base Force, 1989–1992.* Washington, DC: Office of the Chairman of the Joint Chiefs of Staff, Joint History Office, 1993.

Jentleson, Bruce W. *With Friends Like These: Reagan, Bush, and Saddam, 1982–1990.* New York: W. W. Norton, 1994.

Johnson, Robert H. "The Persian Gulf in U.S. Strategy: A Skeptical View." *International Security* 14 (Summer 1989): 122–160.

Joint Military Assessment. Washington, DC: Joint Chiefs of Staff.

Joint Military Net Assessment. Washington, DC: Joint Chiefs of Staff, 1992.

Kagan, Frederick W. "The Army We Have: It's Too Small." *The Weekly Standard* (December 27, 2004): 9-10.

———. "The U.S. Military's Manpower Crisis." *Foreign Affairs* 85 (July–August 2006): 97–110.

———. *Finding the Target: The Transformation of American Military Policy.* New York: Encounter, 2006.

Kagan, Frederick W., and William Kristol. "Men at Work, Children at Play." *The Weekly Standard* (September 24, 2007): 7.

Kagan, Kimberly. "The Tide Is Turning in Iraq." *Wall Street Journal*, September 4, 2007.

Kagan, Robert and William Kristol, eds. *Present Dangers: Crisis and Opportunity in American Foreign and Defense Policy.* San Francisco: Encounter, 2000.

———. "It's Up to Bush." *The Weekly Standard* (December 18, 2006): 9.

Kaplan, Lawrence F., and William Kristol. *The War Over Iraq: Saddam's Tyranny and America's Mission.* San Francisco: Encounter, 2003.

Kaufman, Robert, G. *In Defense of the Bush Doctrine.* Lexington: University Press of Kentucky, 2007.

Keaney, Thomas A., and Eliot A. Cohen. *Revolution in Warfare: Air Power in the Persian Gulf.* Annapolis, MD: Naval Institute Press, 1995.

Keegan, John. *The Iraq War.* New York: Alfred A. Knopf, 2004.

Keller, Bill. "The Sunshine Warrior." *New York Times*, September 22, 2002.

Kilcullen, David. "Countering Global Insurgency." *Journal of Strategic Studies* 28 (August 2005): 597–617.

Kipp, Jacob, Lester Grau, Karl Prinslow, and Don Smith. "The Human Terrain System: A CORDS for the 21st Century." *Military Review* 86 (September–October 2006): 8–15.

Kissinger, Henry. *White House Years.* Boston: Little, Brown, 1979.

———. *Years of Renewal.* New York: Touchstone, 1999.

Kitfield, James. *War and Destiny: How the Bush Revolution in Foreign and Military Affairs Redefined American Power.* Washington, DC: Potomac Books, 2005.

Kohn, Richard K. "Out of Control: The Crisis in Civil-Military Relations." *The National Interest* 35 (Spring 1994): 3–17.

Krauthammer, Charles. "The Unipolar Moment." *Foreign Affairs* 70 (1990–1991): 23–33.

———. "The War: A Roadmap." *Washington Post*, September 28, 2001.

———. "Redefining the War," *Washington Post*, February 1, 2002.

———. "The Unipolar Moment Revisited." *National Interest* 70 (Winter 2002–2003): 5–17.

Krepinevich, Andrew F., Jr. "Cavalry to Computer: The Pattern of Military Revolutions." *National Interest* 37 (Fall 1994): 30–42.

———. "How to Win in Iraq." *Foreign Affairs* 84 (September–October 2005): 87–104.

Kristol, William. "Keep on Surgin'." *The Weekly Standard* (July 25, 2007): 9.

Kristol, William, and Robert Kagan. "Toward a Neo-Reaganite Foreign Policy." *Foreign Affairs* 75 (July–August 1996): 18–32.

Krulak, Charles C. "The Strategic Corporal: Leadership in the Three Block War." *Marines* 28 (May 1999): 28–34.

Lake, Anthony. "The Need For Engagement," address to the Woodrow Wilson School, Princeton University, November 30, 1994.

———. "The Price of Leadership," address before the National Press Club, Washington, DC, April 27, 1995.

Lind, Michael. *The American Way of Strategy.* Oxford: Oxford University Press, 2006.

Locher, James R., III. *Victory on the Potomac: The Goldwater-Nichols Act Unifies the Pentagon.* College Station: Texas A&M University Press, 2002.

Lowry, Richard. "End Iraq." *National Review* (October 15, 2001): 33–34.

Luttwak, Edward N. *Strategy: The Logic of War and Peace.* Cambridge, MA: Belknap, 1987.

Lyons, James. "Multifaceted Strategy for Iraq." *Washington Times,* October 16, 2006.

Maddrell, Debra O. *Quiet Transformation: The Role of the Office of Net Assessment.* Washington, DC: National Defense University, 2003.

Maddy-Weitzman, Bruce. "Islam and Arabism: The Iran-Iraq War." *Washington Quarterly* 5 (Autumn 1982): 181–188.

Mandelbaum, Michael. "Foreign Policy as Social Work." *Foreign Affairs* 75 (January–February 1996): 16–32.

———. *The Case for Goliath: How America Acts as the World's Government in the Twenty-first Century.* New York: Public Affairs, 2005.

Mann, James. *Rise of the Vulcans: The History of Bush's War Cabinet.* New York: Penguin, 2004.

Marshall, Joshua Micah. "The Reluctant Hawk: The Skeptical Case for Regime Change in Iraq." *Washington Monthly* (November 2002): 43–46.

May, Ernest R. *"Lessons" of the Past: The Use and Misuse of History in American Foreign Policy.* London: Oxford University Press, 1973.

Mazarr, Michael. "Middleweight Forces for Contingency Operations." *Military Review* 71 (August 1991): 32–39.

Mazarr, Michael J., Don M. Snider, and James A. Blackwell Jr. *Desert Storm: The Gulf War and What We Learned.* Boulder, CO: Westview, 1993.

Mazarr, Michael, et. al. *The Military Technical Revolution: A Structural Framework.* Washington, DC: Center for Strategic and International Studies, 1993.

McCaffrey, Barry R. Memorandum for Col. Michael Meese, Department of Social Sciences, U.S. Military Academy, December 18, 2007.

McInerney, Thomas G. Testimony in *Hearings to Examine Threats, Responses, and Regional Considerations Surrounding Iraq,* United States Senate Committee on Foreign Relations, 107th Congr., 2d sess., July 31 and August 1, 2002.

McMaster, H. R. Interview by *PBS Frontline,* February 21, 2006.

Mead, Walter Russell. *Power, Terror, Peace, and War: America's Grand Strategy in a World at Risk.* New York: Alfred A. Knopf, 2004.

Mearsheimer, John J., and Stephen M. Walt. "An Unnecessary War." *Foreign Policy* 134 (January–February 2003): 50–59.

Meilinger, Phillip S. "The Origins of Effects-Based Operations." *Joint Force Quarterly* 35 (October 2004): 116–122.

Military Operations in Low Intensity Conflict. Washington, DC: Headquarters, Departments of the Army and the Air Force, December 5, 1990.

Military Transformation: A Strategic Approach. Washington, DC: Department of Defense Office of Force Transformation, 2003.

Miller, James N., and Shawn W. Brimley. *Phased Transition: A Responsible Way Forward and Out of Iraq.* Washington, DC: Center for a New American Security, June 2007.

Monten, Jonathan. "The Roots of the Bush Doctrine: Power, Nationalism, and Democracy Promotion in U.S. Strategy." *International Security* 29 (Spring 2005): 112–156.

Moustakis, Fotios, and Rudra Chaudhuri. "The Rumsfeld Doctrine and the Cost of US Unilateralism: Lessons Learned." *Defence Studies* 7 (September 1997): 358–75.

Mueller, John, and Karl Mueller. "Sanctions of Mass Destruction." *Foreign Affairs* 78 (May–June 1999): 43–53.

Multi-National Forces–Iraq. *Focus Groups on Reconciliation in Iraq,* executive summary of findings, December 2007.

Muravchik, Joshua. *Apply the Reagan Doctrine to Iraq.* Washington, DC: American Enterprise Institute, 1999.

Murray, Williamson, and Robert H. Scales Jr. *The Iraq War.* Cambridge, MA: Belknap, 2003.

Myers, Richard B. Testimony before the Senate Armed Services Committee, Washington, DC, September 29, 2005.

Mylroie, Laurie. *Study of Revenge: Saddam Hussein's Unfinished War Against America.* Washington, DC: American Enterprise Institute Press, 2000.

Nagl, John. *Learning to Eat Soup With a Knife: Counterinsurgency Lessons From Malaya and Vietnam.* New York: Praeger, 2002.

Nance, Malcolm W. *The Terrorists of Iraq: Inside the Strategy and Tactics of the Iraq Insurgency.* Charleston, SC: BookSurge, 2007.

National Defense Strategy of the United States of America. Washington, DC: Department of Defense, 2005.

National Intelligence Council. *Prospects for Iraq's Stability: A Challenging Road Ahead,* January 2007.

———. *Prospects for Iraq's Stability: Some Security Progress but Political Reconciliation Elusive,* August 2007.

National Military Strategy of the United States. Washington, DC: Office of the Chairman of the Joints Chiefs of Staff, 1992.

National Security Strategy of the United States. Washington, DC: The White House, 1988.

National Security Strategy of the United States. Washington, DC: The White House, 1990.

National Security Strategy of the United States. Washington, DC: The White House, 1991.

National Security Strategy of the United States of America. Washington, DC: The White House, 2002.

National Security Strategy of the United States of America. Washington, DC: The White House, 2006.

National Strategy for Combating Terrorism. Washington, DC: The White House, 2003.

National Strategy for Combating Terrorism. Washington, DC: The White House, 2006.

National Strategy for Victory in Iraq. Washington, DC: National Security Council, 2005.

Nixon, Richard. *RN: The Memoirs of Richard Nixon.* New York: Grosset and Dunlap 1978.

Nye, Joseph S., Jr., and Roger K. Smith, eds. *After the Storm: Lessons From the Gulf War.* Lanham, MD: Madison, 1992.

Obaid, Nawaf, and Anthony Cordesman. *Saudi Militants in Iraq: Assessment and the Kingdom's Response.* Washington, DC: Center for Strategic and International Studies, 2005.

Odierno, Raymond. Video news briefing from Baghdad, June 18, 2003.

Office for Reconstruction and Humanitarian Assistance. *A Unified Mission Plan for Post Hostilities Iraq.* Initial working draft, April 21, 2003.

———. *A National Security Strategy for a Global Age.* Washington, DC: The White House, 2000.

———.*A National Security Strategy for a New Century*. Washington, DC: The White House, 1998.

———.*A National Security Strategy for a New Century*. Washington, DC: The White House, 1999.

O'Hanlon, Michael. "Breaking the Army." *Washington Post,* July 3, 2003.

———. "The Need to Increase the Size of the Deployable Army." *Parameters* 34 (Autumn 2004): 4–17.

———. *Defense Policy for the Post-Saddam Era*. Washington, DC: Brookings Institution, 2005.

O'Hanlon, Michael E., and Kenneth M. Pollack. "A War We Just Might Win." *New York Times,* July 30, 2007.

Oliker, Olga, et. al. *U.S. Policy Options for Iraq: A Reassessment*. Santa Monica, CA: RAND Corporation, 2007.

Olson, William J. *US Strategic Interests in the Gulf Region*. Boulder, CO: Westview, 1987.

Operational Maneuver From the Sea. Quantico, VA: U.S. Marine Corps Combat Development Command, 1996.

Orzag, Peter. *Estimated Costs of U.S. Operations in Iraq and Afghanistan and of Other Activities Related to the War on Terrorism*. Testimony before the Committee on the Budget, U.S. House of Representatives, October 24, 2007.

Owens, Bill. *Lifting the Fog of War*. Baltimore, MD: Johns Hopkins University Press, 2000.

Packer, George. *The Assassins' Gate: America in Iraq*. New York: Farrar, Straus, and Giroux, 2005.

———. "The Lesson of Tal Afar." *New Yorker* (April 10, 2006): 9–62.

Palmer, Michael A. *Guardians of the Gulf: A History of America's Expanding Role in the Persian Gulf, 1833–1992*. New York: Free Press, 1992.

Pascual, Carlos. Prepared statement for the Senate Foreign Relations Committee, June 16, 2005.

———. Interview in *Joint Force Quarterly* 42 (2006): 80-85.

Pascual, Carlos, and Kenneth M. Pollack. "The Critical Battles: Political Reconciliation and Reconstruction in Iraq." *Washington Quarterly* 30 (Summer 2007): 7–19.

Pelletiere, Stephen C. *The Iran-Iraq War: Chaos in a Vacuum*. Westport, CT: Praeger, 1992.

Pelletiere, Stephen C., Douglas V. Johnson II, and Leif R. Rosenberger. *Iraqi Power and U.S. Security in the Middle East*. Carlisle Barracks, PA: U.S. Army War College Strategic Studies Institute, 1990.

Peltz, Eric, et. al. *Sustainment of Army Forces in Operation Iraqi Freedom: Major Findings and Recommendations*. Santa Monica, CA: RAND Corporation, 2005.

Perle, Richard. "The U.S. Must Strike at Saddam Hussein." *New York Times*, December 28, 2001.

Perry, William J. "Defense in an Age of Hope." *Foreign Affairs* 75 (November–December 1996): 64–79.

Petraeus, David H. "Learning Counterinsurgency: Observations From Soldiering in Iraq." *Military Review* 84 (January–February 2006): 2–11.

Phillips, David L. *Losing Iraq: Inside the Postwar Reconstruction Fiasco*. New York: Basic Books, 2005.

Pimlott, John, and Stephen Badsey, eds. *The Gulf War Assessed*. London: Arms and Armour, 1992.

Pollack, Kenneth M. "Next Stop Baghdad?" *Foreign Affairs* 81 (March–April 2002): 32–47.
———. *The Threatening Storm: The Case for Invading Iraq.* New York: Random House, 2002.
———. "Spies, Lies, and Weapons: What Went Wrong." *Atlantic Monthly*, January–February 2004, 78–92.
Posen, Barry R. "The Case for Restraint," *The American Interest* 3 (November–December 2007): 6–12.
Possible Costs to the United States of Maintaining a Long-Term Military Presence in Iraq. Washington, DC: Congressional Budget Office, September 2007.
Powell, Colin. "U.S. Forces: Challenges Ahead." *Foreign Affairs* 71 (Winter 1992–1993): 32–45.
———. *My American Journey.* With Joseph E. Persico. New York: Ballantine, 1995.
———. "Address to the U.N. Security Council," New York, NY, February 5, 2003.
———. Interviewed by Bob Schieffer on CBS News *Face the Nation*, December 17, 2006.
Pre-War Planning for Post-War Iraq. Fact sheet from the Office of Near Eastern and South Asian Affairs, Office of the Assistant Secretary of Defense for International Security Affairs, n.d..
Pritchard, Tim. *Ambush Alley: The Most Extraordinary Battle of the Iraq War.* New York: Random House, 2005.
Progress or Peril? Measuring Iraq's Reconstruction. Report of the Post-Conflict Reconstruction Project. Washington, DC: Center for Strategic and International Studies, September 2004.
Quadrennial Defense Review Report. Washington, DC: Department of Defense, 2001.
Quadrennial Defense Review Report. Washington, DC: Department of Defense, 2006.
Rathmell, Andrew. "Planning Post-Conflict Reconstruction in Iraq: What Can We Learn?" *International Affairs* 81 (October 2005): 1026–30.
Record, Jeffrey. *The Rapid Deployment Force and U.S. Military Intervention in the Persian Gulf.* Cambridge, MA: Institute for Foreign Policy Analysis, 1981.
———. *Hollow Victory: A Contrary View of the Gulf War.* Washington: Brassey's, Inc., 1993.
———. *Bounding the Global War on Terrorism.* Carlisle Barracks, PA: U.S. Army War College, 2003.
———. "The Bush Doctrine and the War With Iraq." *Parameters* 33 (Spring 2003): 4–21.
Report of the Independent Commission on the Security Forces of Iraq, September 2007.
Report of the Senate Select Committee on Postwar Findings About Iraq's WMD Programs and Links to Terrorism and How They Compare With Prewar Assessments, 109th Congr., 2d sess., September 8, 2006.
Rice, Condoleezza. "Promoting the National Interest." *Foreign Affairs* 79 (January–February 2000): 45-62.
———. Interviewed by Margaret Warner on PBS *NewsHour*, September 25, 2002.
Ricks, Thomas E. *Fiasco: The American Military Adventure in Iraq.* New York: Penguin, 2006.
Rieff, David. "Blueprint for a Mess." *New York Times Magazine*, November 2, 2003.
Robb, John. *Brave New War: The Next Stage of Terrorism and the End of Globalization.* New York: John Wiley and Sons, 2007.
Romjue, John J. *From Active Defense to AirLand Battle: The Development of Army*

Doctrine, 1973–1982. Fort Monroe, VA: Historical Office, U.S. Army Training and Doctrine Command, 1984.

Rosen, Gary, ed. *The Right War? The Conservative Debate on Iraq.* Cambridge: Cambridge University Press, 2005.

Rubin, Barry. "The Reagan Administration and the Middle East." In *Eagle Defiant: United States Foreign Policy in the 1980s,* edited by Kenneth A. Oye, Robert J. Lieber, and Donald Rothchild. Boston: Little, Brown, 1983.

———. "The Gulf Crisis: Origins and Course of Events." In *Middle East Contemporary Survey,* vol. 14, edited by Ami Ayalon. Boulder, CO: Westview, 1990.

Rumsfeld, Donald H. Prepared testimony for the Senate Armed Services Committee hearings on Iraq, September 19, 2002.

———. Interview with Todd McDermott, WCBS-TV, New York City, May 27, 2003.

———. Prepared testimony for the Senate Armed Services Committee, Washington, DC, July 9, 2003.

———. Interview with *Fox and Friends,* November 11, 2003.

———. "New Model Army," *Wall Street Journal,* February 3, 2004.

Rycroft, Matthew. Memorandum to David Manning, July 23, 2002 (the "Downing Street memo").

Schmitt, Gary. "A Case of Continuity." *National Interest* 69 (Fall 2002): 11–13.

Schwarzkopf, H. Norman. *It Doesn't Take a Hero.* With Peter Petre. New York: Bantam, 1993.

Scowcroft, Brent. "Build a Coalition." *Washington Post,* October 16, 2001.

Seeking a National Strategy: A Concert for Preserving Security and Promoting Freedom, Phase II report of the United States Commission on National Security, 21st Century, 2000.

Sepp, Kalev I. "From 'Shock and Awe' to 'Hearts and Minds': The Fall and Rise of US Counterinsurgency Capability in Iraq." *Third World Quarterly* 28 (2007): 217-230.

Shape, Respond, Prepare Now—a Military Strategy for a New Era. Washington, DC: Joint Chiefs of Staff, 1997.

Shultz, George P. *Turmoil and Triumph: My Years as Secretary of State.* New York: Charles Scribner's Sons, 1993.

Simon, Steven N. *After the Surge: The Case for U.S. Military Disengagement From Iraq.* New York: Council on Foreign Relations, February 2007.

Slocombe, Walter B. "To Build an Army." *Washington Post,* November 5, 2003.

Snider, Don M., and Miranda A. Carlton-Carew, eds. *U.S. Civil-Military Relations: In Crisis or Transition?* Washington, DC: Center for Strategic and International Studies, 1995.

Snider, Don M., Daniel Gouré, and Stephen A. Cambone. *Defense in the Late 1990s: Avoiding the Train Wreck.* Washington, DC: Center for Strategic and International Studies, 1995.

Speed and Knowledge, the annual report on the Army After Next Project to the Chief of Staff of the Army. Fort Monroe, VA: U.S. Army Training and Doctrine Command, 1997.

Stephenson, James. *Losing the Golden Hour: An Insider's View of Iraq's Reconstruction.* Washington, DC: Potomac Books, 2007.

Sterner, Michael. "The Iran-Iraq War." *Foreign Affairs* 63 (Fall 1984): 128–143.

Stevenson, Charles A. *SECDEF: The Nearly Impossible Job of Secretary of Defense.* Washington, DC: Potomac Books, 2006.

Strakes, Jason E. "Fourth Generation Conflict? Local Social Formations and Insurgencies in Post-Ba'ath Iraq." *Journal of Third World Studies* 24 (Fall 2007): 27–44.

Summers, Harry G., Jr. *On Strategy II: A Critical Analysis of the Gulf War.* New York: Dell, 1992.

Suskind, Ron. *The One Percent Doctrine: Deep Inside America's Pursuit of Its Enemies Since 9/11.* New York: Simon and Schuster, 2006.

Talbott, Strobe. "Post-Victory Blues." *Foreign Affairs* 71 (1991–1992): 53–69.

Taylor, William J., Jr., and James Blackwell. "The Ground War in the Gulf." *Survival* 33 (May–June 1991): 230–245.

Tenet, George. "Evolving Dangers in a Complex World." Written testimony for the Senate Select Committee on Intelligence on the Worldwide Threat 2003, February 11, 2003.

————. *At the Center of the Storm: My Years at the CIA.* New York: HarperCollins, 2007.

Terrill, W. Andrew. *The United States and Iraq's Shiite Clergy: Partners or Adversaries?* Carlisle Barracks, PA: U.S. Army War College Strategic Studies Institute, 2004.

Third Infantry Division (Mechanized). *Operation Iraqi Freedom.* After Action Report, Final Draft, May 12, 2003.

Transforming Defense: National Security in the 21st Century, Report of the National Defense Panel, December 1997.

Tritten, James John. *Our New National Security Strategy: America Promises to Come Back.* Westport, CT: Praeger, 1992.

Triumph Without Victory: The Unreported History of the Persian Gulf War. New York: Times Books, 1992.

Troxell, John F. *Force Planning in an Era of Uncertainty: Two MRCs as a Force Sizing Framework.* Carlisle Barracks, PA: U.S. Army War College Strategic Studies Institute, 1997.

Tucker, Robert W. "Oil: The Issue of American Intervention." *Commentary* 59 (January 1975): 21–31.

————. "The End of a Contradiction?" *National Interest* 69 (Fall 2002): 5-7.

United States Institute of Peace. *Who Are the Insurgents? Sunni Arab Rebels in Iraq.* Special Report 134 (April 2005).

United States Marine Corps. *Warfighting Concepts for the 21st Century.* Quantico, VA: Marine Corps Combat Development Command, 1996.

The U.S. Navy In Desert Shield/Desert Storm. Washington, DC: Naval Historical Center, 1991.

"U.S. Policy Toward the Persian Gulf," *National Security Directive 26,* October 2, 1989.

Van Creveld, Martin. *The Changing Face of War: Lessons of Combat From the Marne to Iraq.* New York: Ballantine, 2006.

Vance, Cyrus. *Hard Choices: Critical Years in America's Foreign Policy.* New York: Simon and Schuster, 1983.

Vick, Adam J., et. al. *Air Power in the New Counterinsurgency Era: The Strategic Importance of the USAF Advisory and Assistance Missions.* Santa Monica, CA: RAND Corporation, 2006.

Viorst, Milton. "Iraq At War." *Foreign Affairs* 65 (Winter 1986–87): 349–65.

Vuono, Carl E. "Desert Storm and the Future of Conventional Forces." *Foreign Affairs* 70 (Spring 1991): 49–65.

8

Walker, David M. *Stabilizing Iraq: An Assessment of the Security Situation*, testimony for the Subcommittee on National Security, Emerging Threats and International Relations, House Committee on Government Reform. Washington, DC: General Accounting Office, September 11, 2006.

Walt, Stephen M. *Taming American Power: The Global Response to U.S. Primacy*. New York: W. W. Norton, 2005.

Warden, John A., III. *The Air Campaign: Planning for Combat*. Washington, DC: Pergamon-Brassey's, 1989.

Weinberger, Caspar W. *Fighting for Peace: Seven Critical Years in the Pentagon*. New York: Warner, 1990.

West, Bing. *The March Up: Taking Baghdad With the United States Marines*. New York: Bantam, 2004.

White, Jeffrey. *An Adaptive Insurgency: Confronting Adversary Networks in Iraq*. Washington, DC: Washington Institute for Near East Studies, 2006.

Wilson, Isaiah. "Thinking Beyond War: Civil-Military Operational Planning in Northern Iraq." Paper prepared for delivery, Peace Studies Program, Cornell University, October 14, 2004.

Wilz, John Edward. "The Making of Mr. Bush's War: A Failure to Learn From History?" *Presidential Studies Quarterly* 25 (Summer 1995): 533–54.

———.*A Wiser Peace: An Action Strategy for a Post-Conflict Iraq*. Washington, DC: Center for Strategic and International Studies, January 2003.

Wolfowitz, Paul. Interviewed by Melissa Block on National Public Radio, February 19, 2003.

———. Testimony before the Committee on the Budget, U.S. House of Representatives, 108th Congr., 1st sess., February 27, 2003.

Woodward, Bob. *The Commanders*. New York: Touchstone, 1991.

———. *Bush at War*. New York: Simon and Schuster, 2002.

———. *Plan of Attack*. New York: Simon and Schuster, 2004.

———. *State of Denial*. New York: Simon and Schuster, 2006.

Woolsey, R. James. "The Iraq Connection." *Wall Street Journal*, October 18, 2001.

Zakaria, Fareed. *The Future of Freedom: Illiberal Democracy at Home and Abroad*. New York: W. W. Norton, 2004.

Zinni, Anthony. Testimony before the Senate Armed Services Committee, January 28, 1999.

Zoellick, Robert B. "A Republican Foreign Policy." *Foreign Affairs* 79 (January–February 2000): 63–78.

INDEX

disarmament, 41; and peace-keeping, 63, 64, 65; reinvigorated by the end of the Cold War, 8; role in post-Hussein Iraq, 131; sanctions against Iraq, 50; weapons inspections, 67, 68, 125, 128, 138. *See also* Security Council Resolution
unrestricted warfare: 177
Vance, Cyrus: 4
Vera de Mello, Sergio: 151
Vietnam, effect on American strategy: 1,2, 17, 18, 19-20, 22, 26, 41, 42, 54, 55, 57, 63, 191, 197
Vigilant Warrior. *See* Operation Vigilant Warrior
Voinovich, John: 186
Vuono, Carl: 32
Walt, Stephen: 136
war planning: 25
Warden, John A., III: 26

Warner, John: 184, 186
Warrick, Thomas S.: 131, 132
Waxman, Matthew: 68
way of war, American. *See* American way of war
Weekly Standard: 78, 103, 104
Weinberger, Caspar: principles for the use of military force, 10-11, 20, 31, 63, 76; supporting regime change in Iraq, 69
West Point: Bush speech (2002), 86, 90
Wolfowitz, Paul: 78, 102, 103, 104, 107, 109-10, 115, 120, 130, 131, 135, 160, 192
Woodward, Bob: 24, 104
Woolsey, R. James: 91, 103
Zakaria, Fareed: 95
Zarqawi, Abu Musab al-: 114, 164, 169, 173
Zinni, Anthony: 70, 104, 136

ABOUT THE AUTHOR

Dr. Steven Metz is Chairman of the Regional Strategy and Planning Department and Research Professor of National Security Affairs at the U.S. Army War College Strategic Studies Institute. He has been with SSI since 1993, previously serving as Henry L. Stimson Professor of Military Studies and SSI's Director of Research. Dr. Metz has also been on the faculty of the Air War College, the U.S. Army Command and General Staff College, and several universities. He has been an advisor to political campaigns and elements of the intelligence community, served on many national security policy task forces, testified in both houses of Congress, and spoken on military and security issues around the world. He is the author of more than 100 publications, including articles in journals such as *Washington Quarterly, Joint Force Quarterly, The National Interest, Defence Studies,* and *Current History*. Dr. Metz's research has taken him to thirty countries, including Iraq immediately after the collapse of the Saddam regime. He currently serves on the RAND Corporation Insurgency Board and holds a Ph.D. from Johns Hopkins University.